School & College CURRICULUM DESIGN

Book Three: IMPACT

Matt Bromley

Spark BOOKS

ISBN: 9798722688484

Dedication

I am lucky: my job affords me the opportunity to visit countless schools and colleges both in the UK and overseas. Ostensibly, I do so to share my expertise and experience which, let me tell you, gives me a perpetual sense of imposter syndrome. I'm particularly surprised when a school or college invites me back because they wish to hear more! But in so doing, I get to talk to and learn from so many wonderful colleagues – teachers, leaders, support staff all – who are dedicated to the education profession and determined to make a difference for the young people in their charge.

It is fair to say my thoughts and ideas are continually reshaped and refined as a consequence of these inspiring interactions. Sometimes, my opinions are solidified because I see and hear hard evidence of their truth. At other times, my opinions are challenged and changed as they meet with the hard resistance of reality.

I therefore dedicate this book to the thousands of hard-working people who work in education every day and who have helped shape the ideas I share within these pages. They can take the credit; I will accept the blame for any errors or omissions.

This is Book Three in a three-volume series and I have been overwhelmed by the positive response I've received to the first two books. As a consequence of those books, I've been invited to visit so many schools and colleges and to speak at countless conferences. And with each engagement, I have learned more.

Lots of schools and colleges have used my books as a blueprint for their curriculum developments and it is beyond humbling to see my advice enacted in practice and already making a positive difference to pupils' lives.

Each step I've taken in my career has been about expanding my classroom. As a teacher, I saw the impact I had on the pupils I taught. As a head of department, that class grew a little. It grew again when I became a senior leader and headteacher. Now, and forgive both my hubris and hyperbole, my class spans the globe! I feel I'm having an impact on pupils all over the world. But don't worry, my ego is kept in check by my own children who appear to have no idea what I do for a living except provide them with a personal taxi service!

I'd therefore like to add my thanks here to those colleagues who've bought the first two books – or even bought a set for their staff – and have contacted me to tell me how it's helped them. And I'd also like to thank those colleagues who've approached me at conferences and asked me to sign a copy, thus fulfilling one of my lifelong dreams!

Contents

Front matter

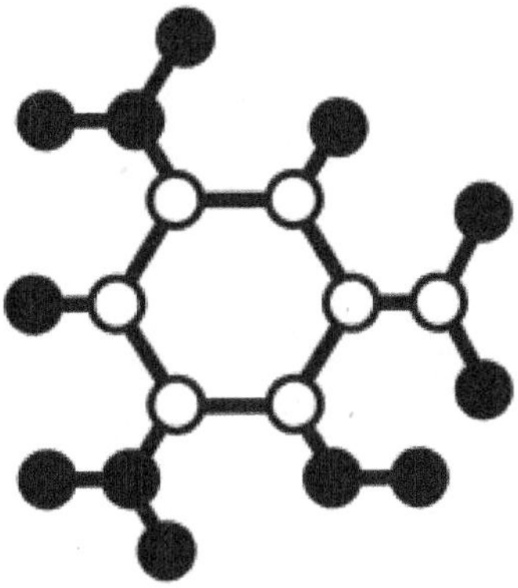

A note on the text

This is Book Three in a three-volume series on the subject of school and college curriculum design. This book tackles 'curriculum impact'. Book One explored 'curriculum intent' whilst Book Two examined 'curriculum implementation'.

The series title is, somewhat convolutedly I know, 'School *and College* Curriculum Design' because it is aimed at leaders and teachers in primary, secondary and further education settings.

At times, as in Books One and Two, I will refer to 'pupils and students' to make clear my advice applies equally to young children *and* older learners. I will also make reference to both the schools inspection handbook and the further education and skills inspection handbook, where it is helpful to articulate the differences between the two.

However, for the sake of brevity, and to avoid unnecessary convolution, I will often default to the terms 'pupils' and 'schools'.

I wish to make clear, therefore, that all of the advice contained within this book – and indeed in the series as a whole – relates to schools *and* further education settings including colleges and training providers, even if the language does not always feel so inclusive of the tertiary sector.

Of course, at times I will talk about strategies specific to schools such as the Pupil Premium Grant but all the advice – if not the illustrated examples – is, I think, relevant to all readers.

I have worked extensively – as a teacher, leader and advisor – in all three phases (primary, secondary and FE), as well as in HE, and have enacted the advice I share in this series of books in all three phases and so I know it can work in all.

Yes, there are clear differences; but all three phases have more in common than that which divides them.

Although this series of books includes reference to the education inspectorate in England, Ofsted, the advice I share is, I think, applicable to educators in other countries both in the UK and overseas.

One further note about the text you're about to read before you do so...

Although I think it likely that many readers of this book will have already enjoyed (or perhaps endured?) Books One and Two in the series, I don't wish to presume that this is the case for all. As such, there will be some repetition from the previous two volumes whenever I think it important to call-back some core ideas before expanding upon them in this volume.

Where there is a significant overlap with the earlier books, I will explicitly note it so you can skip ahead if you so wish. Although I am wary of needless repetition and wish to provide good value for money, I have decided that, when all's said and done, there is no harm in revisiting some of the key ideas I expounded in the first two books in the series. We do so when teaching our pupils, after all, and call it retrieval practice.

Likewise, I know that many readers, busy imparting their daily duties in schools and colleges, dip in and out of a book of this size and take time to work through it. Accordingly, where I think it will help to refresh memories and place content in context, I provide summaries of previous chapters before expanding on those ideas.

The story so far...

This is the third of three guides to the school and college curriculum design process.

Taken together, this series seeks to navigate you through the process of redesigning your school or college curriculum, in order to ensure that it is broad and balanced, ambitious for all, and prepares pupils and students for the next stages of their education, employment and lives.

The journey began in Book One with **curriculum intent** – the ***'Why?'*** and the ***'What?'*** of education.

The second book, meanwhile, tackled **curriculum implementation** – the ***'How?'*** of education.

This book concludes our journey with **curriculum impact** – the ***'How successfully?'***

The story so far...

Book One was about all the planning that happens before teaching happens.

In *Part One* of Book One, we defined that slippery term 'curriculum' and argued that a curriculum is not a single entity; rather, it is a composite of at least four different elements: the national, the basic, the local, and the hidden curriculums.

We also defined the words 'broad' and 'balanced' and explored what a broad and balanced curriculum looked like in practice.

We examined the primacy of the curriculum over teaching, learning and assessment, and defended curriculum's role as the master, as opposed to the servant, of education.

We considered the true purpose of a high-quality education and, by so doing, articulated the intended outcomes of an effective school and college curriculum.

We explored the vital role that senior leaders can play in the curriculum design process whilst also defending the rights of middle leaders and teachers – those with subject specialist knowledge – to create their own disciplinary curriculums with a degree of freedom and autonomy.

We analysed the importance of creating a culture of high aspirations where each pupil is challenged to produce excellence.

We considered the centrality of social justice to effective curriculum design, too; and concluded that a curriculum is a means of closing the gap between disadvantaged pupils and their more privileged peers.

In *Part Two* of Book One, we examined *why* designing a knowledge-rich curriculum was important because, contrary to popular opinion, pupils can't 'just Google it'. We discussed *what* knowledge mattered most to our pupils' future successes and how to identify the 'clear end-points' or 'body of knowledge' of a whole-school or college - and indeed subject-specific - curriculum.

Also in *Part Two*, we discussed ways of ensuring our curriculum is ambitious for all, including by adopting (and possibly adapting) a mastery approach whereby we set the same destination for all pupils and students, irrespective of their starting points and backgrounds, rather than reducing the curriculum offer or 'dumbing down' for some. We talked, too, of modelling the same high expectations of all, albeit accepting that some pupils will need additional and different support to reach that destination, and not all will do so.

In *Part Three* of Book One, we discussed how to assess the starting points of our curriculum, both in terms of what has already been *taught* (the previous curriculum) and what has actually been *learnt* and retained (our pupils' starting points – their prior knowledge, and their knowledge gaps and misconceptions).

We explored the importance of curriculum continuity, too, and considered the features of an effective transition process. And we looked at ways of instilling a consistent language *of* and *for* learning.

In *Part Four* of Book One, having identified both our destination and our starting points, we plotted a course between the two, identifying useful waypoints or checkpoints at which to stop along the way – which might take the form of 'threshold concepts' – through which pupils must travel because their acquisition of these concepts (be they knowledge or skills) is contingent on them being able to access and succeed at the next stage.

We explored the importance of having a planned and sequenced curriculum, ensuring we revisit key concepts several times as pupils travel through the education system but, each time, doing so with increasing complexity, like carving a delicate statue from an alabaster block, each application of hammer and chisel revealing ever finer detail and, in the case of curriculum sequencing, more – and indeed *more complex* - connections to prior learning (or schema) that, in turn, help pupils to learn more and cheat the limitations of their working memories in order to move from novice and towards expert.

We explored how these 'way-points' or threshold concepts might be used as a means of assessment so that curriculum knowledge – rather than something arbitrary such as scaled scores, national curriculum levels, GCSE or A Level grades, or passes/merits/distinctions on vocational qualifications – is what we assess, by means of a progression model.

In *Parts Five* and *Six* of Book One on curriculum intent, we turned to the subject of differentiation – arguing again that all pupils deserve access to the same ambitious curriculum, no matter their starting points and backgrounds, and no matter the opportunities and challenges they face in life.

We accepted that, of course, some pupils need more support and more time in order to reach the designated end-points of our curriculum, or to master the 'body of knowledge' we assign them, and even then not all will do so, but we argued that we should not 'dumb down' or reduce our curriculum offer for disadvantaged or vulnerable pupils, pupils with SEND, or learners with High Needs, because by so doing we only perpetuate the achievement gap and double their disadvantage. Rather, we should ensure that every pupil is plotted a course for the same destination, albeit accepting that the means of transport and journey time may differ.

Accordingly, in *Part Five* we defined excellence and explored the importance of 'teaching to the top'. We looked at how to model high expectations of all pupils. And we looked at ways of 'pitching' learning in pupils' 'struggle zones' (delicately balanced between their comfort zones and their panic zones where work is hard but achievable with time, effort and support).

Then, in *Part Six*, we looked at ways of diminishing disadvantage - accepting that if we want to offer all pupils the same ambitious curriculum, we must also identify any gaps in their prior knowledge and skills and support those pupils with learning difficulties or disabilities to access our curriculum and have a fair – if not equal – chance of academic success.

We looked at the role of cultural capital in closing the gap, arguing that vocabulary instruction (particularly of Tier 2 words) is a useful means of helping disadvantaged pupils to access our curriculum, but that this, in and of itself, is not enough. Rather, we asserted that cultural capital took myriad forms and had different definitions, and, as such, we should also plan to explicitly teach pupils how to speak, read and write in each subject discipline, and fill gaps in their world knowledge.

We also looked at how to make a success of in-class differentiation and additional interventions and support. And we looked at how to develop pupils' literacy and numeracy skills in order to help disadvantaged learners to access our curriculum. Finally, we examined ways of developing pupils' metacognition and self-regulation skills to help them become increasingly independent and resilient as learners.

In short, Book One in this three-volume series followed a six-step process of curriculum design which went as follows:

1. Agree a vision
2. Set the destination
3. Assess the starting points
4. Identify the waypoints
5. Define excellence
6. Diminish disadvantage

Book One – as I said earlier – was about all the planning that happens before teaching happens.

Book Two, meanwhile, was about all the teaching that happens next...

In other words, it dealt with curriculum implementation, the way in which teachers translate curriculum plans into classroom practice with pupils and students.

We began *Part One* of Book Two by asking the question, 'What is implementation?'

In the schools' inspection handbook, we said, Ofsted defines implementation as the way in which "the curriculum is taught at subject and classroom level".

Accordingly, during an inspection, Ofsted will want to see how teachers enable pupils to understand key concepts, presenting information clearly and promoting appropriate discussion, how teachers check pupils' understanding effectively, identifying and correcting misunderstandings, and how teachers ensure that pupils embed key concepts in their long-term memory and apply them fluently.

Further, Ofsted will want to see if the subject curriculum that classes follow is designed and delivered in a way that allows pupils to transfer key knowledge to long-term memory and if it is sequenced so that new knowledge and skills build on what has been taught before and towards defined end points.

In the further education and skills inspection handbook, Ofsted argues that teachers need sufficient subject knowledge, pedagogical knowledge and pedagogical content knowledge to be able teach learners effectively.

Effective teaching and training should, Ofsted argues, ensure that learners in further education and skills settings know more and remember what they have learned within the context of the approach that teachers have selected to serve the aims of their curriculum. Consequently, learners will be able to apply vocational and technical skills fluently and independently.

In short, effective curriculum implementation is high quality teaching which leads to long-term learning.

In *Part Two* of Book Two, we turned our attention to the matter of evidence-informed teaching...

We said that one of the best ways to ensure we implement the curriculum effectively – that is to say, in a way that leads to long-term learning – is to follow the evidence. These days, there's a surfeit of research evidence about what works and what doesn't. From the darkness there is light.

Evidence tells us, for example, that feedback is a highly effective teaching strategy. It tops the Educational Endowment Foundation's (EEF) chart as the most impactful tool at a teacher's disposal and so it would follow that schools should invest time and money in improving the effectiveness of feedback...

However, caution should be exercised, we said, because the term 'feedback' is a somewhat slippery one and can mean many different things.

The EEF say that feedback is "information given to the learner or teacher about the learner's performance relative to learning goals or outcomes. It should aim towards (and be capable of producing) improvement in students' learning. Feedback redirects or refocuses either the teacher's or the learner's actions to achieve a goal, by aligning effort and activity with an outcome."

Feedback, say the EEF, can be about "the output of the activity, the process of the activity, the student's management of their learning or self-regulation, or them as individuals (which tends to be the least effective)."

According to the EEF, studies tend to show very high effects of feedback on learning. However, some studies show that feedback can have negative effects and make things worse. It is therefore important, the EEF say, to understand the potential benefits and the possible limitations of feedback as a teaching and learning approach. In general, research-based approaches that explicitly aim to provide feedback to learners, such as Bloom's 'mastery learning', tend to have a positive impact.

One thing to note is that, just because the EEF toolkit says that feedback is good, this does not imply that teachers should do lots more of it. It does mean that, when done well, it can really benefit pupils and so feedback should be done better, which is to say that feedback should be meaningful and helpful to pupils.

In practice, effective feedback tends to:

- Be specific, accurate and clear (e.g., "It was good because you..." rather than just "correct")
- Compare what a learner is doing right now with what they have done wrong before (e.g., "I can see you were focused on improving X as it is much better than last time's Y...")
- Encourage and support further effort
- Be given sparingly so that it is meaningful
- Provide specific guidance on how to improve and not just tell students when they are wrong
- Be supported with effective professional development for teachers

Broader research suggests that feedback should be about complex or challenging tasks or goals as this is likely to emphasise the importance of effort and perseverance as well as be more valued by the pupils.

It's also worth remembering that feedback can come from peers as well as adults.

In order to ensure marking and feedback don't become behemoths, we must sense-check our assessments for their purpose, process and validity, and ensure marking is always meaningful, manageable and motivating.

In *Part Two* of Book Two, we also noted that evidence tells us that metacognition and self-regulation are as impactful as feedback.

Indeed, they take equal top-billing on the EEF toolkit and, like feedback, are said to add an extra eight months of learning per year.

Also akin to feedback, though, metacognition can mean different things to different people.

The EEF say that metacognitive approaches aim to help pupils think about their own learning more explicitly, often by teaching them specific strategies for planning, monitoring and evaluating their learning.

Metacognition gifts pupils a repertoire of strategies to choose from and the skills to select the most suitable strategy for any given learning task.

Metacognition, then, describes the processes involved when learners plan, monitor, evaluate and make changes to their own learning behaviours. Metacognition is often considered to have two dimensions:

1. Metacognitive knowledge, and
2. Self-regulation.

Metacognitive knowledge refers to what learners know about learning. This includes:

- The learner's knowledge of their own cognitive abilities (e.g., 'I have trouble remembering key dates in this period of history')
- The learner's knowledge of particular tasks (e.g., 'The politics in this period of history are complex')
- The learner's knowledge of the different strategies that are available to them and when they are appropriate to the task (e.g., 'If I create a timeline first it will help me to understand this period of history').

Self-regulation, meanwhile, refers to what learners do about learning. It describes how learners monitor and control their cognitive processes. For example, a learner might realise that a particular strategy is not yielding the results they expected so they decide to try a different strategy.

Put another way, self-regulated learners are aware of their strengths and weaknesses, and can motivate themselves to engage in, and improve, their learning.

We approach any learning task or opportunity with some metacognitive knowledge about:

- Our own abilities and attitudes (knowledge of ourselves as a learner)
- What strategies are effective and available (knowledge of strategies)
- This particular type of activity (knowledge of the task)

When undertaking a learning task, we start with this knowledge, then apply and adapt it. This is metacognitive regulation. It is about "planning how to undertake a task, working on it while monitoring the strategy to check progress, then evaluating the overall success".

Next in *Part Two* of a Book Two, we explored the importance of creating an effective learning environment...

Once we've used research evidence to help us determine which teaching strategies will lead to long-term learning, we said, we need to attend to the learning environment because we know with some degree of certainty that the physical, social and emotional conditions in which pupils learn really do matter.

Pupils need to feel comfortable if they are to accept the challenge of hard work, and their basic needs must be met if they are to attend to teacher instruction. And the environment must help ensure pupils focus on the curriculum content we need them to learn and avoid unhelpful distractions or detractions.

How we use our classroom space and the rules, routines and expectations we establish are therefore crucial considerations.

In terms of the physical learning environment, we said, we should consider factors such as room temperature, light, noise, layout, and the use of displays.

In terms of the social learning environment, we said, we should consider how we create a whole school culture which promotes good behaviour and positive attitudes to learning, tackles poor behaviour including low-level disruption, and protects all staff and pupils from harassment and harm.

In terms of the emotional environment, we said, we should consider how to create a classroom culture in which pupils feel safe and secure enough to willingly take risks and make mistakes from which they can learn. Here, the first few days spent in a new learning environment are perhaps the most pivotal in determining a pupil's academic progress. We explored five ways to create a 'growth mindset' culture, these were: 1. Use frequent formative feedback, 2. High levels of challenge for every pupil, 3. Explicitly welcome mistakes, 4. Engaging in deliberate practice, and 5. Reward effort not attainment.

Then, in *Part Three* of Book Two, we explored the three steps of teaching for long-term learning...

There are myriad factors that determine a pupil's success, not least their own hard work, diligence and, yes, innate intelligence. Environmental factors play their part, too, as does the amount of support and influence that a pupil receives from their community of friends and family.

However, we said, there is a 3-step learning process that teachers can follow in order to maximise the chances of pupils acquiring and retaining knowledge over the longer term so that it can be applied in multiple contexts.

The act of acquiring new knowledge and skills is the start of the learning process, it is what happens (or begins to happen) in the classroom when a teacher - the expert - imparts their knowledge or demonstrates their skills (perhaps through the artful use of explanations and modelling) to their pupils - the novices.

Next, pupils store this new information in their long-term memories (via their working memories) where it can be recalled and used later.

The process of storing information in the long-term memory is called 'encoding'. The process of getting it back out again is called 'retrieval'.

A pupil could demonstrate their immediate understanding of what they've been taught by repeating what the teacher has said or by demonstrating the skill they've just seen applied. But this immediate display is not necessarily 'learning'. Rather, it is a 'performance'. It is a simple regurgitation of what they've just seen or heard and takes place in the working memory, without any need for information to be encoded in the long-term memory.

We can all repeat, rote-like, something someone else has just said or mimic a skill they've just demonstrated. But unless we can retain that knowledge or skill over time, we haven't really learnt it. And if we can't apply that knowledge or skill in a range of different situations, then - similarly - we haven't really learnt it, or at least not in any meaningful sense.

However, if we simply repeat the information over and again verbatim, we will only really improve pupils' surface knowledge of that information. To improve and deepen pupils' understanding, we need to teach curriculum content in different domains. We need to model examples of its use in a range of contexts. And when we repeat learning we should do so in different ways.

The process of learning, then, is the interaction between one's sensory memory and one's long-term memory.

Our sensory memory is made up of:

- What we see - this is called our **iconic** memory
- What we hear - this is called our **echoic** memory
- What we touch - our **haptic** memory

Our long-term memory is where new information is stored and from which it can be recalled when needed, but we cannot directly access the information stored in our long-term memory. As such, the interaction that takes place between our sensory memory and our long-term memory occurs in our working memory, or short-term memory, which is the only place where we can think and do.

In summary, there are - to my mind, as I explained in Book Two - three steps to improve the process of teaching for long-term learning:

1. Stimulate pupils' senses to gain the attention of working memory
2. Make pupils think hard but efficiently to encode information into long-term memory
3. Embed deliberate practice to improve pupils' storage in and retrieval from in long-term memory

Coupled with this 3-step process of teaching for long-term learning, I recommend that we also use a 4-step teaching sequence whenever pupils are introduced to new information...

I explained in *Part Three* of Book Two that research by Kirschner, Sweller and Clark (2006) compared guided models of teaching, such as direct instruction, with discovery learning methods, such as problem-based learning, inquiry learning, experiential learning, and constructivist learning, and found that the latter methods didn't work as well as the former. It didn't matter, they argued, if pupils preferred less guided methods, they still learned less from them (see also Clark, 1989).

In his book, Visible Learning, Professor John Hattie found that the average effect size for teaching strategies which involved the teacher as a "facilitator" was 0.17, whereas the average effect size for strategies where the teacher acted as an "activator" was 0.60. Direct instruction had an effect size of 0.59 compared to problem-based learning with an effect size of just 0.15.

Therefore, direct instruction – it seems – is more effective than discovery learning approaches. But what, exactly, does good direct instruction look like in practice?

Personally, as I set out in Book Two, I think direct instruction works best when it follows this four-step sequence:

1. Telling
2. Showing
3. Doing
4. Practising.

Telling – or teacher explanation – works best when the teacher presents new material to pupils in small "chunks" and provides scaffolds and targeted support.

Showing – or teacher modelling – works best when the teacher models a new procedure by, among other strategies, thinking aloud, guiding pupils' initial practice and providing pupils with cues.

Doing – or co-construction – works best when the teacher provides pupils with "fix-up" strategies – corrections and "live" feedback.

Practising – or independent work – works best when the teacher provides planned opportunities in class for extensive independent practice.

Next in *Part Four* of Book Two, we turned our attentions to the subject of differentiation and explored ways of ensuring equal access to teaching for long-term learning...

When we talk about differentiation, we said, we often have in mind ways of scaffolding learning for our 'less able' pupils. But pupils – like learning – are complex and no pupil is uniformly 'less able' than another. Rather, some pupils have acquired more knowledge and skills in one area than another pupil or have practised a task more often. Of course, some pupils have additional and different needs – such as those young people with learning difficulties or disabilities – and they sometimes require a different approach. But to say they are 'less able' is, I think, an unhelpful misnomer.

What's more, the term 'less able' infers an immovable position – if you are 'less able' you are destined to remain so ad infinitum, living your life languishing in the left-hand shadow of the bell-curve.

As I explained in Book Two, I'm not suggesting that every pupil performs the same – or has the same capacity to do so. We are not all born equal. But defining someone as less able as a result of a test – whether that be Key Stage 2 SATs, Year 7 CATs or GCSE outcomes - means we are in danger of arbitrarily writing off some pupils by means of a snapshot taken through a pinhole lens.

We said that when approaching differentiation, therefore, we would be wise to remember that all pupils – like all human beings – are different, unique, individual. Differentiation, therefore, should not be about treating 'less able' pupils – or indeed those with SEND or eligible for Pupil Premium funding – as a homogenous group. Rather, we should treat each pupil on an individual basis.

Nor should we assume that what works with one pupil will work with all and that what was proven to work with 'less able' pupils in another school, in another district, in another country, (according to research evidence and meta-analyses) will work in our classroom.

To promote challenge in the classroom for all pupils, we need to reduce the threat level, we need to ensure no one feels humiliated if they fall short of a challenge. Rather, they need to know that they will learn from the experience and perform better next time.

Once we've created a positive learning environment in which pupils willingly accept challenge, we need to model high expectations of all. Having high expectations of pupils is not only a nice thing to do, but it also leads to improved performance.

It's common practice to talk about three waves of intervention for disadvantaged pupils and those with SEND.

According to the now-defunct National Strategies, Wave 1 is "quality inclusive teaching which takes into account the learning needs of all the pupils in the classroom". As such, if we do not first provide pupils with quality classroom teaching, then no amount of additional intervention and support will help them to catch up.

But even with the provision of 'quality first teaching', some pupils will require more - and more tailored - support in the guise of Wave 2 in-class differentiations and Wave 3 additional interventions which take place outside the classroom and off the taught timetable.

Such intervention strategies may take the form of one-to-one support from a teaching assistant (TA) or additional learning support (ALS), small group targeted teaching by a SEND or High Needs specialist, or support from external agencies such as speech and language therapists.

The ultimate aim of such additional support, in most cases, is for it to become redundant over time. In other words, we want pupils with SEND to become increasingly independent and for the scaffolds to fall away. Indeed, this is the stated aim of Education Health and Care Plans (EHCPs) and High Needs funding: over time, discrete funding should be reduced as its impact is felt and pupils require less and less support.

With this aim in mind, it is important to ensure that all strategic interventions aimed at pupils with SEND are monitored whilst they are happening and are:

- Brief (20– 50mins)
- Regular (3–5 times per week)
- Sustained (running for 8–20 weeks)
- Carefully timetabled
- Staffed by well-trained TAs (5–30 hours' training per intervention)
- Well-planned with structured resources and clear objectives
- Assessed to identify appropriate pupils, guide areas for focus and track pupil progress
- Linked to classroom teaching

Also in *Part Four* of Book Two, we explored ways to motivate pupils to learn...

As well as supporting pupils to access our curriculum, we said, we need to motivate them so that they *want* to learn. Motivation, we said, requires:

1. *A destination to aim for* – knowing what the outcome looks like and not giving up until you reach it.
2. *A model to follow* – an exemplar on which to base your technique provided by someone who is regarded as an expert and who sets high expectations.
3. *Regular checkpoints* – waypoints to show what progress has been made and what's still to do, coupled with regular celebrations of ongoing achievements and timely messages about upcoming milestones.
4. *Personalisation* – the ability to make choices about how to carry out tasks in order to increase enjoyment and engagement.

In the classroom, there are two types of motivation that matter most: intrinsic and extrinsic.

1. Intrinsic motivation – this is the self-desire to seek out new things and new challenges, in order to gain new knowledge. Often, intrinsic motivation is driven by an inherent interest or enjoyment in the task itself. Pupils are likely to be intrinsically motivated if they attribute their educational results to factors under their own control, also known as *autonomy*, they believe in their own ability to succeed in specific situations or to accomplish a task – also known as a sense of *self-efficacy,* and they are genuinely interested in accomplishing something to a high level of proficiency, knowledge and skill, not just in achieving good grades – also known as *mastery*.

2. Extrinsic motivation – this is the performance of an activity in order to attain a desired outcome. Extrinsic motivation comes from influences outside an individual's control, a rationale, a necessity, a need. Common forms of extrinsic motivation are rewards (for example, money or prizes), or – conversely – the threat of punishment. We can provide pupils with a rationale for learning by sharing the 'big picture' with them. In other words, we can continually explain how their learning fits in to the module, the course, the qualification, their careers and to success in work and life.

We said we can also motivate pupils to learn if we engender a culture of excellence in our classrooms because the first step towards motivating pupils to produce high-quality work is to set tasks which inspire and challenge them, and which are predicated on the idea that every pupil will succeed, not just finish the task set but produce work which represents personal excellence.

We also said that we can ensure *classwork is personally meaningful* – for example by triggering pupils' curiosity and by posing a big question that captures the heart of a topic in clear, compelling language, and we can give pupils some choice about how to conduct the work and present their findings.

We can also ensure that *classwork fulfils an educational purpose* – for example by providing domain-specific opportunities to build metacognition and character traits such as resilience, collaboration and communication, as well as study skills such as note-taking, critical thinking and self-study, and by emphasising the need to create high-quality products and performances through the formal use of feedback and drafting.

We then focused on ways of supporting disadvantaged pupils...

In order to help disadvantaged pupils to learn, we said, we can follow a three-point plan:

1. Identify the barriers
2. Plan the solutions
3. Agree the success criteria

Identify the barriers

Before we can put in place intervention strategies aimed at supporting disadvantaged pupils, we must first understand why a gap exists between the attainment of disadvantaged pupils and non-disadvantaged pupils. In short, we need to ask ourselves: What are the barriers to learning faced by our disadvantaged pupils? Are these barriers always in place or only for certain subjects, topics, skills, etc?

Plan the solutions

Once we have identified the barriers our disadvantaged pupils face towards learning, we need to plan the solutions. And one of the most effective solutions, though by no means the only one, is to focus on developing pupils' cultural capital...

Cultural capital takes myriad forms and is highly complex. There is not one single solution, but we have to start somewhere, and in Book Two of this series I suggested we start with vocabulary because we know with some certainty that a lack of early language and literacy skills is a major cause of disadvantage. The explicit instructions of tier 2 and 3 vocabulary – as defined by Isabel Beck – is therefore advisable but this must be done in domain-specific ways and only when relevant to disciplinary learning.

In addition, I suggested that strategies aimed to helping disadvantaged pupils work best when they focus on the following:

1. Improving pupils' transitions between the key stages and phases of education
2. Developing pupils' cross curricular literacy skills
3. Developing pupils' cross curricular numeracy skills

Agree the success criteria

The third and final action on our three-point plan is to *agree the success criteria*. Once we've identified the barriers to learning faced by our disadvantaged pupils and have planned the best solutions to help them overcome those barriers, we need to be clear about what success will look like. We need to ask ourselves: What is my aim here? For example, is it to: raise attainment; expedite progress; improve attendance; improve behaviour; reduce exclusions; improve parental engagement; or expand upon the number of opportunities afforded to disadvantaged pupils?

Whatever our immediate goal is, we said, ultimately, we should be seeking to diminish the difference between the attainment of disadvantaged pupils in our school and non-disadvantaged pupils nationally, as well as narrowing our within-school gaps. As such, if our initial aim is pastoral in nature, for example to improve behaviour and attendance, or reduce exclusions, then we must take it a step further and peg it to an academic outcome.

In *Part Five* of Book Two, we set out ways of creating the *culture* for implementation...

In Book One we said that senior leaders in schools and colleges have five key roles in terms of creating the right culture to implement an effective curriculum: firstly, they need to agree the vision for their whole school or college curriculum which involves defining what is meant by the term 'curriculum' and making decisions about the national, basic, local and hidden curriculums; secondly, they are key to determining how broad and balanced the whole school or college curriculum will be and why; thirdly, they need to articulate the purpose of education in their school or college – and therefore guide middle leaders in determining the broad 'end-points' (schools) or 'body of knowledge' (FE) to be taught; fourthly, they need to create the culture in which a curriculum can flourish; finally, they need to be the gatekeepers and defenders of staff skills and time.

Then, in Book Two, we said that the fourth and fifth roles were critical because, if we are not careful, curriculum intent and implementation are in danger of becoming a fad to which a considerable amount of time is dedicated.

As I explained in *Part Five* of Book Two, I am not suggesting improving curriculum design and ensuring teaching leads to long-term learning are not important endeavours and deserving of more of our time – I think they are – but I am saying that, if we decide we need colleagues to dedicate more time to these important processes, then we must also decide what they can stop doing in order that their overall workload does not increase; rather, that they focus their time on doing the things that will have the biggest impact on pupils.

As well as protecting our colleagues' workloads, we need to ensure they are helped to develop the knowledge and skills required to engage in effective curriculum thinking, design and delivery. This includes designing programmes of CPD that perform a dual function: firstly, that they help teachers and middle leaders to develop their pedagogical content knowledge so that they know more about effective teaching strategies and approaches; and secondly, that they help teachers and middle leaders to develop their subject-specific knowledge so that they know more about their chosen disciplines.

As well as creating the culture, in *Part Five* of Book Two, we explored ways of creating the *systems* for implementation... because a school, we said, also needs to attend to the following systems if their curriculum is to be effectively implemented: performance management and quality assurance.

Designing an effective *performance management* system, we said, might start by agreeing a set of expectations or standards against which teachers can be measured for the purposes of appraisal. One solution is the professional portfolio approach, not to be confused with a tick-box approach which mandates teachers to self-assess against a fixed set of criteria, but rather about teachers taking genuine responsibility for their own professional development and taking their professional practice seriously. Another possible solution is the 'balanced scorecard' approach – this works when criteria are quantifiable rather than qualitative – which is a means of aggregating a range of data.

Designing a *quality assurance* system, meanwhile, might start by consulting upon, agreeing and communicating a vision for the quality of education in our schools or colleges. This vision is unique to each institution because it reflects its local context. The next stage might be to write a short mission statement which articulates how that vision will be realised. The third stage might be to set the priorities for the next three years. These priorities should help focus the school or college on the actions it needs to take in order to achieve its vision and mission. Next might come the 'quality standards', the everyday behaviours and values you need your school or college to embody.

The purpose of quality assurance, we said, is to critically reflect on past performance in order to improve future performance. Self-evaluation requires subject leaders to state their position at the end of each academic year, the actions they took in the previous year to get there, the positive impact of those actions on pupils, each with supporting evidence, and the areas for improvement that remain and that they therefore need to focus on in the year ahead. The areas for improvement contained within the self-evaluation document, we said, should then be carried forward to the curriculum improvement plan and form the objectives for the year ahead. The curriculum improvement plan should be a live document used to record the actions required in-year in order to improve the quality of education each subject discipline provides. Each action taken to improve the quality of provision should be added to the plan alongside emerging evidence of its impact on pupils.

To quality assure each subject's provision and to support their curriculum improvements, subject leaders might take part in around three curriculum reviews during the academic year, roughly one per term. Each curriculum review, we said, should be a professional process used to support and challenge leaders. The process should begin and end with a curriculum improvement plan. The plan should be used to determine the nature of the review and to identify key areas of focus for the review. The outcome of the review process should, in turn, be an updated plan.

Our systems also need to promote *classroom consistency* – to help pupils avoid cognitive overload – and *collective autonomy* - whereby teachers plan together.

We also need to address the issues of teacher recruitment and retention if we are to have qualified subject specialists teaching all our pupils. In addition to dealing with the issue of workload, we said we could start to do this by:

- Addressing the nature of teachers' workloads
- Providing more opportunities for flexible working
- Improving pay and rewards
- Improving the quality of school facilities
- Improving the support leaders give to staff
- Providing more encouragement to teachers and make expectations clearer
- Improving the quality of initial teacher training
- Improving the availability of continuing professional development
- Improving the quality and relevance of CPD
- Tailoring the support offered to new teachers
- Providing opportunities for career progression including into leadership positions
- Improving the professional recognition and social standing of teachers

And that whistle-stop tour of Books One and Two in this series brings us to the here and now...

This book, Book Three – Impact, is, at least in part, about how we assess all of the above. We will return to this point more explicitly in Part One, Chapter Three of this book but, in order to ensure that we can have an informed discussion on the matter, let us first do two things:

Firstly, let us take a sideways step to explore the Ofsted context so that we can place our curriculum discussions in perspective and so that we can use a shared language thereafter. As I said above, we do so not because Ofsted are important but simply because their inspection document provides a useful framework for our exploration of the curriculum. Although readers from outside of England, including those colleagues I work with in Wales whose inspectorate is Estyn not Ofsted, may feel this section of the book is irrelevant, I still think the Ofsted inspection framework and methodology are of interest so please do bear with me. Alternatively, feel free to skip ahead.

Secondly, let us set out the central tenets of intent and implementation so that we can reflect on the final 'I' in our holy trinity: impact. This will involve some repetition but, again, I plead with you to bear with me because, even if you have read Books One and Two recently, I think a further examination of those first two I's of intent and implementation will help activate your prior knowledge in these areas which will, in turn, help you appreciate the interconnectedness of our three I's.

The Ofsted context

As I say above, if you are not based in England, have recently read Books One and Two in this series, or already have an in-depth knowledge of the Ofsted inspection process, feel free to skip this chapter although, if you have the time and inclination, you may still find it of use...

Ofsted, the schools and college inspectorate in England, published a new education inspection framework which came into effect in September 2019.

The purpose of this new framework, Ofsted says, is to discourage schools from narrowing their curriculum offer – perhaps in the form of running a three-year GCSE or closing down certain subjects.

The EIF is also intended to end practices such as teaching to the test – being blinkered by what the Chief Inspector of Schools, Amanda Spielman, calls the 'stickers and badges' of qualification outcomes at the expense of a more rounded education that better prepares pupils for the next stages of their education, employment and lives.

Finally, the EIF aims to tackle social justice issues, ending educational disadvantage and affording every child, no matter their starting point and background, an equal opportunity to access an ambitious curriculum and to succeed in school and college. This final aim is, in part, achieved by providing disadvantaged children with the knowledge and cultural capital they need to succeed in life.

So, before we progress further along our own curriculum journey towards 'impact', let us take a short pitstop to consider the Ofsted context...

The new key inspection judgments

There are four key judgment areas in the new EIF:

1. Quality of education
2. Behaviour and attitudes
3. Personal development, and
4. Leadership and management

In addition, as before, schools and colleges will receive an 'overall effectiveness' grade.

The old judgment pertaining to 'outcomes for pupils' has therefore been scrapped, making clear that test and/or exam results are no longer paramount and that schools in difficult circumstances which might not achieve good headline outcomes can nevertheless provide a good quality of education and serve their pupils well.

The 'teaching, learning and assessment' judgment has also gone. This implies that the focus will be on a whole school's provision – its curriculum – and how that curriculum is delivered and assessed, not so much on an individual teacher's classroom practice.

Both 'outcomes for pupils' and 'teaching, learning and assessment' have been subsumed within a new judgment called 'quality of education' which places the quality of the school curriculum centre-stage.

For the purposes of this series of books, we are focusing on the 'quality of education' judgment and its definition of curriculum according to its **intent, implementation** and **impact**...

Intent is "a framework for setting out the aims of a programme of education, including the knowledge and understanding to be gained at each stage".

Implementation is a means of "translating that framework over time into a structure and narrative within an institutional context".

Impact is the means of "evaluating what knowledge and understanding pupils have gained against expectations.

We might therefore conclude that:

- Intent is concerned with *curriculum design* and provision, the emphasis being on providing a broad and balanced curriculum for all pupils

- Implementation, meanwhile, is about *curriculum delivery*, in other words on teaching, assessment and feedback, crucially that which leads to long-term learning

- Impact is about *pupil progress and achievement* as assessed by external test and/or exam results and by using progression and destinations data, recognising that good outcomes are not just measured in qualifications but in how well pupils are developed as rounded citizens of the world

Earlier, I went even further and defined the 3I's simply as:

- Intent = *why and what?*
- Implementation = *how?*
- Impact = *how successfully?*

Each of the 3I's, Ofsted says, will not be graded separately but evidence for each will be aggregated into an overall grade for the 'quality of education'.

It is worth noting that 'quality of education' is considered a leading judgment – in other words, it will form the bulk of inspection activity, provide the majority of the evidence used to grade a school, and as such – put simply – if the quality of education is not judged to be 'good' then every other judgment and indeed 'overall effectiveness' are unlikely to be, though of course it's not impossible.

Before we home in on what more Ofsted has to say about the curriculum, let's examine some of the mechanics of inspection...

Preparation for inspection

In the draft handbook, Ofsted proposed that, for section 5 (i.e. full) inspections, inspectors would arrive on site the day before inspection activity began in order to prepare. But, following feedback from senior leaders, Ofsted has said that, rather than be on site, all preparation will continue to be carried out off site and the notice of inspection will remain at half a day.

However, Ofsted also said that the pilot inspections convinced them that inspectors could enhance the way that they prepared for inspection. Accordingly, under the 2019 EIF inspectors will increase considerably the amount of time they spend speaking to leaders about the education provided by the school or college during the normal pre-inspection telephone call.

Indeed, this phone call – which will take place in the afternoon before an inspection, after '*the* call' (I.e., the one giving notice) has been made, will now last for approximately ninety minutes.

Inspectors will use this conversation to understand:

- The school or college's context, and the progress that's been made since the previous inspection, including any specific progress made on areas for improvement identified at previous inspections
- The headteacher's or college quality nominee's assessment of the school's or college's current strengths and weaknesses, particularly in relation to the curriculum, the way teaching supports pupils to learn the curriculum, the standards that pupils achieve, pupils' behaviour and attitudes, and personal development
- The extent to which all pupils have access to the school's or college's full curriculum
- A discussion of specific areas of the school (subjects, year groups, and so on; and in the case of FE colleges, the types of provision on offer) that will be a focus of attention during inspection.

This call will, Ofsted says, give inspectors and headteachers/nominees a shared understanding of the starting point of the inspection. It will also help inspectors to form an initial understanding of leaders' view of the school's progress and to shape the inspection plan.

The method of inspection

In tandem with the final EIF, Ofsted outlined its methodology for inspection. Inspection activity will, it said, take three forms:

1. **Top-level view**: inspectors and leaders will start with a top-level view of the school's curriculum, exploring what is on offer, to whom and when, leaders' understanding of curriculum intent and sequencing, and why these choices were made.

2. **Deep dive**: next, they will be a 'deep dive' which will involve gathering evidence on the curriculum intent, implementation and impact over a sample of subjects, topics or aspects. This, Ofsted says, will be done in collaboration with leaders, teachers and pupils. The intent of the deep dive is to seek to interrogate and establish a coherent evidence base on the quality of education.

3. **Bringing it together:** finally, inspectors will bring the evidence together to widen coverage and to test whether any issues identified during the deep dives are systemic. This will usually lead to school leaders bringing forward further evidence and inspectors gathering additional evidence.

Top level view

This will largely take place during the initial 90-minute phone call between the lead inspector and headteacher/nominee and, as I say above, will focus on the school's context, the headteacher's assessment of the school's current strengths and weaknesses, the extent to which all pupils have access to the full curriculum, and specific areas of the school (subjects, year groups, aspects of provision, and so on) that will be a focus of attention during inspection.

Deep dive

The deep dive, meanwhile, will take place throughout the inspection visit and will include the following elements:

- An evaluation of senior leaders' intent for the curriculum in any given subject or area, and their understanding of its implementation and impact

- An evaluation of curriculum leaders' long- and medium-term thinking and planning, including the rationale for content choices and curriculum sequencing
- Visits to a deliberately and explicitly connected sample of lessons
- The work scrutiny of books or other kinds of work produced by pupils who are part of classes that have also been (or will also be) observed by inspectors
- A discussion with teachers to understand how the curriculum informs their choices about content and sequencing to support effective learning
- A discussion with a group of pupils from the lessons observed.

Ofsted says that, during deep dives, context will matter. Carrying out lesson visits or work scrutiny without context will, they accept, limit the validity of their judgments.

It is important that, in order to make lesson visits and work scrutiny more accurate, inspectors know the purpose of the lesson (or the task in a workbook), how it fits into a sequence of lessons over time, and what pupils already knew and understood before the lesson began. Conversations with teachers and subject leads will, they say, provide this contextual information.

Ofsted also says that a sequence of lessons, not an individual lesson, will be their unit of assessment – accordingly, inspectors will need to evaluate where a lesson sits in a sequence, and leaders'/teachers' understanding of this.

As has been the case for some years – though perhaps not as widely known as some of us would like – inspectors will not grade individual lessons or teachers.

Ofsted says that work scrutiny will form a part of the evidence inspectors will use to judge whether or not the intended curriculum is being enacted. They'll ask: Do the pupils' books support other evidence that what the school set out to teach has, indeed, been covered?

Work scrutiny activities, Ofsted says, can provide part of the evidence to show whether pupils know more, remember more and can do more, but only as one component of the deep dive which includes lesson visits and conversations with leaders, teachers and pupils.

Coverage is a prerequisite for learning, Ofsted says; but simply having covered a part of the curriculum does not in itself indicate that pupils know or remember more.

Work scrutiny activities cannot be used to demonstrate that an individual pupil is working 'at the expected standard' or similar, and it is not always valid – Ofsted admits – to attempt to judge an individual pupil's individual progress by comparing books from that pupil at two points in time.

Ofsted says that inspectors can make appropriately secure judgments on curriculum, teaching and behaviour across a particular deep dive when four to six lessons are visited, and inspectors have spoken to the curriculum lead and teachers to understand where each lesson sits in the sequence of lessons.

The greater the number of visits, therefore, the more that inspectors can see the variation in practice across a deep dive. However, there is a point after which additional visits do little to enhance the validity of evidence. Since an inspection evidence base will include multiple deep dives, the total number of lessons visited over the course of the inspection will substantially exceed four to six.

Ofsted says that inspectors should review a minimum of six workbooks (or pieces of work) per subject per year group and scrutinise work from at least two-year groups in order to ensure that evidence is not excessively dependent on a single cohort. Normally, inspectors will repeat this exercise across each of the deep dives, subjects, key stages or year groups in which they carry out lesson visits.

Bringing it together

At the end of day one, the inspection team will meet to begin to bring the evidence together. The purpose of this important meeting is to:

- Share the evidence gathered so far to continue to build a picture of the quality of education, identifying which features appear to be systemic and which are isolated to a single aspect

- Allow the lead inspector to quality assure the evidence, and especially its 'connectedness'
- Establish which inspection activities are most appropriate and valid on day 2 to come to conclusions about which features are systemic
- Bring together evidence about personal development, behaviour and attitudes, safeguarding, wider leadership findings, and so on, in order to establish what further inspection activity needs to be done on day 2 to come to the key judgments.

Inspecting the curriculum

According to the inspection handbooks, inspectors will take a range of evidence, including that held in electronic form, into account when making judgments.

This, Ofsted says, will include official national data, discussions with leaders, staff and pupils, questionnaire responses and work in pupils' books and folders.

Gathering evidence

Before we consider what inspectors will want to do and see both before and during an inspection, I think it equally valuable to clarify what inspectors will not do and see because this can bust some unhelpful myths...

What Ofsted does NOT want

Ofsted makes clear that inspectors will not grade individual lessons, create unnecessary workload for teachers, routinely check personnel files (although inspectors may look at a small sample), or advocate a particular method of planning, teaching or assessment.

Likewise, Ofsted will not require schools to provide any written record of teachers' verbal feedback to pupils, individual lesson plans, predictions of attainment and progress scores, assessment or self-evaluation (other than that which is already part the school's business processes).

Ofsted will not require performance and pupil-tracking information, monitoring of teaching and learning and its link to teachers' professional development and the teachers' standards (other than that which is already part of the school's normal activity), specific details of the pay grade of individual teachers who are observed during inspection, or processes for the performance management arrangements for school leaders and staff.

What's more, Ofsted does not expect schools or colleges to carry out a specified amount of lesson observations, use the Ofsted evaluation schedule to grade teaching or individual lessons, ensure a particular frequency or quantity of work in pupils' books or folders, take any specific steps with regard to site security (in particular, inspectors do not have a view about the need for perimeter fences), or carry out assessments or record pupils' achievements in any subject, including foundation subjects in primary schools, in a specific way, format or time.

Ofsted does not expect secondary schools to be at similar stages of EBacc implementation as any other schools. They do not expect any schools or colleges to provide additional information outside of their normal curriculum planning, or to produce a self-evaluation document or summary in any particular format.

Ofsted does not specify that tutor groups/form time must include literacy, numeracy or other learning sessions, nor does it dictate the frequency, type or volume of marking and feedback, or the content of, or approach to, headteacher/principal and staff performance management.

So far so pragmatic. It is, I think, helpful that Ofsted has set out – and so explicitly – what it does not want or expect to see in order to dispel myths and prevent unhelpful leadership practices from emerging.

What Ofsted does want

As well as any publicly available information about the school, inspectors will look at a summary of any school self-evaluations (usually called the SEF, or, in the case of FE settings, the self-assessment report or SAR) and the current school improvement plan (the SIP or SDP which, as I'm sure you know, stands for school development plan) including any planning that sets out the longer-term vision for the school, such as the school or academy trust's strategy (or, in FE settings, the college strategy and quality improvement plan or QIP).

They will expect schools and colleges to have to hand at the start of an inspection the single central record, a list of staff and whether any relevant staff are absent, whether any teachers cannot be observed for any reason (for example, where they are subject to capability procedures), whether there is anyone working on site who is normally employed elsewhere (such as at a different school in a MAT or on a different site of a merged college group), and maps and other practical information.

They'll also want copies of the school's timetable, a current staff list and times for the school day, the Pupil Premium strategy, any information about previously planned interruptions to normal school routines during the period of inspection, records and analysis of exclusions, pupils taken off roll, incidents of poor behaviour and any use of internal isolation, records and analysis of bullying, discriminatory and prejudiced behaviour, either directly or indirectly, including racist, sexist, disability and homophobic/biphobic/transphobic bullying, use of derogatory language and racist incidents.

Ofsted also wants a list of referrals made to the designated person for safeguarding in the school or college and those who were subsequently referred to the local authority, along with brief details of the resolution, a list of all pupils who have open cases with children's services/social care and for whom there is a multi-agency plan, up-to-date attendance analysis for all groups of pupils, documented evidence of the work of those responsible for governance and their priorities, including any written scheme of delegation for an academy in a MAT and details of governance within a merged college group, and any reports from external evaluation of the school or college.

What Ofsted will do

During an inspection, inspectors will gather further evidence by observing lessons, scrutinising pupils' work, talking to pupils about their work, gauging both their understanding and their engagement in learning, and obtaining pupils' perceptions of the typical quality of education in a range of subjects.

Discussions with pupils and staff will also be used as evidence (as will – in primary schools – listening to pupils read), and inspectors will look at examples of pupils' work for evidence of progress in knowledge, understanding and skills towards defined endpoints.

The lead inspector will invite the headteacher or nominee, curriculum leaders and other leaders to take part in joint observations of lessons. Inspectors will not take a random sample of lesson observations. Instead, they will connect lesson observation to other evidence. Lesson observation will be used for gathering evidence about 'implementation' and how lessons contribute to the quality of education. And observations will provide direct evidence about how behaviour is managed within individual classrooms.

The lead inspector will also invite curriculum leaders and teachers to take part in joint scrutiny of pupils' work. Inspectors will not evaluate individual workbooks or teachers. Inspectors will connect work scrutiny to lesson observation and, where possible, conversations with pupils and staff. Work scrutiny will be used for gathering evidence about the 'impact' of the quality of education. Inspectors may also use work scrutiny to evaluate pupils' progression through the curriculum.

Those are the mechanics of inspection under the 2019 EIF. Now let's focus on the role that the curriculum will play in inspections...

What Ofsted say about the curriculum

As I said earlier, Ofsted defines the curriculum in terms of its intent, implementation and impact. Let's take a closer look at what Ofsted has to say about each of those '3I's'...

1. Intent

When inspecting 'intent' in <u>schools</u>, inspectors will look to see whether or not the curriculum builds towards **clear 'end points'**. In other words, they will want to see clear evidence of what pupils will be expected to know and do by each of these end points, be they the end of a year, key stage or phase.

In <u>FE</u> settings, rather than clear end-points, inspectors will look to see if curriculum managers and teachers have identified the **'body**

of knowledge' students will be expected to acquire. Ofsted defines this 'body of knowledge' as the technical, vocational and life skills that a learner needs so that they will thrive in the future and not be left behind. It's worth a college considering how this body of knowledge has been influenced by the provider's local context and by the typical gaps in learners' knowledge and skills. It's also worth considering the extent to which the college takes account of the knowledge, skills and behaviours that learners bring with them.

Inspectors will also want to see evidence that a school's or college's curriculum is **planned and sequenced** so that new knowledge and skills build on what has been taught before, and towards those defined end points.

As well as being clearly sequenced and building towards a clear end-point, Ofsted says that a curriculum should also **reflect the provider's local context** by addressing typical gaps in pupils' and students' knowledge and skills.

The curriculum should remain as broad as possible for as long as possible, too, and, in schools, pupils should be afforded the opportunity to study a strong academic core of subjects, such as those offered by the English Baccalaureate (EBacc). In colleges, we might assume that inspectors will want to see that students are afforded the opportunity to study a well-rounded study programme which includes English and maths, employability and enrichment opportunities.

In schools, inspectors will want to see evidence that there are **high ambitions for all pupils**, whether they are academic, vocational or technical in nature. And Ofsted will want to see that the school does not offer disadvantaged pupils or pupils with SEND a reduced curriculum.

In FE settings, meanwhile, inspectors will seek to assure themselves that the provider intends to **include all its learners in its high academic, technical and vocational ambitions**. They will also seek to assure themselves that the provider offers disadvantaged learners or those with SEND, including those who are eligible for High Needs funding, a curriculum that remains ambitious and meets their needs.

In FE, it is also expected that the provider's curriculum intent will have regard to the needs of learners, employers, and the local, regional and national economy as necessary.

Curriculum narrowing

Talking of a reduced curriculum, inspectors will be particularly alert to signs of narrowing in the key stages 2 and 3 curriculums in primary and secondary schools respectively. In other words, if a school has shortened key stage 3, inspectors will look to see that the school has made provision to ensure that pupils still have the opportunity to study a broad range of subjects in Years 7 to 9.

At the heart of an effective key stage 4 curriculum, Ofsted says, is a strong academic core: the EBacc. On this point, the schools' inspection handbook invites contention. It restates the government's response to its EBacc consultation, published in July 2017, which was a commitment that a large majority of pupils should be expected to study the EBacc. Indeed, it is therefore the government's ambition that 75% of Year 10 pupils in state-funded mainstream schools should be starting to study EBacc GCSE courses nationally by 2022, rising to 90% by 2025. Including this information in the handbook implies that Ofsted will expect schools to be working towards these goals and will have some explaining to do if they fall short. However, as I said above, Ofsted will not expect all schools to be at similar stages of implementation.

Cultural capital

There are several explicit mentions of 'cultural capital' in the schools' inspection handbook. Ofsted says that inspectors will judge the extent to which schools and colleges are equipping pupils with the knowledge and cultural capital they need to succeed in life. Ofsted's definition of this knowledge and cultural capital matches that found in the aims of the national curriculum: namely, that it is "the essential knowledge that pupils need to be educated citizens, introducing them to the best that has been thought and said and helping to engender an appreciation of human creativity and achievement".

In FE settings, Ofsted argues that the curriculum is a powerful means to address social disadvantage, giving learners access to the highest levels of knowledge, skills and experience. As such, the curriculum should be based on a firm agreement about what education and training should be provided for each learner.

2. Implementation

Under curriculum implementation, inspectors will seek evidence of how the school curriculum is taught at subject and classroom level. They will want to see how teachers enable pupils to understand key concepts, presenting information clearly and promoting appropriate discussion, how teachers check pupils' understanding effectively, identifying and correcting misunderstandings, and how teachers ensure that **pupils embed key concepts in their long-term memory** and apply them fluently.

Further, they will want to see if the subject curriculum that classes follow is designed and delivered in a way that allows pupils to transfer key knowledge to long-term memory and it is sequenced so that **new knowledge and skills build on what has been taught before** and towards defined end points.

In FE settings, Ofsted argues that teachers need sufficient subject knowledge, pedagogical knowledge and pedagogical content knowledge to be able teach learners effectively. Ofsted recognises that there will be areas in which staff are not yet experts, so inspectors will explore what leaders are doing to support staff to ensure that no learner receives poor teaching.

Effective teaching and training should, Ofsted argues, ensure that learners in FE settings **know more and remember what they have learned** within the context of the approach that teachers have selected to serve the aims of their curriculum. Consequently, learners will be able to apply vocational and technical skills fluently and independently.

In both schools and FE settings, inspectors will want to see evidence that teachers use assessment to check pupils' understanding, and they will evaluate how assessment is used in the school or college to support the teaching of the curriculum, but – crucially – not in a way that substantially increases teachers' workloads. By including reference to the report of the Teacher Workload Advisory Group, 'Making data work', which recommends that school leaders should not have more than two or three data collection points a year,

Ofsted rather implies – I think – that it will expect schools to follow this advice or have a solid rationale for not doing so.

In practice, I would argue that effective curriculum implementation involves high quality teaching which leads to long-term learning. Talking of which...

John Sweller's 'Cognitive Load Theory' (2011) posits that, "If nothing has altered in long-term memory nothing has been learned." The educational psychologist Paul Kirschner, meanwhile, defines learning as a change in long-term memory.

For its part, Ofsted argues that:

- Progress means knowing more and remembering more
- Knowledge is generative (or 'sticky'), i.e., the more you know, the easier it is to learn
- Knowledge is connected in webs or schemata
- Knowledge is when humans make connections between the new and what has already been learned

We might, therefore, meaningfully define long-term learning as the acquisition of new information (knowledge, skills and understanding) and the application of that information at a later time and in a range of contexts. The theory being this: for pupils to succeed, particularly on linear courses with terminal assessments after a year or two, they must be able to retain information over the long-term. They must also be able to apply what they've learnt in one context to other contexts such as in an exam, in the workplace and in life.

Now let's turn to the third and final 'I' of the Ofsted framework and the subject of this book...

3. Impact

Under impact, inspectors will gather evidence to help them judge whether the most disadvantaged pupils in a school or college – as well as pupils with SEND or those eligible for High Needs funding – are given the knowledge and cultural capital they need to succeed in life.

Ofsted says that national assessments and examinations are useful indicators of the outcomes pupils in the school achieve, but that they only represent a sample of what pupils have learned. As such, inspectors will balance these with their assessment of the standard of pupils' work from the first-hand evidence they gather on inspection.

Ofsted says that learning in schools must build towards a goal. As such, at each stage of pupils' education, they will want to see evidence that they're being prepared for the next stage of education, training or employment, and will consider whether pupils are ready for that next stage.

In FE settings, inspectors will make clear that there need be no conflict between teaching a broad, rich curriculum and achieving success in examinations and tests. A well-constructed, well-taught curriculum will lead to good results because those results will reflect what students have learned.

In FE, as in schools, national tests and examinations are therefore a useful indicator of the outcomes that learners achieve, and inspectors will balance these with their assessment of the achievement of learners drawn from the first-hand evidence they gather on inspection about non-qualification activity and the progress that learners make from starting points.

As in schools, Ofsted says that learning in further education settings must build towards a goal. At each stage of learners' education, they are being prepared for the next stage of education, training or employment or independence. Inspectors of FE provision will consider whether learners are ready for the next stage by the time they leave the provider or provision that they attend. Inspectors in FE will also consider whether learners are ready for the next stage and are going to appropriate, high-quality destinations.

If, having read the last few paragraphs, you're getting a strange sense of déjà vu, then you should: Ofsted, like me, believe schools and FE have more in common than that which divides them, and so apply the same rationale and indeed the same high standards to all phases of education – hence the eerily similar language used in both inspection handbooks.

Measuring outcomes

In terms of the evidence of impact, inspectors say they will use nationally-generated performance information about pupil progress and attainment – that which is available in the IDSR – as well as first-hand evidence of how pupils are doing, drawing together evidence from the interviews, observations, work scrutinies and documentary review described above. They will use nationally-published information about the destinations to which its pupils and students progress when they leave the school or college, and – in primary schools – they will listen to a range of pupils read.

Ofsted will not want to see internal assessment data such as that used to track progress in-year. Ofsted says that this is because inspectors do not want to add to school leaders' and teachers' workload by having them produce lots of data for the purposes of inspection. Unsaid but also a probable factor in this decision, is the belief that some schools and colleges will present 'massaged' data that isn't accurate or helpful.

In the final version of the inspection framework and handbooks, Ofsted softened its position with regards a school's and college's internal data. They clarified that they would be interested in hearing the conclusions headteachers/principals, nominees, and school and college leaders had drawn from their own data but would not want to see the data itself.

As such, I'd recommend that senior leaders extrapolate their own data and have clear findings to share.

What has Ofsted previously opined about curriculum?

Before we move away from Ofsted and begin our deeper exploration of curriculum impact, I think it worthwhile mining some recent inspection evidence because this might prove useful when considering what Ofsted regards as strengths and weaknesses of school and college curriculums...

Evaluations of inspection reports show that, in the past, Ofsted has regarded the following – which I have taken the liberty of paraphrasing – as strengths:

- Leaders review the curriculum regularly and check the impact on outcomes for all pupils, then remodel it to help all pupils perform well
- Leaders are attuned to research findings, as well as reforms to national curriculum and qualifications, and use this to inform how their local curriculum is developed to improve outcomes and pupils' personal development
- Careers education, information, advice and guidance (CEIAG) is integral to the curriculum and pupils' progression, and the curriculum helps pupils to experience and learn about their options for their future
- There is a recognition that challenge is for all not just the most able pupils.

Conversely, Ofsted has noted the following – which, again, I have paraphrased – as weaknesses:

- Coordination of numeracy and literacy across the curriculum is poor and, as such, pupils struggle to read and access learning
- Support from middle leaders to develop pedagogy is poor – notably in mixed ability classes in Key Stage 3
- Pupils in Key Stage 3 repeat work from primary school which leaves them bored and frustrated by the lack of challenge
- There is a lack of understanding and coherence in assessment, and a lack of oversight
- Expectations of pupils are low
- The timetable is fragmented and poorly planned, leading to a lack of coherence across the curriculum
- Leaders are slow to tackle issues as a result of teacher vacancies and lack innovation to sustain a good curriculum despite teacher shortages.

Part One: The curriculum design process

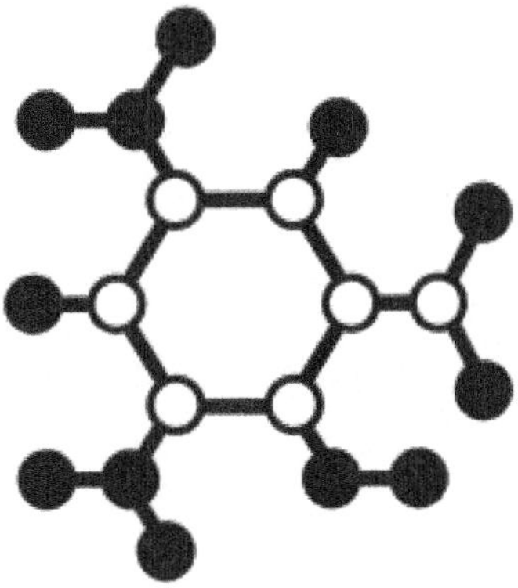

Chapter 1: What is curriculum intent?

As I explained in the chapter entitled 'the story so far' when summarising the content of Book One in this series, I advocate a 6-step process of curriculum *intent*...

1. Agree a vision
2. Set the destination
3. Assess the starting points
4. Identify the waypoints
5. Define excellence
6. Diminish disadvantage

For the benefit of those who have read Book One, or not done so recently, let us now take a look at each of those six steps in turn, albeit briefly, because we will return to these ideas later in this book when we consider the purposes of assessment...

Step 1: Agree the vision

The first step towards designing an effective curriculum is to agree the vision. This requires each school and college to consult on and then communicate a shared definition of what is meant by the word 'curriculum', as well as a working definition of what that curriculum encompasses in practice within the context of that school or college. This working definition might include, where relevant, aspects of the national, basic, local and hidden curriculums.

Agreeing the vision is also about defining what a school or college interprets as being a 'broad and balanced' curriculum. It means deciding upon and articulating the purpose of education within that school or college (why do we exist, what is our hope for all pupils and students?) and using this to write a vision against which all future curriculum decisions can be measured.

Talking of measurements, agreeing the vision is also about designing a meaningful assessment system which uses the curriculum as the progression model rather than relying on arbitrary grades, levels or numbers. This progression model should clearly show where each pupil and student is at any point in time by cataloguing what they know and can do, and what they do not yet know and cannot yet do – in other words, which aspects of the curriculum they have mastered and which they have not.

Senior leaders have several roles to play at this stage of the curriculum design process including working hard to create a whole-school or -college culture in which the curriculum can thrive. This culture, I argued, has three layers: the staff culture; the pupil and student culture; and the learning culture.

Senior leaders must also ensure their middle leaders and teachers are afforded sufficient time to engage in the curriculum planning process and are equipped with the knowledge and skills required for this complex task, including through the provision of quality professional development that performs the dual functions of developing subject knowledge *and* pedagogical content knowledge.

Step 2: Set the destination

The second step towards designing an effective curriculum is to set the destination which is about identifying what we want all pupils and students to know and be able to do at the end of their curriculum journeys – be that at the end of a module or topic, at the end of a year, key stage or phase, at the end of their school or college studies, or indeed in ten years' time.

This stage begins by developing a shared understanding of the importance of knowledge – including cultural capital – and then agreeing, within subject disciplines or curriculum areas, *what* knowledge matters most to our pupils' and students' future successes.

Knowledge is needed, not simply to pass qualifications, but also to enable pupils and students to be genuinely prepared for the next stages of their education, employment and lives. As such, the knowledge base must be broad, encompassing employability and enrichment skills, cross-curricular skills such as literacy and numeracy, and research and study skills such as note-taking, and approaches to learning such as metacognition and self-regulation. What's more, the knowledge base must be suitably challenging for all.

A part of the process of setting the destination is identifying the key concepts that must be taught – and learnt – in each subject discipline. These 'foundational' concepts – a combination of knowledge *and* skills – provide the 'end points' or 'body of knowledge' towards which all pupils are headed.

Step 3: Assess the starting points

The third step towards designing an effective curriculum is to assess the starting points and this, broadly speaking, takes two forms: the starting points of the *taught* curriculum and the starting points of the *learnt* curriculum.

The taught curriculum is that which is written down in curriculum plans (national curriculum documents, awarding body specifications, schemes of work, and so forth) and taught by teachers. The learnt curriculum, meanwhile, is that which each pupil or student has actually acquired, what they really know and can do – including their misconceptions and misunderstandings.

In terms of the *taught* curriculum, it's important to know the end points of the previous curriculum – what pupils are expected to know and be able to do by the time they begin studying your curriculum because you need to ensure, as far as is possible, that there is curriculum continuity – that each stage of education flows smoothly and naturally into the next and that each new year, key stage and phase of education consolidates and builds upon what has gone before rather than needlessly repeating prior content. This can be achieved, in part, by ensuring that transition arrangements are improved and that teachers and middle leaders in each phase work more closely with their counterparts in the preceding and succeeding phases in order to share data and engage in joint professional development and curriculum planning.

In terms of the *learnt* curriculum, it's important to understand what each pupil knows and can do and what they do not yet know and cannot yet do. This can be achieved, in part, through better data-sharing but also by using ongoing assessments such as class discussions, hinge questions, multiple-choice quizzes, and exit tickets in order to ascertain where each pupils' 'struggle zone' is positioned as well as to activate their prior learning.

Step 4: Identify the waypoints

The fourth step towards designing an effective curriculum is to identify the waypoints. Once the destination and the starting points are known, the curriculum must carve a path between the two and this path must grow ever steeper as pupils near the end. In other words, the curriculum needs to be increasingly complex and challenging as pupils travel through it, and it must help pupils to develop as independent learners, too. One way to do this is to identify the threshold concepts that pupils must acquire at each stage – the checkpoints through which they must pass on the way to their destination. These thresholds concepts can also act as a source of meaningful assessment – a progression model – which measure pupils' progress.

Step 5: Define excellence

The fifth step towards designing an effective curriculum is to define excellence so that our curriculum is ambitious for all but that each pupil and student is afforded equal access to the curriculum and is supported to travel through it and achieve.

This is, in part, about developing a growth mindset, believing that every pupil and student is capable of achieving excellence, no matter their starting points and backgrounds. But it is also about 'teaching to the top' for all pupils and not dumbing down or reducing the curriculum offer for disadvantaged pupils for that is only to double their disadvantage.

Defining excellence and providing equal access to an ambitious curriculum is also about having high expectations of every pupil and about explicitly teaching them the study and research skills – including how to take notes and revise – that they need to succeed.

Delivering excellence requires the curriculum – and teachers – to pitch learning at the appropriate level, which is to say hard but achievable because if the work is too easy or too difficult then pupils simply will not learn.

Step 6: Diminish disadvantage

The sixth and final step towards designing an effective curriculum is to diminish disadvantage because if we are to provide an ambitious curriculum for all we must also accept that not all pupils and students start from the same point and that some will require more support and more time to reach their destination.

We diminish disadvantage by closing the gap between disadvantaged pupils – including those with SEND or High Needs – and their peers. This can, in part, be achieved by identifying the academic barriers that each pupil and student faces, then choosing the appropriate strategies to support them to overcome those barriers, and finally setting the success criteria for them. Intervention strategies work best when they are short term, intensive, focused and tailored. What's more, there is no substitute for quality first teaching and so improving teacher and teaching quality must always take precedence.

One way to support disadvantaged pupils is to use research evidence such as the EEF toolkit which posits that feedback and metacognition are the most impactful strategies at a teacher's disposal. But the application of such evidence must be carried out carefully because each pupil is different, just as each teacher, each class and each school or college is different, and so what works for one might not necessarily work for others.

We can also help to diminish the disadvantage by better understanding the root cause of that disadvantage. One such cause – though by no means the only cause – is a lack of cultural capital. One of the most tangible forms that cultural capital takes is vocabulary and so our curriculum should be a means of explicitly teaching vocabulary – the language *of* and *for* learning – in order to equip pupils and students with the tools they need to access the curriculum and achieve.

The journey's end

And those are the six steps I recommended you follow in Book One of this series when embarking upon your 'curriculum intent' journey but it is also worth using this process when *reviewing* the effectiveness of your existing curriculum – which is a part of 'impact', hence me summarising it again here.

Of course, curriculum intent is only really the start... pupils and students experience the curriculum, not through specifications, schemes of work and lesson plans, but through the teaching, learning and assessment that takes place in the classroom and, as such, it is crucial that our broad, balanced and ambitious curriculum is taught in a way that's effective and leads to long-term learning...

Teaching for long-term learning

Once we've designed a broad, balanced, and ambitious curriculum to which all our pupils and students have access and are supported to achieve its destinations, we must translate it into classroom practice for this is how pupils encounter a curriculum: in the interactions that take place between teachers and learners, and between different learners, in the classroom, on the sports field, and in workshops and labs.

As I explained in Book Two, the secret to teaching our curriculum in a way that leads to long-term learning is to follow three steps, namely:

1. Create a positive learning environment in order to stimulate sensory memory

2. Make pupils think hard but efficiently in order to gain the attention of - but cheat - working memory

3. Plan for deliberate practice in order to improve storage in, and retrieval from, long-term memory

I first articulated my 3-step approach to long-term learning in my book, How to Learn, and included an updated and abridged version of this in Book Two if this series.

Allow me to briefly explain this process for you now...

We learn by means of an interaction between our sensory memory (sometimes referred to as our 'environment') and our long-term memory. Our sensory memory is made up of: what we see – this is called our iconic memory; what we hear – this is called our echoic memory; and what we touch – our haptic memory. Our long-term memory is where new information is stored and from which it can be recalled when needed, but we cannot directly access the information stored in our long-term memory. As such, the interaction that takes place between our sensory memory and our long-term memory occurs in our working memory, or short-term memory, which is the only place where we can think and do.

It might be helpful to think of our sensory memory as a haulage truck, our long-term memory as a warehouse, and our working memory as the holding bay where new deliveries are received, processed and labelled ready for stowing. The payload cannot be passed directly into the warehouse, it must first pass through the holding bay to be sorted.

In order to stimulate our pupils' sensory memories and thus engage the active attention of their working memories and make them think, we need to create classroom conditions conducive to learning, conditions that stimulate pupils' iconic, echoic and haptic memories. In other words, we need to engage pupils' senses in order to gain their attention.

It might sound like common sense - and indeed it is - to say that, for our pupils to learn, we must first gain their attention, but it's all too easy for learning to fail simply because we haven't stimulated our pupils' senses and therefore gained their attention, or because we have focused their attention on the wrong things.

I'm sure you're familiar with the Dancing Gorilla Awareness Test. If not, briefly: observers are asked to watch a video of a group of about eight people playing basketball and are told to count the number of passes made by the players dressed in white, ignoring the players in black. In the middle of the game, a man or woman in a gorilla suit dances across the court, weaving his or her way through the players. Most observers count the number of passes correctly but utterly fail to spot the gorilla. Their attention is not grabbed by the gorilla because they don't expect to see such an incongruous thing and are only focused on the ball as it passes from one player in white to another.

Sadly, this happens in our lessons all the time: our pupils miss what is right at the ends of their noses because either we've failed to gain the active attention of their working memories or have focused that active attention on the wrong things. For example, if I wanted a class to research the origins of two online encyclopaedias, Wikipedia and Microsoft's Encarta, and find out why Wikipedia – with no money and a reliance on volunteers to act as contributors – proved more successful than the encyclopaedia backed by big business, boasting an army of well-paid, qualified staff including Bill Gates, and asked them to do so on the internet, there's a danger that they would focus their attention on the act of researching rather than on the topic they'd been asked to research.

In other words, if I didn't explicitly teach them the skills needed to carry out the task and learn about Wikipedia, they would use all their working memory capacity on acquiring and using these skills and none, or very little, on the content.

They'd have to think about where to search, what search terms to use, how to sift information and make decisions about what was relevant and what was not, what was reliable and what was not. However, if I'd explicitly taught them how to conduct independent research - such as the use of three independent sources, skimming and scanning for key facts and names and dates, how to use quotations, how to detect inference and bias, etc., then modelled the process and got them to practice the skills until they become automatic – then they could have focused their attentions on the information they'd found out about Wikipedia (such as: In 2009, the year Encarta closed, only 1.27% of encyclopaedia searches in America were carried out using Encarta; Wikipedia meanwhile accounted for 97%) not on how to research that information.

This is important because if you don't think, you don't learn. We must gain pupils' active attentions and make them think hard in order for information to be processed in their working memories and then encoded in their long-term memories. And if we get them thinking hard about *how* to research, then they will process and encode this and learn nothing – or too little – about *what* they researched.

In short, stimulating pupils' sensory memories and focusing their attention on the right things is essential if our pupils are to engage their working memories.

Talking of which...

In order to help pupils to utilise their limited working memories (depending on which research you read, it's thought that we can only handle between five and nine concepts in working memory at any one time - see, for example, Miller 1956), we need to ensure they are made to think hard - are challenged with work that is difficult but achievable.

If the work is too easy, pupils will be able to complete it through habit and without thinking - this is called 'automaticity'. For example, if I asked you to calculate 2 x 10, you would do so automatically, through habit, without having to think about it because you likely mastered your times tables many years ago.

If the work's too hard, pupils will be unable to complete it because they will overpower their limited working memories with too much information (what's called 'cognitive overload') and the learning process will fail. For example, if I asked you to calculate 367 x 2892 in your head in a minute, you wouldn't be able to do so. Chances are, you'd do one of two things instead: Either you'd not attempt it because you'd quickly assess the task to be beyond your reach and therefore a pointless waste of energy; or you'd attempt it but be unable to hold so much information in your working memory and so would fail. Either way, you would be demotivated by your failure and, more importantly, you wouldn't have learnt or practised anything, so the task would have been pointless.

Like Goldilocks, you need to find the bowl of porridge that's neither too hot nor too cold but is just right. In other words, you need to pitch your curriculum in the 'struggle zone', or what Robert Bjork calls the 'sweet spot' at the edge of pupils' current knowledge and abilities, albeit just within their reach. Lev Vygotsky defined this as the 'zone of proximal development' which is sandwiched between what pupils can do unaided and cannot yet do, in the area which is hard but achievable with time, effort and support.

But, in making pupils think hard, we also need to help them think efficiently. Thinking, as we have seen, will fail if pupils overload their working memories. As such, we need to help pupils cheat the limited space in their working memories (to mitigate cognitive overload) by learning new things within the context of what they already know (allowing them to 'chunk' information together to save space) and by teaching the requisite knowledge and skills before they are applied because, as Daniel Willingham puts it in his book Why Students Don't Like School, "memory is the residue of thought".

Once pupils have been made to think hard but efficiently and have processed information in their working memories, we need to ensure they encode that information into their long-term memories and can easily retrieve it again later.

In order to help pupils store information in their practically limitless long-term memories (long term memory is so big, it will take more than a lifetime to fill it), we need to plan opportunities for deliberate practice, and we need to use two teaching strategies called spacing and interleaving.

Only by repeating learning and by doing so in a range of contexts, will we increase the storage strength of the information in long term memory. The better the storage strength, the more readily available will be our knowledge and skills.

Repeating learning - the very act of recalling prior knowledge and skills from long term memory - also improves their retrieval strength. The better the retrieval strength, the more easily, quickly and efficiently are knowledge and skills recalled from long term memory and brought into the working memory where they can be used.

The best form of repetition is purposeful practice which has well-defined, specific goals, is focused, involves feedback, and requires pupils to get out of their comfort zones because, if they don't push themselves beyond their comfort zones, they'll never improve. Getting out of their comfort zones means trying to do something that they couldn't do before. In this respect, the secret is not to "try harder" but rather to "try differently."

And so, in summary, there are – as I explained in Book Two in this series - three steps that we should take in order to ensure that our broad, balanced and ambitious curriculum is implemented in a way that leads to long-term learning:

1. Create a positive learning environment in order to stimulate sensory memory

2. Make pupils think hard but efficiently in order to gain the attention of - but cheat - working memory

3. Plan for deliberate practice in order to improve storage in, and retrieval from, long-term memory

Again, this is a useful process to bear in mind when evaluating the effectiveness of the way in which we teach our curriculum – a part of our 'impact' discussions, hence why I have summarised the process for you here.

Chapter 2: What is curriculum implementation?

As I explained earlier, in the schools' inspection handbook, Ofsted defines implementation as the way in which "the curriculum is taught at subject and classroom level".

Accordingly, during an inspection, Ofsted will want to see how teachers enable pupils to understand key concepts, presenting information clearly and promoting appropriate discussion, how teachers check pupils' understanding effectively, identifying and correcting misunderstandings, and how teachers ensure that **pupils embed key concepts in their long-term memory** and apply them fluently.

Further, Ofsted will want to see if the subject curriculum that classes follow is designed and delivered in a way that allows pupils to transfer key knowledge to long-term memory and if it is sequenced so that **new knowledge and skills build on what has been taught before** and towards defined end points.

We will unpack those two paragraphs in a moment.

In the further education and skills inspection handbook, meanwhile, Ofsted argues that teachers need sufficient subject knowledge, pedagogical knowledge and pedagogical content knowledge to be able teach learners effectively.

Effective teaching and training should, Ofsted argues, ensure that learners in further education and skills settings **know more and remember what they have learned** within the context of the approach that teachers have selected to serve the aims of their curriculum. Consequently, learners will be able to apply vocational and technical skills fluently and independently.

In both schools and FE settings, Ofsted says that inspectors will want to see evidence that teachers use assessment to check pupils' understanding, and they will evaluate how assessment is used in a school or college to support the teaching of the curriculum, but – crucially – not in a way that substantially increases teachers' workloads. As I explained earlier, by including reference to the report of the Teacher Workload Advisory Group, 'Making data work', which recommends that school leaders should not have more than two or three data collection points a year, Ofsted implies – I think – that it will expect schools to follow this advice or have a solid rationale for not doing so.

In short, then, Ofsted's definition of effective curriculum implementation is, I think, high quality teaching which leads to long-term learning.

So, let's unpack those ingredients...

How the curriculum is taught at subject level

Here, we might consider how curriculum plans are written to ensure the subject is taught in a planned and sequenced manner, and in a way that ensures all teachers within a department are consistent in the content they deliver, as well as in the broad pedagogical approaches they apply to teach their subject.

It might help to consider the following questions:

What makes our subject different to other subjects on the timetable? For example, how do scientists think, as distinct from mathematicians? How do scientists speak, read and write? How is this explicitly taught to pupils?

What shape does the subject curriculum take? Is it linear or spiral? What does progress look like in this subject? Can it be extrapolated by assessing pupils' knowledge and skills at two points in time? Or is it more complex than this? Can some skills be observed? What about knowledge, how do you know when pupils have acquired it securely and can apply it in a meaningful way? Indeed, can you know this?

What form do the key concepts (end points or body of knowledge) take in this subject? For example, are they worded as big questions, ideas, concepts, values, behaviours, facts, or skills? Or a combination of all these and more?

How do these key concepts develop other time? Do they get reinforced each term and year? Do they get built upon and added to as pupils progress through the curriculum and as subject content is returned to with increasingly complexity? How are explicit links made between what pupils already know and can do, and what they need to learn next?

Is the subject content the same regardless of which teacher a pupil has? What value judgments are made about what knowledge and skills are most important and which aspects of the subject can be dropped? Are such decisions made as a department or by individual teachers? Is subject content taught in the same or broadly similar ways by all teachers in the department? For example, where appropriate, do all teachers use the same presentation slides, textbooks and worksheets? Do they all use the same schemata or aide memoire?

What cross-curricular links are made? Do subject teachers work with other departments to identify commonalities and themes where relevant? Do subjects liaise on their sequencing to maximise the potential to support each other's delivery? When maths is needed in science, do science teachers use the same mathematical methods as maths teachers? Do all teachers ensure they teach tier 2 vocabulary in ways that do not contradict other subjects but that make explicit the differences that exist in the meanings of, say, command words such as 'analyse' between subject disciplines?

How the curriculum is taught at classroom level

Here, we might consider the way curriculum plans are translated into classroom practice by individual teachers. In so doing, the following questions may prove useful:

What does our subject-specific learning environment, including classrooms and corridors, look and sound like? What makes the teaching of this subject different to the teaching of other subjects? How is the learning environment organised? What do all classrooms contain? How are the walls used? What layout is optimal? How is the space utilised including the use of displays to aid learning? What of the social environment? What do interactions look like and why? Does the way the classroom is run mirror expectations in the subject field? Are explicit links to the subject discipline made?

What rules and routines are particular to this subject? How are they articulated, reinforced, enforced? In subjects with a practical element, such as design and technology, engineering, and construction, how are health and safety taught and high standards upheld?

What does the teacher do in this subject? What is the balance between teacher-led and pupil-led activities? What do teacher explanations look like in practice? How does the teacher make use of modelling and thinking aloud? How do they make their subject expertise explicit to pupils so what is invisible to the novice learner becomes visible?

Is pair and group work used in this subject? How and why? What guidelines are established? How and how often? Are they routinely upheld? Does self- and peer-assessment and feedback feature in this subject? How is this managed?

What does assessment look like in our subject? What is assessed, by whom, when and how? How is feedback given? What is done with it?

How teachers enable pupils to understand key concepts

Here, we might consider the ways in which teachers articulate the end points or body of knowledge to be learned in their subject discipline. In so doing, we might pose the following questions:

What are the key concepts? Who decides? When are they taught? How and how often are they returned to and expanded upon? Do key concepts feature in learning objectives or intended outcomes? Do key concepts feature in knowledge organisers or unit summaries? Are they used in low-stakes quizzes, hinge questions, exit tickets, homework tasks and so on in order to ensure they form part of retrieval practice activities?

How do teachers in our subject discipline routinely – and unobtrusively – assess pupils to ensure they have understood the key concepts they've taught? Do they return to this to ensure that what pupils know today, they still know tomorrow?

How teachers present information clearly

Here, we might consider what effective teacher instruction looks like in each subject discipline. In some subjects, teacher explanations might be the most effective and efficient means of imparting information, whereas in other subjects a more hands-on approach for pupils (such as pair or group work, or problem-based learning etc.) might be preferable. In many subjects, of course, a combination of the two approaches probably works best because it provides a varied diet for learning activities for pupils and moves them towards independence.

The following questions may be helpful here:

Where teacher explanations are used, do teachers present information with clarity? Do they explicitly teach the vocabulary that pupils need to know, and do they 'front load' their explanations with the key facts or ideas pupils need?

Do teachers made good use of modelling, constructing and deconstructing examples of excellence for pupils rather than showing 'one I made earlier'? Do they accompany these models with 'thinking aloud' to ensure pupils are exposed to an expert's decision-making processes and to ensure they can see that producing work of high quality is rarely easy and without error, rather it is an iterative process that involves learning from mistakes, taking two steps forward and one step back?

Do teachers check their pupils' understanding of these key concepts routinely and regularly and use the information this gleans to adapt their teaching pace and style?

How teachers promote appropriate discussion

Here, we might consider how class discussion and debate are managed. As such, the following questions may be of use:

When are classroom discussions used? Does the teacher use whole-class, group or pair discussion, or a combination? When group work is used, is this is the best means of promoting discussion and are guidelines established to ensure all pupils are engaged and that no one gets a 'free ride'? Are roles assigned to ensure each pupil has a responsibility and is accountable to the group for its success?

Does the teacher explicitly teach effective debating skills and is this within a subject-specific context? Are the rules and routines for effective debate and discussion regularly and consistently reinforced? Are these rules the same in each classroom and with each teacher in a department? What about across the whole school or college curriculum? Do these rules help pupils to comment on others' contributions without it becoming a personal attack? Are active listening skills taught?

Do pupils know there is no hiding place in the classroom and that they will be expected to contribute? But is the classroom a safe place for pupils to take risks and make mistakes, and are reluctant speakers helped to develop confidence and resilience over time? Is there a safety net to catch pupils when they fall? Do discussions help pupils to make progress? Are discussions and question-and-answer sessions inclusive of all pupils?

How teachers check pupils' understanding effectively, identifying and correcting misunderstandings

In addition to what I say above about enabling pupils to understand key concepts including through assessment and by routinely returning to concepts to ensure that what pupils know today, they still know tomorrow, it's important that teachers also discover and unpack any misunderstandings and misconceptions that pupils develop. Assessment therefore needs to identify when pupils get it wrong or when gaps remain, and the results of these assessments need to be used to inform the teacher's planning and teaching.

Accordingly, I would add the following questions:

Do teachers ensure that any misconceptions and gaps are addressed? Do they ensure that pupils have acquired the requisite key concepts to enable them to move on to the next part of the curriculum? Do they use this information to inform their planning and teaching?

How teachers ensure that pupils embed key concepts in their long-term memory

Information has only been learned if it has been encoded in long-term memory. Indeed, the educational psychologist Paul Kirschner defines learning simply as a change in long-term memory. Information is encoded in long-term memory (in other words, it is transferred from the short-term or working memory into the long-term memory from where it can be accessed and used later) when pupils have actively attended to the information.

Pupils are more likely to attend to information if it is stimulating and if it requires them to think – in other words, the work must be challenging. However, as working memory is very small, it is also important that pupils are helped to make good use of that limited space and avoid overloading it with too much information at once.

As such, here we might consider the following questions:

How do teachers in each subject discipline 'hook' pupils and gain the active attention of their working memories? How do teachers ensure pupils focus on the curriculum content they need to encode and avoid unhelpful distractions?

How do teachers pitch learning so that it falls within pupils' struggle zones, meaning it is hard and requires thinking, but is also within their capability and does not overload their working memories?

How teachers ensure that pupils can apply key concepts fluently

Once information has been encoded in long-term memory, it has been learned. However, this is not enough if we are to achieve long-term learning. If information is left dormant, it will become increasingly hard to recall later. In other words, pupils may learn something today but be unable to recall it and apply it tomorrow.

Here, therefore, we might consider the following questions:

How and how often do teachers return to prior learning to keep it active and accessible? What do teachers do with that prior learning when they do return to it? As long-term memory is practically limitless, it is helpful for pupils to do something different with their prior learning each time they return to it, thereby encoding new information in long-term memory.

How are pupils helped to apply prior learning in different ways and in different contexts so that learning becomes transferable? How do teachers help pupils to see connections within and across the curriculum so that they can apply what they learn in one topic to another related topic, or what they learn in one subject to another related subject, and so on?

Above all else, it is important that pupils are afforded the opportunity to apply their newfound knowledge and skills – to do something with it beyond sitting exams. As such, we should ask:

How are knowledge and skills placed within a wider context so pupils can see why that knowledge and those skills are useful and usable both now and in the future? Do teachers articulate the purpose of learning in each subject and each topic, because with purpose comes motivation?

How the subject curriculum is designed and delivered in a way that allows pupils to transfer key knowledge to long-term memory

In addition to what I say above about encoding information in long-term memory, it is important that – at a subject level and in long- and medium-term teaching plans – opportunities for pupils to engage in retrieval practice activities are baked into the curriculum and not left to chance or to individual teachers' discretion.

One way to do this well is to adopt a progression model such as the one I outlined in Book One in this series which makes use of threshold concepts. A progression model is not only a useful means of assessing pupils' progress, but also a way to ensure that concepts are returned to often and are built upon with increasingly complexity.

How the subject curriculum is sequenced so that new knowledge and skills build on what has been taught before

Another advantage of the progression model is that it helps to ensure the curriculum is planned and sequenced. Sequencing is a means of ensuring that curriculum content is taught in a logical order and that concepts are returned to and developed over time.

Here, therefore, we might consider the following:

In what order is subject content taught and how is the subject curriculum taught over time?

Is there curriculum continuity, including between the different phases and key stages of education?

Do teachers in each year group and key stage know what went before and what follows?

In this sense, we might regard the subject curriculum as a novel and each teacher as being responsible for writing one or two chapters. Each teacher must know the plot arc of the whole book and must understand how their chapters fit in, how they will develop character, theme and plot. They must ensure their chapters are also consistent in both language and tone.

The current state of curriculum planning in some schools and colleges reminds of an old parlour game called Consequences whereby the first player writes a word or a sentence, folds the page (if it's a single word, they follow guidelines such as 'write an adjective to describe a man' followed by 'write the name of a man' and so on; if it's a sentence, they usually write freely but leave the last word or so of their sentence visible for the next player to see, onto which they can adjoin their sentence) and passes it on to the next player who adds a sentence of their own, folds the page and passes it on to the third player and so on. At the end, the paper is unfolded, and someone reads the story aloud. Invariably, it is nonsensical but amusing. Our curriculum is in danger of being nonsensical if we do not do more to remove the creases and ensure greater continuity – and there is nothing amusing about that.

How the subject curriculum is sequenced so that new knowledge and skills builds towards defined end points

In Book One in this series, as I have already explained, I articulated a six-step process of curriculum design. Having articulated the broad vision and purpose of each subject curriculum, the process began by setting the destination. In other words, the act of planning a curriculum begins at the end. What do you want pupils to know and be able to do at the end that they didn't know and couldn't do at the beginning?

Where you plant the flag is up to you, but the key is starting with the destination in mind rather than starting from where pupils are now. Why? Because starting from where pupils are now might encourage you to dumb down or lower your expectations. Starting at the end, with 'the best that has been thought and said' in your subject discipline, ensures you have high expectations and aspirations and set pupils on a journey towards excellence.

As such, planning and sequencing a subject curriculum means building towards a defined destination, the clear end points or body of knowledge you have agreed upon as a department. Curriculum continuity, therefore, is not simply about building upon what went before, it is also about building towards a shared destination, an aspirational goal.

In further education and skills setting, implementation is also about...

How learners apply vocational and technical skills fluently and independently

Here, we need to recognise that the application of some practical skills can be observed and assessed. We also need to be mindful of the fact that some vocational qualifications are not built to support teaching for long-term learning. For example, some qualifications allow you to teach something, assess it, then move on and never return to it.

Here, I would caution against using the qualification specification as your guiding star. Of course, we need to teach the specification to enable learners to gain good qualifications that will open doors to future success, but the qualification is not the be-all and end-all of an FE college education. Rather, we need to do what is in the best interests of our learners and prepare them for the next stage of their training, employment and lives. This means keeping all the plates spinning throughout the course regardless of whether those plates will be assessed again as part of the qualification. If something was worth teaching and worth learning in the first place, then it must not be allowed to gather dust in our learners' long-term memories;

rather, it must be kept alive and accessible so that our learners can apply that learning in college, in work and in life.

So, if that is what intent and implementation are, what about impact...?

Chapter 3: What is curriculum impact?

As we saw earlier, according to Ofsted's new education inspection framework, the school curriculum is defined according to its **intent, implementation** and **impact**...

Intent is "a framework for setting out the aims of a programme of education, including the knowledge and understanding to be gained at each stage".

Implementation is a means of "translating that framework over time into a structure and narrative within an institutional context".

Impact is the means of "evaluating what knowledge and understanding pupils have gained against expectations.

In Book One of this series, and summarised above, I shared a process for approaching curriculum *intent*. I argued that a curriculum is not a single entity; rather, it is a composite of at least four facets: the national, the basic, the local, and the hidden curriculums. I explored what a broad and balanced curriculum might look like in practice. I considered the true purpose of education and, by so doing, articulated the intended outcomes of an effective school curriculum.

I also examined *why* designing a knowledge-rich curriculum was important and discussed *what* knowledge mattered most to our pupils' future successes and how to identify the 'clear end-points' of a whole-school – and indeed subject-specific – curriculum. I discussed ways of ensuring our curriculum was ambitious for all, including by adopting a mastery approach rather than reducing the curriculum offer or 'dumbing down' for some. I talked, too, of modelling the same high expectations of all, albeit accepting that some pupils will need additional and different support to reach that destination.

In Book Two, and again summarised above, I turned my attention to curriculum *implementation.* I explained that Ofsted want to see how teachers enable pupils to understand key concepts, presenting information clearly and promoting appropriate discussion; how teachers check pupils' understanding effectively, identifying and correcting misunderstandings; and how teachers ensure that pupils embed key concepts in their long-term memory and apply them fluently.

I apologise if the introductory chapters of this book, and this chapter so far, are a little repetitive but I emphasise these key points yet again because it's important to bear them in mind as we complete the trilogy and analyse what curriculum *impact* means in practice.

Why?

Because, at its heart, I think that 'impact' is about evaluating the extent to which we achieve all the above aims and ambitions.

Ofsted, for its part, says that, under impact, inspectors will gather evidence to help them judge whether the most disadvantaged pupils in school – as well as pupils with SEND – are given the knowledge and cultural capital they need to succeed in life.

In judging impact, Ofsted says that national assessments and examinations are useful indicators of the outcomes pupils in school achieve, but that they only represent a sample of what pupils have learned. As such, inspectors will balance these with their assessment of the standard of pupils' work from the first-hand evidence they gather on inspection.

Ofsted says that learning in schools must build towards a goal. As such, at each stage of pupils' education, inspectors are likely to want to see evidence that pupils are being prepared for the next stage of education, training or employment, and will consider whether pupils are ready for that next stage.

Measuring outcomes

In the old Common Inspection Framework (CIF), one of the key judgments was 'Outcomes for pupils' but this is notable by its absence from the EIF. It's culling signals – I would argue – that test or qualification outcomes are no longer paramount; rather, schools and colleges should focus on the real substance of education: the curriculum. And, in so doing, schools and colleges should ensure that every pupil and student is genuinely and holistically prepared for what comes next. Qualifications remain vital, of course, because they open doors to future success, but certification is not the be-all-and-end-all of an effective education.

As such, outcomes are no longer the sole lens through which our 'impact' is judged. Inspectors will still use nationally-generated performance information about pupil progress and attainment – that which is available in the IDSR – but they will triangulate this with first-hand evidence of how pupils are doing, drawing together their findings from the interviews, observations, work scrutiny and documentary review they gather on inspection, in order to make some judgments about impact. And even then, this evidence will only form a part of the evidence inspectors use to reach a judgment. For example, inspectors will also use nationally-published information about the destinations to which pupils progress when they leave school, and – in primary schools – they will listen to a range of pupils read.

Measuring wider impact

For me, one of the key lines from all the Ofsted documentation is this: Inspectors will judge the extent to which "learners are ready for the next stage of education, employment or training". This is key, I think, because it sums up the purpose of education: it is not solely to get pupils through qualifications, though these are clearly important; but rather to genuinely prepare pupils for what comes next.

In practice, this means that schools and colleges need to provide for pupils' broader development, enabling them to discover and develop their interests and talents. It means that the school curriculum needs to develop pupils' character including their resilience, confidence and independence, and help them keep physically and mentally healthy. It means that at each stage of education, schools need to prepare pupils for future success in their next steps and prepare them for adult life by equipping them with the knowledge and skills to be responsible, respectful, active citizens who contribute positively to society, developing their understanding of fundamental human values, their understanding and appreciation of diversity, celebrating what we have in common and promoting respect for all.

It stands to reason, I would suggest, that if the purpose of education is to prepare pupils for the next stage of their education, employment and lives, then the ways in which we measure 'impact' must go beyond mere outcomes.

Indeed, if we are to focus on the real substance of education, provide a broad and balanced curriculum that's ambitious for all and tackles social justice issues, then we should measure the impact of all this.

As such, I would argue that the purpose of 'impact' is at least threefold:

1. To evaluate the effectiveness of the way in which the curriculum is designed
2. To evaluate the effectiveness of the way in which the curriculum is taught
3. To evaluate the pace of pupil progress, pupil outcomes, and pupils' preparedness for their next steps

In Part Two of this book, we will explore each of these purposes in turn...

Part Two: Counting what counts

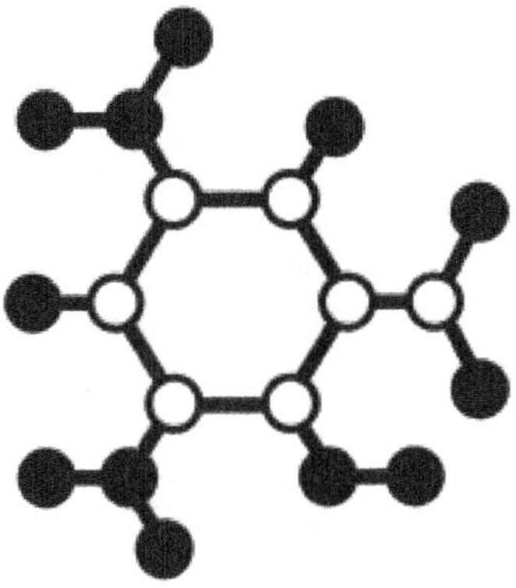

Chapter 4: Evaluating the impact of curriculum planning

A good curriculum is a living organism, forever changing in response to reality. Curriculum design, therefore, should be a cyclical process. A curriculum should not be designed then left to stagnate. Rather, we should design a curriculum, teach it, assess it to see if it's working as well as we had hoped, then redesign it in light of our findings and so on.

To help oil the wheel, so to speak, I think we should use assessment data to answer the following questions about our curriculum:

Is our curriculum ambitious enough?

Does our curriculum teach the knowledge and skills pupils need in order to take advantage of the opportunities, responsibilities and experiences of later life? Does our curriculum reflect our school's local context? For example, does it address typical gaps in pupils' knowledge and skills? Does it bring the local community into school and take pupils out into the community? Does it respond to our pupils' particular life experiences?

Is our curriculum sufficiently broad so as to ensure pupils are taught as many different subject disciplines as possible for as long as possible? Is it sufficiently balanced so that each subject discipline has a fair amount of space on the timetable to deliver both breadth and depth? Are pupils able to study a strong academic core of subjects but also afforded a well-rounded education including in the arts?

Do we account for the hidden curriculum and ensure there are no inconsistencies or contradictions between what we explicitly teach in lessons and what we teach by way of the values, behaviours and attitudes all our staff display daily, and by the quality of the learning environment and our rules and routines?

Have we identified the right end points?

Is it clear what 'end points' we are building towards as a school and in each subject discipline that we teach? Is it clear what our pupils need to know and be able to do at each stage in order to reach those end points? Will the end points we set all our pupils on course towards fully prepare them for the next stage of their education, employment and lives?

Do we make explicit links between related end points within and across subject disciplines? As well as subject-specific knowledge and skills, do we also identify the research and study skills – and indeed other cross-curricular skills – that our pupils need in order to succeed? Are these skills explicitly taught and reinforced? Are they taught consistently across all subjects where applicable?

Do we ensure that the end points of each part of our curriculum seamlessly join to the starting points of the next and so on, so that we achieve curriculum continuity and so that transitions between the various years, key stages and phases of education are as smooth as they can be?

Have we planned and sequenced our curriculum effectively?

Does our planning ensure that new knowledge and skills build on what has been taught before and towards these clearly defined end points?

Is there an appropriate pace that allows for sufficient breadth and depth?

Is content taught in a logical progression, systematically and explicitly enough for all pupils to acquire the intended knowledge and skills?

Is there an appropriate level of challenge for all?

Does our progression model allow for a mastery approach where the higher-performing pupils are sufficiently stretched and lower-performing pupils are effectively supported, and yet the integrity of our teaching sequence is still maintained so that no pupil runs too far ahead or falls too far behind?

Do we bake retrieval practice into our curriculum to ensure we activate prior knowledge as and when appropriate and keep that prior knowledge accessible to pupils so that they can make connections between what they learned yesterday, what they're learning today, and what they will learn tomorrow? Does this enable pupils to forge ever-more complex schemata in long-term memory and aide automaticity?

Does our curriculum help to tackle social justice issues?

Have we planned to teach the knowledge and cultural capital our pupils need in order to access and understand our curriculum and go on to thrive in later life?

Are there high academic ambitions for all pupils, and do we offer disadvantaged pupils and pupils with SEND the same curriculum experience as their peers rather than 'dumb down' or reduce the offer?

Do we identify the barriers some pupils face in school and within each subject discipline, including though not solely a potential vocabulary deficit, and do we plan effective support strategies to help overcome those barriers? Whenever we use additional intervention and support strategies to help disadvantaged pupils and those with SEND, do we monitor their effectiveness as they're happening rather than wait to evaluate their eventual success once they've ended?

...The above is by no means an exhaustive list but at its heart is a simple self-evaluative question: Is our curriculum working for all our pupils?

I would argue that our assessment practices need, among other things, to answer this crucial question. And the outcomes of those assessments should be used to tweak our curriculum when – as will inevitably be the case from time to time – the answer is 'no'.

So, when considering 'curriculum impact', we should ask ourselves: how do we assess the effectiveness of our curriculum and what do we do with the findings?

In the next chapter, I will explore ways of evaluating the effectiveness of the way in which our curriculum is taught and then, in Chapter 6, I will explore ways of evaluating the pace of our pupils' progress, eventual pupil outcomes, and pupils' preparedness for their next steps.

Chapter 5: Evaluating the impact of curriculum teaching

As well as using assessment to evaluate the effectiveness of our curriculum planning – or *intent* – we should also learn from our impact assessments how well the curriculum is translated into practice in the classroom – in other words, its *implementation.*

Assessment is an integral – indeed, one might argue, an *essential* – component of effective teaching and learning.

Broadly speaking, there are two ways in which the outcomes of an assessment can be used: **summatively** – the focus of which is on what a pupil has achieved at the end of a unit, year or course; and **formatively** – the focus of which is on diagnosing a pupil's next steps.

Summative assessment usually takes the form of high-stakes tests; formative assessment can take many forms including class discussions, multiple-choice quizzes, peer-teaching and so forth.

Whereas summative assessment is the assessment *of* learning, formative assessment is often referred to as 'assessment *for* learning' (or AfL for short) because it's a way of providing pupils with feedback about the progress they've made thus far and about what they need to do next to make further such progress.

But I would argue that formative assessment is not solely assessment *for* learning, it's also assessment *as* learning and indeed assessment *as teaching…*

Why 'assessment *as* learning'? Well, formative assessment is a means by which pupils actually learn, not just a guide to future learning. For example, by engaging in classroom discussions and questioning (one of the five key formative assessment strategies expounded by Marnie Thompson and Dylan Wiliam in 2007, on which more later), pupils deepen their knowledge and understanding and therefore learn.

Why 'assessment *as teaching*'? Well, formative assessment is not only a method of providing information to pupils on which they can act, or indeed a means through which pupils can actually learn; it's also a mechanism for providing information to the teacher on which they too can act – after all, teachers use the outcomes of formative assessment to guide their planning and teaching; formative assessment tells them what pupils know and can do and what they do not yet know and cannot yet do, and therefore, at its simplest, proffers intelligence about whether to re-teach, recap or move on.

We should therefore use our impact assessments to evaluate the effectiveness of our teaching. To achieve this aim, it might help to ask the following questions:

Do teachers have expert knowledge of the subjects they teach? If not, are they being supported to address gaps in their knowledge so that pupils are not disadvantaged by ineffective teaching? Does the school support an effective programme of subject-specific professional development as well as training on generic pedagogy? Do the teachers assigned to each cohort, each year group and each level and type of qualification have the knowledge and experience to teach it well? Thus: is timetabling as effectiveness as it could be?

Do teachers enable pupils to understand key concepts, presenting information clearly? Are teacher explanations effective – for example, do they make use of dual coding? Do teachers also model thinking aloud for pupils to make the invisible visible and the implicit explicit? Do they explicitly teach the language – including tier 2 and 3 vocabulary – that pupils need in order to understand the curriculum?

Do teachers articulate clear learning outcomes and make explicit what pupils should know and be able to do at the end of each sequence of lessons? Do teachers establish routines for classroom discussions so that all pupils contribute fairly and in order that debate deepens pupils' understanding?

Do teachers make use of 'live' low-stakes assessment practices such as hinge questions and exit tickets to assess pupils' understanding and to identify the gaps in their knowledge and skills, as well as their misunderstandings? Do they use these assessments to inform their planning and teaching so that lesson planning is fluid and responsive, rather than something to stick to religiously?

Do teachers ensure that pupils embed key concepts in their long-term memory and apply them fluently? Is the subject curriculum taught in such a way that helps pupils to transfer key knowledge to long-term memory?

Do teachers gain the active attention of pupils' working memories and make them think hard but efficiently about curriculum content? Once encoded into long-term memory, do teachers provide plenty of opportunities for retrieval practice to ensure the knowledge in long-term memory is brought back into the working memory so that it remains accessible, and so as to encourage pupils to apply that knowledge in different contexts? Is prior learning linked to new learning, so that what is taught today builds upon what was taught yesterday and so forth?

Are explicit links made between different parts of the curriculum and indeed across curriculum areas to help make knowledge transferable and useable? Is teaching sequenced in practice not just in lesson plans so that pupils acquire the knowledge and skills needed to complete each task before they are asked to complete it, and so that new knowledge and skills logically build on what has been taught before enabling pupils to make progress towards clearly defined end points?

Do teachers use formative assessment to check pupils' understanding in order to inform their planning and their teaching, and to help pupils embed and use knowledge fluently and develop their understanding? Do all these assessments have a clear purpose? Do they provide valid data on which the teacher can and does act? Is the feedback garnered from assessments meaningful and motivating to pupils? Does it help them to close the gap between their current performance and their desired performance? Is time set aside every time feedback is given to pupils so that they can process it, question it if needed, and act upon it in class whilst the teacher is present to provide support, challenge and encouragement?

In evaluating the effectiveness of the way in which the curriculum is taught, we would do well to consider the question, 'What is learning?' If we define the complex process of learning as an alteration in long-term memory, as do many cognitive scientists and educational psychologists, then we might conclude that if nothing has altered in long-term memory, nothing has been learned.

However, transfer to long-term memory depends on a number of factors. In order to develop understanding, pupils must connect new knowledge with existing knowledge. Pupils must also develop fluency and unconsciously apply their knowledge as skills. This process must not be reduced to, or confused with, simply memorising lists of facts. Rather, learning has to be meaningful, which is to say both useful and usable.

So, in addition to the above, I would suggest you also ask yourselves: how do we assess the effectiveness of the way in which our curriculum is taught so that pupils transfer key concepts into long-term memory and can apply them fluently and what do we do with the findings?

In the next chapter we will explore the third and final purpose of impact assessments: ways of evaluating the pace of pupil progress, pupil outcomes and their preparedness for the next stages of their education, employment and lives.

Chapter 6: Evaluating pupil outcomes and preparedness for the next stage

As well as evaluating the effectiveness of our curriculum planning and teaching, we want our impact assessments to measure eventual outcomes so that we can determine what pupils have achieved and also the extent to which our curriculum planning and the way in which we have translated those curriculum plans into classroom practice have enabled pupils to achieve what we intended for them to achieve and that we have not perpetuated or opened any attainment gaps.

To be clear, by 'outcomes' I do not solely mean test and exam results, of course; and nor do I solely mean *qualification* outcomes in the sense of certification.

As I argued above, the purpose of education is not just certification but to genuinely prepare pupils for the next stage of their education, employment and lives. So, what does this look like? What might we assess in order to make a judgment about the impact of our curriculum on pupil outcomes?

Here, it might be helpful to take a look at the 'personal development' judgment in the Ofsted schools inspection handbook which says that 'preparedness' includes:

- Developing pupils as responsible, respectful and active citizens who are able to play their part and become actively involved in public life as adults
- Developing and deepening pupils' understanding of the fundamental British values of democracy, individual liberty, the rule of law and mutual respect and tolerance

- Promoting equality of opportunity so that all pupils can thrive together, understanding that difference is a positive, not a negative, and that individual characteristics make people unique
- Promoting an inclusive environment that meets the needs of all pupils, irrespective of age, disability, gender reassignment, race, religion or belief, sex or sexual orientation
- Developing pupils' character, which we define as a set of positive personal traits, dispositions and virtues that informs their motivation and guides their conduct so that they reflect wisely, learn eagerly, behave with integrity and cooperate consistently well with others. This gives pupils the qualities they need to flourish in our society
- Developing pupils' confidence, resilience and knowledge so that they can keep themselves mentally healthy
- Enabling pupils to recognise online and offline risks to their well-being – for example, risks from criminal and sexual exploitation, domestic abuse, female genital mutilation, forced marriage, substance misuse, gang activity, radicalisation and extremism – and making them aware of the support available to them
- Enabling pupils to recognise the dangers of inappropriate use of mobile technology and social media
- Developing pupils' understanding of how to keep physically healthy, eat healthily and maintain an active lifestyle, including giving ample opportunities for pupils to be active during the school day and through extra-curricular activities
- Developing pupils' age-appropriate understanding of healthy relationships through appropriate relationship and sex education
- Providing an effective careers programme in line with the government's statutory guidance on careers advice that offers pupils:
    - unbiased careers advice
    - experience of work, and
    - contact with employers
    - to encourage pupils to aspire, make good choices and understand what they need to do to reach and succeed in the careers to which they aspire
- Supporting readiness for the next phase of education, training or employment so that pupils are equipped to make the transition successfully.

Ultimately, we should measure the impact of our curriculum by the extent to which we prepare all our pupils for their next steps – do they make good progress through our curriculum and go on to achieve positive destinations? Do our pupils leave us as well-rounded, cultured, inquisitive, caring, kind, resilient, knowledgeable human beings ready to make their own way in the world? And do we, as a consequence, make the world a better place one pupil at a time – for this surely is a measure of true success?

Preparing pupils for the next stage of their lives

Some of the stated aims of the new Education Inspection Framework (EIF) are to prevent the narrowing of the curriculum, to stop schools 'teaching to the test', and to promote social justice.

With this framework, HMCI Amanda Spielman said she wants schools to focus on what she calls 'the real substance of education'. In other words, she wants schools to move beyond the 'stickers and badges' of qualifications – though I would argue that achieving a good set of qualifications is clearly still important – and focus on preparing all pupils, irrespective of their starting points and backgrounds, for the next stages of their lives.

This 'next stage' might be the next level of qualification or it might be meaningful employment, but irrespective, it will be to prepare pupils as active citizens and happy, healthy people.

The importance of preparing pupils for the next stage of their lives runs through the EIF like the letters in a stick of seaside rock. It is referenced – explicitly or implicitly – in all the key judgments. Let's take a look at what it says in each...

Quality of education

Curriculum intent

Here, inspectors will be alert to signs of narrowing in the key stages 2 and 3 curriculums - the notion being that pupils should be afforded the opportunity to study as broad a range of subjects as possible for as long as possible to order to help them develop a well-rounded education, thus keeping open as many doors to the future as possible.

Also under 'curriculum intent', Ofsted says inspectors will judge the extent to which schools are equipping pupils with the knowledge and 'cultural capital' they need to succeed in life. Ofsted says its definition of 'cultural capital' matches that found in the aims of the national curriculum: namely, that it is "the essential knowledge that pupils need to be educated citizens, introducing them to the best that has been thought and said and helping to engender an appreciation of human creativity and achievement".

Curriculum implementation

Here, inspectors will want to see if the subject curriculum is designed and delivered in a way that allows pupils to transfer key knowledge to long-term memory and that it is sequenced so that new knowledge and skills build on what has been taught before and towards defined end points.

It is this focus on transferring knowledge into long-term memory that once again signals the importance of preparing pupils for their next steps and moving beyond qualifications. By ensuring schools teach for long-term learning, they enable their pupils not only to acquire new knowledge and skills, but to apply that knowledge and those skills in a meaningful way at a later time and in a range of contexts, including in work and in life.

Curriculum impact

Ofsted says that learning must build towards a goal. As such, at each stage of pupils' education, inspectors will want to see evidence that pupils are being prepared for the next stage of education, training or employment, and will consider whether pupils are ready for the next stage.

Behaviour and attitudes

This judgment has been stripped out of 'personal development, behaviour and welfare'. Under the EIF, inspectors will gather evidence about pupil motivation and about their positive attitudes to learning as important predictors of attainment. Overall, judgments will be made on the extent to which schools have fostered a positive, respectful culture in which staff know and care about pupils. Not only does this help prepare pupils for the next stage of their lives, it models the value and behaviours expected of active citizens.

Personal development

Here, inspectors will focus on the impact of a school's provision for personal development but accept – rather refreshingly, I think – that personal development will often not be assessable during pupils' time at school. As such, it is the process not the outcome, the journey not the destination, that will be inspected.

Inspectors will, for example, look at how – and how effectively – schools help build pupils' confidence and resilience. They say that, although schools cannot make children active, engaged citizens, they can help pupils understand how to engage with society. And they can develop and deepen pupils' understanding of the fundamental British values of democracy, individual liberty, the rule of law and mutual respect and tolerance.

Measuring pupils' preparedness for the next stage of their lives

In order to make judgments about the extent to which pupils are being prepared for the next stage of their lives, inspectors are likely to place emphasis on progression and destinations data, understanding where pupils go next and whether or not this represents a positive step in the right direction and is ambitious and challenging. Inspectors are also likely to assess a school's provision for character education, RSE, PSHE, and fundamental British Values.

Enrichment opportunities such as the Duke of Edinburgh award and other outward-bound schemes, as well as the development of oracy skills perhaps through debating societies, will form part of this picture, demonstrating how seriously a school takes the holistic education of its pupils.

Primary schools may find the government's 'activity passport' a useful starting point in considering the kinds of experiences young people should be afforded, though it is best to avoid this becoming a box-ticking exercise.

Here are some further considerations...

The hidden curriculum

Although it is tempting to focus on how the taught curriculum (that which takes place in lessons) helps pupils prepare for the next stage of their lives, schools must not forget that pupils are also informed by messages sent through the 'hidden' curriculum, those parts of the educational experience that occur in the spaces between lessons. In other words, what do the words and actions of all the adults in a school say to pupils about what values and attitudes matter most in life, and about how to behave as a citizen and employee?

Explicit or implicit

Schools should also consider whether or not the skills that pupils need in order to be prepared for the next stage of their lives should be taught explicitly or implicitly, in isolation as 'transferable skills' or through a subject discipline as a domain-specific skill.

Critical thinking is not, for example, a transferable skill because it is impossible to be critical about something on which you have little or no background knowledge. You must first acquire deep knowledge on a subject before you can be taught how to think critically about that subject. However, a school may decide that some skills are indeed transferable because they are used in many subjects across the curriculum and in similar ways. Take, for example, structuring an argument, working in a team, giving feedback to a peer, internet research, note-taking, and so on.

Information, advice and guidance

A further point to note here is the importance of IAG including impartial careers guidance and guidance on which qualifications to study. If pupils are not appropriately and expertly advised about the paths they can take, how can they be expected to take the right paths and be prepared for whatever awaits them around the next corner?

Transitions

Finally, schools and colleges need to consider what they do to help pupils and students adjust to all the changes they face whilst in education. This includes the transition between schools as well as between the various phases, stages and years of education.

Now that we have set out the three broad purposes of our impact assessments, let us consider how we can sense-check any assessments we carry out in order to ensure they have a clear purpose, follow a workable and efficient process, and proffer valid and reliable data on which we can and indeed do act in order to hasten the pace of pupil progress and improve their eventual outcomes...

Part Three: Sense-checking assessments

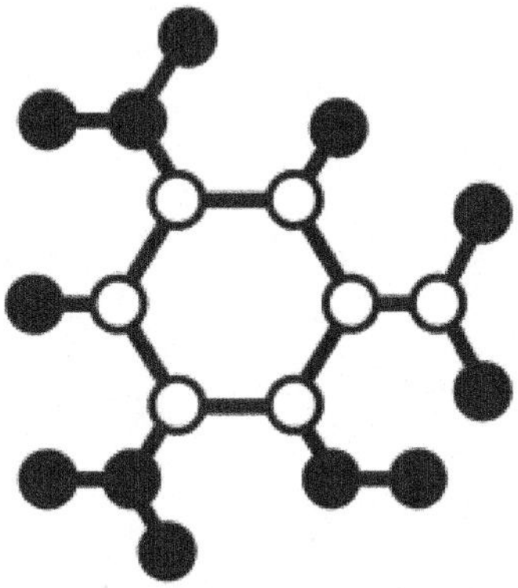

Chapter 7: Purpose, process, and validity

When we are clear *why* we assess, we need to ensure *how* we assess is the best possible way of doing so and that it results in useful and useable data.

As we explored in Part One of this book, broadly speaking, I would suggest that there are three possible reasons for engaging in assessment activity:

1. To evaluate the effectiveness of the way in which the curriculum is designed
2. To evaluate the effectiveness of the way in which the curriculum is taught
3. To evaluate the pace of pupil progress, pupil outcomes, and pupils' preparedness for their next steps

Once we are clear on that, I would suggest we then need to ensure that all our assessment decisions in school or college are sense-checked for three things:

1. Purpose
2. Process
3. Validity

Let us take a look at each in turn...

Purpose

As a handy rule of thumb, whenever we ask teachers to engage in any form of assessment, we should ask ourselves: Why? What is the point of this assessment? How will this assessment - and the data we collect from it - help pupils to make better progress and improve the quality of education at our school?

If an assessment or data collection exercise is solely for management purposes (to produce a report to governors, say; or to generate pretty graphs to impress in meetings) rather than to actually help pupils to make progress, then in all good conscience it should stop.

Of course, I know that it's not always as simple as this...

A teacher's time is finite and sometimes we also need to stop doing things that are indeed in pupils' best interests rather than for management purposes in order to do other things that are more impactful to pupils, or in order to cut a teacher's workload and make their jobs more manageable. As Dylan Wiliam says, the essence of effective leadership is stopping teachers doing good things to give them time to do even better things.

Process

As well as considering the purpose of assessment, we should think about the process by which teachers are expected to assess, input data, and report the outcomes of assessment.

Here, it is useful to ask ourselves whether the process is as efficient as it can be or if it is unnecessarily burdensome.

Consider also: when and how often are teachers expected to assess and input data? Are teachers expected to engineer a test for pupils or can data be gathered in a more holistic, synoptic way? How is the data inputted, directly into software or can teachers supply it in written form for the admin team to input? If it requires the use of technology, do all teachers have easy access to it? What will be the outcome of this data collection exercise? What will be done with the data afterwards and by whom?

As well as considering the time implications of data collection, it is wise to consider the extent to which teachers are trained in using the systems – including what you might consider basic spreadsheets as well as commercial software – and the extent to which they have the requisite skills to assess, record and analyse data, as well as act upon that data. Again, think about the opportunity cost, too. How long will it take a teacher to input this data and what else could they be doing with their time that might have a bigger impact on our pupils?

Validity

Finally, we should consider how valid the data we garner from assessments will be. By this, I don't mean how useful the data will be (we covered this under 'purpose') but rather how accurate and useable it will be.

In other words, although we may have confidence that the data will be very useful in helping pupils to make better progress (for example, by identifying 'at risk' pupils who require additional interventions, and by 'stretching' higher-performing pupils to high grade achievement), the actual data we mine might not be as accurate as we hope and so all our subsequent actions may be futile or misguided.

To help answer this question of accuracy, we may wish to consider once again whether or not teachers have the requisite skills to be able to assess and provide data. Have we triangulated previous teacher assessments with actual validated outcomes? Have teacher assessments proven accurate in the past? Were some teachers' predictions way off-mark and, if so, have we identified any training needs? Have teacher assessments helped to predict eventual outcomes and therefore been useful in terms of identifying those pupils who are at risk of underachievement? Did the subsequent interventions prove effective? Sometimes we keep doing what we've always done because that is easy but, sometimes, we keep doing the wrong things. We should not be afraid to be bold and to question seemingly unquestionable practices.

We may also wish to consider what is actually being assessed and if indeed that thing is assessable in a meaningful way.

What, for example, are we comparing a pupil outcome to? Are those two things indeed comparable? Is the data we draw reliable and defensible? Is it, for example, possible at this stage to assess progress, or might we be measuring a poor proxy for progress instead?

If assessments are used to measure progress over time, such as on a 'flight-path', is progress in this topic and subject actually linear? Should we be able to see nice, neat contrails heading for the skies? Or is progress messier than this because pupils need to go backwards before they can go forwards? Or because different things are being assessed in different topics at different times? Succeeding in topic 1 might not, for example, mean that pupils will do even better in topic 2 because the knowledge and/or skills being taught may be different and/or unrelated.

Horses for courses

As well as considering the purpose, process and validity of assessment practices, I would argue that thought should be given to the varying demands of different subjects if we are to ensure a teacher's workload is fair and manageable. For example, marking in essay-based subjects such as English and History is often more time-consuming than tick-marking in subjects with short, right/wrong answers such as... well, I wouldn't want to alienate readers by saying!

Furthermore, the timing of assessment points will differ depending to the subject and topic. If our whole school assessment policy dictates that every teacher of every subject must assess at set points of the term and year, they may find that they have nothing meaningful to assess at that time and simply make it up to fulfil your expectations or do their best to provide helpful data but it's unlikely to be meaningful.

Here, it may be wise to set wide 'assessment windows' and allow subjects to determine when they assess without that broad timeframe. That way, individual subject teams can ensure that they hold assessments at logical points of a year, key stage or course, when they will be most accurate and helpful to pupils, rather than shoehorn in a test simply for the sake of management accountability.

Chapter 8: Making marking meaningful, manageable and motivating

Once we have sense-checked our assessment practices for their purpose, process and validity, I think we need to ensure that all the marking and feedback that takes place in our schools and colleges are meaningful, manageable and motivating.

Whilst there are, as I explained in Part One of this book, three broad purposes of assessment, we might say that there are two ways in which the outcomes of an assessment might be used in the classroom:

1. ***Summatively*** – to identify what a pupil has achieved at the end of a unit, year, course or school, and to compare pupils and cohorts; and

2. ***Formatively*** – to inform a teacher's planning and instruction, and to diagnose a pupil's next steps and provide them with feedback on which they can act to improve.

Whereas summative assessment is the assessment *of* learning, formative assessment is assessment *for* learning because it's a way of providing pupils with feedback about the progress they've made thus far and about what they need to do next in order to make further such progress.

Formative assessment is also a means through which pupils might actually learn, not just a guide to future learning. For example, by engaging in classroom discussions, pupils can deepen their knowledge and understanding and therefore enact a change in their long-term memory (one common definition of learning).

Formative assessment is also a mechanism for providing information to the teacher on which they too can act – after all, teachers use the outcomes of assessments to guide their planning and teaching; formative assessment provides useful and useable data that tells them what pupils know and can do and what they do not yet know and cannot yet do, and therefore proffers intelligence about whether to re-teach, recap or move on. Assessment data might provide information about the pace of learning and about the order in which learning is sequenced, as well as about the appropriate level of task difficulty.

It's worth noting before we move on that 'assessment *for* learning' only truly becomes *formative* when evidence of pupils' learning is used to adapt teaching to better meet pupils' needs. To say that 'assessment for learning' and 'formative assessment' are synonymous is therefore slightly misleading, albeit a common claim.

Dylan Wiliam and Marnie Thompson (2007) posit that there are five key strategies for formative assessment:

1. Clarifying and understanding learning intentions and criteria for success
2. Engineering effective classroom discussions, questions and tasks that elicit evidence of learning
3. Providing feedback that moves pupils forward
4. Activating pupils as instructional resources for each other, and
5. Activating pupils as owners of their own learning.

We will explore each of these five strategies in the course of the next few chapters and consider what they might look like in practice. And, in order to ensure our assessment practices are effective and do not become a behemoth, we'll also look at how to ensure our current approaches result in marking and feedback that are meaningful, manageable and motivating.

In 2020 Dylan Wiliam and I co-wrote a special supplement for *SecEd Magazine* on the subject of formative assessment. In that supplement, we suggested that school leaders should ask themselves four questions in order to become critical consumers of educational research:

1. Does this solve a problem I have?
2. Can it be implemented here?
3. How much additional achievement will we get?
4. How much will it cost?

We know that many of the central features of formative assessment rank highly in meta-analyses of teaching strategies. For example, and as Wiliam has pointed out, the three most effective strategies identified by the EEF are feedback, metacognition and self-regulated learning, and peer tutoring. These happen to be three of the five 'key strategies' of formative assessment Wiliam and Thompson outlined. The other two are eliciting evidence of achievement and clarifying learning intentions and criteria for success.

It would surely follow, then, that taken together these five strands of formative assessment represent the most effective approach to teaching. Indeed, one might argue that they are common-sense, the 'bread and butter' of good teaching.

An effective teacher starts by articulating what she wants her pupils to learn and shares the criteria against which that learning will subsequently be measured. Then she provides opportunities for pupils to actively engage in the learning process, as well as to support each other's learning. She uses classroom discussions and questioning both to deepen pupils' understanding and to determine how well pupils are progressing; and she provides feedback to help guide pupils on their journey.

But, even if we accept that formative assessment is just common-sense, we need to be careful not to regard it as a panacea and not to focus on the *what* at the expense of the *how*. We also need to remember that the five key strategies of formative assessment do not represent the entirety of good teaching; rather, teachers need to do other things unrelated to assessment such as attend to their instructional design, too.

In terms of focusing on the *how* as much as the *what*, in a moment, as an example, we will explore **feedback**.

But first permit me a sideways step to explore meta-analyses in general and the EEF toolkit in particular because it is thanks to these meta-analyses that feedback has become the 'go to' strategy for raising attainment and yet this can be problematic...

What are meta-analyses and are they reliable?

One criticism aimed at summaries of educational research such as the EEF toolkit and John Hattie's Visible Learning concerns the way in which they conduct meta-analyses then rank strategies by effect size and/or months of extra progress.

A meta-analysis is a way of collating the outcomes of similar studies and converting the data into a common metric, then combining these in order to report an estimate which represents the impact or influence of interventions in that given area.

There are a number of advantages of meta-analyses when conducted as part of a systematic review. For example, they allow large amounts of information to be assimilated quickly. They also help reduce the delay between research 'discoveries' and the implementation of effective strategies. Meta-analyses enable the results of different studies to be compared, and in so doing highlight the reasons for any inconsistencies between similar studies.

However, meta-analyses are not without their problems...

Firstly, it is a misconception that larger effect sizes are associated with greater educational significance.

Secondly, it is a misconception that two or more different studies on the same interventions can have their effect sizes combined to give a meaningful estimate of the intervention's educational importance.

Why?

Because original studies that used different types of 'control group' cannot be accurately combined to create an effect size (not least because what constitutes 'business as usual' in each control group will be different).

Likewise, unless the studies used the same range of pupils, the combined effect size is unlikely to be an accurate estimate of the 'true' effect size of a particular strategy.

Also, the way in which researchers measure the effect can influence the effect size. For example, if you undertake an intervention to improve pupils' ability to, say, decode words, you could choose to use a method specifically designed to 'measure' decoding, or you could use a measure of general reading competence that includes an element of decoding. The effect size of the former will be greater than the latter, due to the precision of the measure used.

Put simply, the original effect sizes we combine to calculate an average (or meta-analysis), in order to be meaningful, must relate to the same outcomes and similar conditions and pupils, including in the control groups.

What's more, increasing the number of test items can influence the effect size. If the number of questions used to measure the effectiveness of an intervention is increased, this may significantly increase the effect size.

Finally, trials are often carried out without first analysing and understanding the barriers that pupils face. When random controlled trials (RCTs) are used in medicine, they only take place *after* intensive theorisation. In education, the process often begins with the trial and subsequent measurements. For example, if it is identified that pupils eligible for the Pupil Premium are not doing as well as their peers in literacy, say, then a trial is launched to test an intervention and the outcome is measured and – if the results are positive – the intervention is recommended for all to use.

However, rarely is there any theorising first about precisely <u>why</u> some pupils are not doing as well as their peers and rarely is there any detailed analysis of the barriers some of these pupils actually face in school. For example, for some pupils it may be that English is an additional language or it may be that their attendance is low. The intervention may work for some pupils but not all, and the meta-analysis may mask the complexity of the issue and send us down the wrong path.

So, should we ignore meta-analyses, effect sizes and the EEF toolkit altogether and go back to doing what we've always done? Of course not. We are finally becoming an evidence-informed profession that uses data to ensure we get better at what we do and, ultimately, improve pupils' life chances. But we should always exercise caution.

We should not regard the data as an oracle; rather, we should contest it and balance what the evidence suggests works with what we know from our own experiences of our own contexts.

We should also dig beneath the meta-analyses and analyse the original studies on which the effect sizes are based because the averages may hide huge variations depending on the nature of the intervention and the context in which it was used.

In conclusion, and as I am often wont to say, teaching is a highly complex, nuanced art-form and we would do well not to reduce it to basic statistics or league tables of 'what works' for only madness that way lies.

So, with these caveats in mind, let us now take a look at what the EEF says about feedback...

The EEF on feedback

Feedback tops the EEF chart – alongside metacognition – as the most impactful strategy at a teacher's disposal and so it seems logical that schools invest time and money in improving the effectiveness of feedback.

However, 'feedback' is a slippery term and can mean many different things. So, before we continue, let's be clear how the EEF defines feedback...

The EEF says that feedback is "information given to the learner or teacher about the learner's performance relative to learning goals or outcomes. It should aim towards (and be capable of producing) improvement in students' learning. Feedback redirects or refocuses either the teacher's or the learner's actions to achieve a goal, by aligning effort and activity with an outcome."

Feedback, says the EEF, can be about "the output of the activity, the process of the activity, the student's management of their learning or self-regulation, or them as individuals (which tends to be the least effective)."

Likewise, this feedback can be "verbal or written, or can be given through tests or via digital technology. It can come from a teacher or someone taking a teaching role, or from peers."

According to the EEF, studies tend to show very high effects of feedback on learning. However, some studies show that feedback can actually have negative effects and make things worse. It is therefore important, the EEF says, to understand the potential benefits and the possible limitations of feedback as a teaching and learning approach. In general, research-based approaches that explicitly aim to provide feedback to learners, such as Bloom's 'mastery learning', tend to have a positive impact.

It's important to note, therefore, that just because the EEF toolkit says that feedback is good, this does not imply that teachers should do lots more of it. Rather, it means that, when done well, it can really benefit pupils and so feedback should be done better not more often, which is to say that feedback should be meaningful and helpful to pupils and given sparingly.

A useful maxim to obey is this: only give feedback to pupils when they are afforded time in class to process it and do something with it.

Broader research suggests that feedback should be about complex or challenging tasks or goals as this is likely to emphasise the importance of effort and perseverance as well as be more valued by the pupils.

Let's move away from the EEF and look more widely at what the evidence tells us about effective feedback...

Other findings on feedback

Although meta-analyses tend to show very high effects of feedback on learning, some studies show that feedback can have negative effects and can actually make things worse (see, for example, Kluger and DeNisi (1996).

It is therefore important to understand the possible limitations, as well as the potential benefits of feedback as a formative assessment tool. In general, research-based approaches that explicitly aim to provide feedback to pupils, such as Bloom's 'mastery learning', tend to have a positive impact.

As I say above, we need to be mindful, therefore, that just because meta-analyses suggest feedback is good, this does not imply that we should do lots more of it.

In practice, we need to carefully consider when we give feedback, what form that feedback takes, and what pupils are expected to do with it. We need to consider how quickly after a task has been attempted, we should give feedback, and whether to do so verbally or in writing, whether to do so in narrative or code form, and whether to do so with marks, marks and comments, or just comments. It is the *how* not just the *what* that we need to consider. In short, meta-analyses can only take us so far.

Beyond the meta-analysis, we know that effective feedback tends to:

- Be specific, accurate and clear (e.g., "It was good because you..." rather than just "correct")
- Compare what a pupil is doing now with what they've done wrong before (e.g., "I can see you were focused on improving X as it is much better than last time's Y...")
- Encourage and support further effort
- Be given sparingly so that it is meaningful
- Provide specific guidance on how to improve and not just tell pupils when they are wrong

There's another health warning before we move on...

Marking and feedback are perhaps the most time-consuming activities in which teachers regularly engage outside of actual classroom teaching.

In their 2016 report, 'Eliminating unnecessary workload around marking', the Independent Teacher Workload Review Group said, "Written feedback has become disproportionately valued by schools and has become unnecessarily burdensome for teachers."

The group also argued that quantity should not be confused with quality: "The quality of the feedback, however given, will be seen in how a pupil is able to tackle subsequent work."

The group recommended that all marking should be meaningful, manageable and motivating...

So, what might this look like in practice?

1. Meaningful marking and feedback

To my mind, marking and feedback have but one purpose: to help pupils make better progress and achieve good outcomes. As I explained earlier, they might do this directly by providing cues to the pupil about what to improve, and they might do it indirectly by providing assessment information to the teacher to guide their planning and teaching.

Marking and feedback carried out for any other purpose are not, in my view, meaningful activities and - as well as being a waste of a teacher's precious time - can distract and indeed detract from this important goal.

The best person to decide which type of marking and feedback to use and when to use it is, of course, the teacher because it is her who will use the assessment information to aid her planning and to support her pupils to make progress.

Although a school's assessment policy may set broad guidelines about how often pupils' work should be marked in order to ensure no pupil falls through the net, it also needs to build in sufficient flexibility so that teachers can decide *how* to do it.

Consistency is important but this does not mean unvarying practice. Whilst having a set of shared expectations regarding marking and feedback will help everybody to be clear about what is required of them, each subject discipline should be allowed to determine the detail of the policy for their areas, responding to the different workload demands of their subject and to the differences inherent in each phase and key stage of education.

The nature and volume of marking and feedback necessarily varies by age group, subject, and what works best for the individual pupil and for the particular piece of work being assessed. As such, teachers should be encouraged to be pragmatic, adjusting their approach according to context.

In practice, this might mean school leaders avoid asking teachers to mark at set times of the year because those times might not always be the best times for that subject and that teacher. Instead, schools might ask teachers to mark a set number of times through the year but allow them or their departments to choose precisely when this would be.

Schools also need to remember that marking looks different in different subjects. As such, departments should be allowed to decide what effective marking and feedback looks like for them. Each subject team may collate examples of best practice to help new staff and to reinforce expectations for existing teachers. But these examples should not be regarded as 'the only way' to do things and should not acquire mythic status.

2. Manageable marking and feedback

A teacher's job is a complex one and it would be possible to work twenty-four hours a day, seven days a week and still not feel that the job is done. And yet there are only so many hours in the day. It is important that, whatever approach schools take to marking and feedback, they ensure they protect teachers' wellbeing because tired teachers do not perform as well and burn-out can lead to issues with teacher retention, and staff shortages seriously impede pupils' progress.

Marking and feedback should, therefore, be proportionate. Any expectation on the frequency of marking should take into account the complexity of marking and the volume of marking required in any given subject, qualification type, and phase and key stage of education.

There is no doubt that feedback is valuable, as we have seen, but we need to decide which one of all the valuable things teachers do is more worthwhile than the others and focus on the areas of biggest impact for the smallest investment of teacher time and energy.

Put simply, if teachers are spending more time marking and giving feedback than pupils are spending on a piece of work then your priorities are somewhat skewed.

School leaders need to ensure teachers are selective in what they mark, rather than expecting them to mark every piece of work a pupil produces and 'tick and flick' every page of their exercise books. Marking everything is time-consuming and counterproductive. Feedback becomes a single grain of sand on a beach, ignored by the pupil because of its sheer ubiquity.

Subject teams and teachers should identify the best assessment opportunities in each topic, module or scheme of work - this might be a synoptic piece that demonstrates pupils' knowledge and understanding across a range of areas, or it might be the exam questions that garner the most marks (for example, the teacher may only assess the 6+ marks questions, whilst pupils and their peers assess the 1 - 5 marks questions).

3. Motivating marking and feedback

Marking can help motivate pupils to make progress. Short verbal feedback is often more motivational than long written comments on pupils' work. Indeed, some pupils find written comments demotivating because they ruin the presentation of their work and are confusing or overwhelming.

Too much feedback is not only harmful to teacher workload, but it can also become a disincentive for pupils because there is too much information on which to focus and respond. What's more, too much feedback can reduce a pupil's long-term retention and harm resilience.

To build retention and resilience, pupils need to be taught to check their own work and make improvements *before* the teacher marks it and gives feedback. Feedback should also prompt further thinking and drafting, perhaps by posing questions on which the pupil has to ruminate and act, as opposed to ready-made suggestions and solutions.

Feedback can be more motivating if it requires pupils to think. For example, we might use comment-only marking more often as this engages pupils because it requires them to take action. Rather than correcting a pupil's spelling, punctuation and grammar, for instance, the teacher might place a letter in the margin for each error in that line using G for grammar, S for spelling, P for punctuation, and so forth. For the higher-performing pupils, the teacher could simply put a dot in the margin for each error. Feedback of this kind gives pupils something to do and therefore makes them think. By thinking, they are more likely to remember the feedback and avoid repeating the same mistakes.

Feedback - the beast of burden?

In their 2016 report, 'Eliminating unnecessary workload around marking', the Independent Teacher Workload Review Group said that "Effective marking is an essential part of the education process. At its heart, it is an interaction between teacher and pupil: a way of acknowledging pupils' work, checking the outcomes and making decisions about what teachers and pupils need to do next, with the primary aim of driving pupil progress. This can often be achieved without extensive written dialogue or comments."

The report went on to say that the group's "starting point is that marking – providing written feedback on pupils' work – has become disproportionately valued by schools and has become unnecessarily burdensome for teachers."

There are a number of reasons for this, the report explained, including the impact of government policy and what has been promoted by Ofsted, as well as decisions taken by school leaders and teachers. This is not to say that all marking should be eliminated, they accepted, but that it must be proportionate.

In short, the group argued that quantity should not be confused with quality. "The quality of the feedback, however given, will be seen in how a pupil is able to tackle subsequent work."

In practice, this means that there can be no 'one-size-fits-all' approach. Rather, a balance must be struck between ensuring consistency and equality of opportunity for all pupils in every curriculum subject and trusting teachers to focus on what they know is in the best interests of their pupils in their context.

Health warnings

The government's teacher workload survey found that 53% of respondents thought that, whilst marking pupils' work was necessary and productive, the excessive nature, depth and frequency of marking was burdensome.

In 2015, a NUT and YouGov survey found that more than half of teachers were considering leaving the profession, with 61% citing "volume of workload" as the main cause of their disquiet.

A recent 'Secret Teacher' column in The Guardian newspaper sought to put some meat on the bones of this debate... The anonymous diarist explained with painful honesty how his school's insistence that he engage in detailed dialogic marking and mark set after set of mock exam papers was endangering his mental and physical health.

Dialogic marking, sometimes called triple marking, is - as I said above - the practice whereby teachers provide written feedback to pupils and pupils are expected to respond in writing to the guidance which, in turn, is then verified by the teacher. Sometimes pupils use different colour pens to indicate the nature of their response with terms like 'green for growth' and 'the purple zone' becoming increasingly commonplace.

So why has dialogic feedback become so popular?

There is, to my knowledge, no government or Ofsted guidance or policy making dialogic feedback a requirement or even an expectation of schools. Although Ofsted did name-check dialogic marking in some of its reports, the inspectorate has since published a handy myth-buster making clear that it does not expect to see a particular frequency or quantity of work in pupils' books or folders (recognising that the amount of work in books and folders will depend on the subject being studied and the age and ability of the pupils), and that it does not expect to see any specific frequency, type or volume of marking and feedback.

Ofsted inspectors have been explicitly told that they are not to comment on marking and feedback in their inspection reports – because the evidence of what works best is as yet inconclusive – beyond stating whether or not what they see corresponds with the school's own assessment policy.

The Teachers' Standards, meanwhile, say only that teachers should "give pupils regular feedback, both orally and through accurate marking, and encourage pupils to respond to the feedback". This is a vague statement which can be interpreted in myriad ways, not necessarily through detailed, dialogic marking.

Who are we marking for?

Some schools I've visited insist on dialogic feedback because it provides a tangible source of evidence for their quality assurance and performance management processes. In other words, it serves a managerial purpose rather than an academic one. However, in so doing, written feedback becomes a poor proxy for good teaching and is reduced from a pupil-led strategy to a box-ticking exercise.

As well as dialogic feedback, teacher workload has been unnecessarily impacted by some schools' insistence that verbal feedback is recorded in books, for example with a stamp. If we insist on such an approach, we need to ask who are we doing it for? Is it a means of control exerted on teachers by senior leaders – another box-ticking exercise to ensure teachers are towing the line – or is it for parents to prove their child is being taught well?

I can see no benefit for the pupil of recording verbal feedback in this way because the pupil already knows they've been given verbal feedback because they were in receipt of it. If it's for control purposes, then school leaders need to ask why they do not trust their teachers and what can be done to remedy that situation. If it's for parents, then school leaders need to communicate their assessment policy more effectively and have bold conversations about what's in the best interests of pupils.

As with any questionable teaching strategy, I always recommend we ask ourselves what impact it would have on our pupils if we suddenly stopped doing it. Would pupils notice? Would they make less progress as a result? I suspect not, thus proving it is a misuse of teachers' time for very little, if any, impact. In fact, as with many of these time-consuming approaches to assessment, it can actually have an adverse impact because it leaves teachers tired and diverts their time and attention away from an alternative strategy that is more worthwhile and impactful.

So, if dialogic feedback and verbal feedback stamps do not pass the 'energy versus impact' test, what does? How can we ensure marking and feedback are made meaningful, manageable and motivating?

More recommendations

In 2016, the Independent Teacher Workload Review Group recommended that, in order to improve the effectiveness of marking and feedback, governors and school leaders should:

- Use the three principles of meaningful, manageable and motivating to review their school's marking practice as part of an overall and proportionate assessment policy in partnership with their teachers
- Evaluate the time implications of any whole school marking and assessment policy for all teachers to ensure that the school policy does not make unreasonable demands on any particular members of staff
- Monitor their marking practice as part of their regular monitoring cycle, and in partnership with their teachers and governing boards, and evaluate its effectiveness on pupil progress
- Challenge emerging fads that indirectly impose excessive marking practices on school

The group also recommended that teachers should:

- Seek to develop a range of assessment techniques to support their pedagogy
- Actively review current practice to ensure marking adheres to the three principles of meaningful, manageable, and motivating

Chapter 9: Whole school v subject specific assessment

In Book One of this series, I explained that, once we have set the destination of our curriculum – what we might call our 'end points', and once you have assessed the starting points of ur curriculum (both in terms of the starting points of the *taught* curriculum and the starting points of the *learnt* curriculum, on which more in a moment), we must plot a course between the two...

In Book One I used an analogy. I said that, if we wanted to find directions using Google Maps, say, we would need to input the destination first then our current location. In other words, Google would ask 'where to?' and then 'where from?'

Once these two pins have been dropped onto the map, Google can begin to find the right path.

In terms of curriculum design, the destination is the intended outcomes of our curriculum, or to use Ofsted's parlance 'the clear end-points' or 'body of knowledge' to be learnt. These end points articulate what knowledge, skills and understanding we expect our pupils and students to have acquired by the time they have finished their curriculum journeys with us. The destination can be positioned at the end of a topic or module, at the end of a year, key stage or phase of education, or indeed many years into the future – say five or ten years – when pupils are applying their knowledge to life and work.

I said that we can think of the starting points of our curriculum in two ways: the starting points of the *taught* curriculum; and the starting points of the *learnt* curriculum.

Put another way, the taught curriculum is what is written in the curriculum plans for the stage or phase immediately preceding that which we teach. This might be the national curriculum or the local curriculum of the schools our pupils come from. We can think of this as the intended curriculum (written down) and the enacted curriculum (actually taught in the classroom).

The learnt curriculum, meanwhile, is what pupils actually know and can do. We can think of this as the real curriculum (what pupils encoded into and can now retrieve from long-term memory). The real curriculum must be assessed on a pupil-by-pupil basis in order to understand what each pupil actually knows and can do, and what gaps remain in their knowledge and skills.

Once we know the destination and starting points, I said, we must carve a path from one to the other. This path is what populates curriculum plans, assessment schedules, and schemes of work.

However – and this is the crucial point for the purposes of our present discussion about assessment – the shape of the path taken in each subject discipline will be different. Some curriculums are linear, following a neat line between the starting point and the destination as pupils build on prior knowledge and make progress. But many curriculums are neither linear nor neat. They may be spiral or helical in shape; they may zigzag.

Let us put a pin in that point for a moment longer, though, whilst we dig deeper into the idea and application of threshold concepts...

Threshold concepts

Irrespective of their shape, most subjects will however find it useful to identify threshold concepts or waypoints that provide a useful checkpoint on the way towards the destination.

Threshold concepts have several advantages: firstly, they provide manageable and achievable stepping-stones for pupils to aim for along the way rather than setting pupils a goal they cannot hope to hit; secondly, they provide a useful pitstop – a means of assessing, recognising and celebrating pupils' progress to date.

When these threshold concepts are used well, they can also become a means of meaningful assessment.

Key concepts are the foundations on which our curriculum is built and the destination to which our pupils are headed. In Book One of this series, I modelled one way of identifying these concepts – albeit with caveats – by using GCSE assessment objectives and learning outcomes. (Those caveats concerned the importance of looking beyond exam specifications and considering the longer-term goals of studying any given subject... For example, though awarding bodies change their specifications every few years, there are some concepts our pupils must know in order for a study of our subject to prove useful to them once they've left school. To help, I suggested we ask ourselves: what do we expect pupils to know and be able to do in our subject in ten years' time?)

By way of example, I homed in on the concept of 'explicit and implicit meanings', concepts pupils must acquire if they are to succeed in their study of English Language at secondary school.

I said that we needed to repeatedly return to these concepts all the way through pupils' schooling and, each time, do so with increasing complexity and anchored in different contexts in order to create more schemata – or mental maps.

As we return to these foundational concepts at increasingly complex levels, I said we could make use of 'threshold assessments' which encourage pupils to move up the reading comprehension 'ladder' from:

Identifies – whereby a pupil shows a simple awareness of language, identifies and gives a simple explanation, identifies literal meanings, and shows some understanding of what is going on...

To:

Explains – whereby a pupil understands language and how it works – for example, they can talk about effects on the reader and use appropriate quotations...

To:

Analyses – whereby a pupil explains the effects of language, goes beyond the literal, analyses words and sentences, and shows an awareness of different meanings, both implicit and explicit...

And, finally, to:

Evaluates – whereby a pupil evaluates the writer's choice of language or impact on the reader and offers their own opinion which is supported by appropriate evidence.

Or, more simply, I said, we could write a sequence of 'can do' statements such as these:

- I can define the words explicit and implicit
- I can identify an explicit and implicit meaning in a non-fiction text
- I can identify both explicit and implicit meanings in a range of different text types
- I can explain why a writer has implied rather than explicitly stated something
- I can comment on the effect of both explicit and implicit meanings on the reader
- I can analyse a writer's use of explicit and implicit meanings

...and so on

There are several advantages to this approach, including – in no particular order:

- The statements make sense to pupils – they're concrete not abstract, simple not lofty
- Pupils can be assessed easily against each statement with a 'yes/no'
- The assessment will inform us what each pupil knows and can do, and what they do not yet know and cannot yet do
- The individual assessment outcomes can be aggregated to provide a percentage of 'mastery' for any given cohort (e.g., 80% of pupils in this class can define both explicit and implicit meanings)
- Both the individual and aggregated assessment outcomes can be used to inform our teaching, notifying us if we need to re-teach or re-cap a concept or concepts, or if can we move on
- Pupils' journeys through this hierarchy of statements can provide tangible evidence of progress – to pupils, parents and schools

- The statements can also be used as learning objectives to provide a clear focus to a lesson or sequence of lessons which can be revisited in the plenary or used on an exit ticket

Of course, learning is neither easy nor neat. Pupils do not often make linear progress and our curriculum is not often linear in shape.

Rather, learning is messy; learners can go backwards as well as forwards, and not all assessments can be used to extrapolate progress over time because what is being assessed at various points through the year may be very different.

As such, 'can do' statements may work for some curriculum content in some subjects but may not – indeed, probably will not – work for everything. Sometimes, the key concepts and their various layers of accomplishment may take the form of questions, factual statements, key features, schools of thought, or exemplars.

Accordingly, to return to that earlier point in which we popped a pin, it is crucial that subject specialists are afforded autonomy in deciding what their key concepts look like and how these might be planned and sequenced over time and then used as a form of assessment.

Designing an assessment system that works for each subject

The Commission for Assessment Without Levels, in their 2015 report, claimed that the use of national curriculum levels led to a curriculum driven by targets which, in turn, came to dominate all forms of in-school assessment and had a profoundly negative impact on teaching and learning.

As a result, progress – they said – became synonymous with moving up to the next 'level' or 'sub-level'. But this posed a problem: progress - in real terms - involves developing a deeper and broader understanding of subject matter, not simply moving on to work that affords a greater level of difficulty. As I have already argued, learning and progress are not always neat and linear.

The Commission also said that, as a consequence of national curriculum levels becoming synonymous with assessment, the more informal, everyday formative assessment that should always have been an integral part of effective teaching at key stage 3 was largely abandoned. Instead, teachers were simply tracking pupils' progress towards target levels rather than engaging in genuine dialogue with pupils about what they had mastered and what they still needed to practice.

One of the other problems with this approach was that the language of levels did not lend itself to assessing the underpinning knowledge and understanding of a concept. Level descriptors offered pseudo-scientific and ostensibly precise measurements which, when analysed, actually offered little help to pupils in their quest to know how to improve.

Removing the 'label' of levels, the Commission suggested, could help to improve pupils' mindsets about their own ability...

Once levels have been removed, argued the Commission, teachers – in reviewing their teaching and assessment strategies – could then aim to ensure that they used methods that allowed all pupils full access to the curriculum.

The Commission also claimed that the expectation placed on teachers to collect data in order to track pupils' progress towards target levels and sub-levels considerably increased teachers' workloads. Without levels, the Commission said, teachers would gradually increase their confidence in using a wider range of formative assessment strategies without the burden of unnecessary recording and tracking.

Removing levels would also shine a brighter spotlight on high quality formative assessment, thereby improving the quality of teaching, as well as contributing to raising standards and reinforcing schools' freedoms to deliver a quality education in the way that best suits the needs of their pupils and the strengths and skills of their staff.

The Commission therefore recommended that schools developed an alternative to levels that marked a definitive departure from the prevailing culture rather than replicated the existing system in all but name. They strongly hinted that schools should base their new assessment systems on the mastery learning approach developed by

Benjamin Bloom in the 1960s. This makes some sense because the new national curriculum also has mastery learning at its core.

In Bloom's version of 'mastery', learning is broken down into discrete units and is presented in a logical order. Pupils are required to demonstrate a comprehensive knowledge of each unit before being allowed to move on to the next unit, the assumption being that all pupils will achieve this level of mastery if they are appropriately supported: some may take longer and need more help, but all will get there in the end.

Inspired by this, in a moment we will explore how a subject discipline might build a new assessment system to measure progress through their curriculum based on the concept of mastery learning but first we must take a step back...

Before we can agree a new subject-specific assessment system, we should write, consult upon and agree and articulate an assessment policy. From this point forwards, the assessment policy should be our guiding light; everything we do to develop an assessment system should support the delivery of our policy. Indeed, as we saw earlier, Ofsted has made clear that they will not comment on how and how often teachers assess pupils, only whether or not they do in line with the school's assessment policy so it's important to get the policy right.

Once a new assessment policy is in place, each subject team needs to decide what unit of measurement they will use. In other words, how will teachers describe pupils' learning and progress in that subject? Whatever measure a team decides to use, it must successfully quantify learning and progress in that subject and must do so in a meaningful way.

So where should we start?

Some schools I've worked with or spoken to have made the mistake of developing a new assessment system that has been a system of 'levels' in all but name.

Rather, subject teams should start by engaging in a process of detailed curriculum planning before they set about designing a system of assessment. Assessment should be the servant and not the master; the curriculum should be king. After all, how can you decide on your assessment criteria before you know what it is that you're assessing? How we teach our curriculum and how pupils respond to it should form the basis of any new assessment system.

What's more, assessment systems which simply recreate grading similar to national curriculum levels and sub-levels are, to my mind, missing the point.

The national curriculum is a description of the content that must be taught in each subject and might, therefore, prove a useful starting point in deciding upon the units of measurement a subject will use to quantify learning and progress. For key stage 4 and post-16 curriculums, we might use awarding body specifications or assessment objectives.

A team's first task, therefore, should be to design a curriculum with clear end-points or bodies of knowledge which describes what will be taught and when, and what learning will result. This kind of detailed curriculum planning – perhaps using my six steps of curriculum intent as a guide – is necessary if a subject team is to successfully develop assessment criteria. Teams should not make the mistake of rushing into designing a new assessment system before they've considered how their curriculum will be taught in practice.

A subject team's second task, then, is to understand how a pupil's knowledge and skills in those parts of the subject covered in a particular module or scheme of work will accumulate over the course of a term, year or key stage into a holistic understanding of the concepts, key ideas, and capabilities learnt in the subject. As such, curriculum plans need to be progressive in nature, developing gradually over time.

Only once everyone is clear about how pupils' knowledge and skills will develop over the course of time can a subject team move on to the third and final task: to develop a means of describing and quantifying what pupils are learning as they move through the curriculum.

Let's now turn our attentions to how this will work in practice and to how we might quantify pupils' learning...

The Commission for Assessment Without Levels were clear in their report that 'life after levels' should be less bureaucratic for teachers. Teachers should spend more time engaged in formative classroom assessments with pupils and less time tracking and recording data. As such, a majority of the assessments that take place should be informal, leading to diagnostic feedback given to pupils and students either in writing in their books or verbally in lessons. Naturally, this data will either be unrecorded or held locally in teachers' mark-books.

Diagnostic feedback should be comment-only and should be specific about what pupils need to do in order to improve. The best feedback addresses faulty interpretations and comments on rather than grades work. The best feedback also provides cues or prompts for further work, is timely, specific and clear, and is focused on task and process rather than on praise. Feedback also works best when it is explicit about the marking criteria, offers suggestions for improvement, and is focused on how pupils can close the gap between their current and their desired performance; it does not focus on presentation or quantity of work.

Occasionally, however, it will be necessary for teachers to reflect on how well their pupils are responding to what is being taught and to share this information more formally with their subject leaders, senior leaders, and other colleagues who teach the same class. This more formal assessment will need to take the form of progress against or towards targets – or perhaps age-related expectations – so what should it look like in practice?

The use of levels and sub-levels assumed that pupils scaled the mountain of progress in a uniform manner in response to teaching, and that we could measure each step with accuracy then categorise and label each pupil accordingly.

Mastery learning replaces this rush to hike up the mountainside with the belief that all pupils will comprehensively know and understand the core content from each topic or module before moving on to the next. Progress, therefore, tends to be non-linear and tailored to meet the needs of each pupil. At the very least, it is likely to look different to how progress looks in other subject disciplines and thus must be bespoke.

'Progress' is a complex concept – a dotted line used to summarise the overall path taken along the mountainside, snaking towards the peak, which may go up as well as down as pupils find the right terrain and get a solid foothold in the rock. However, statistically speaking, we can estimate the average grade that a pupil is capable of achieving based on their prior performance and this information can be used to notify us if pupils fall below expectations.

Intended learning outcomes or objectives (of which more in Chapter 10) provide a good starting point – a foundation, if you like – for tracking pupil progress because they summarise what is taught in each lesson or unit and they are already widely used in lesson planning and delivery. Teachers routinely write and share objectives with pupils at the start of lessons and use them to measure progress in lesson plenaries.

As long as intended learning outcomes cover all the key concepts (end points) that must be learnt, then tracking and recording pupils' acquisition of them should provide a cumulative assessment log which will quantify their progress at any given point.

As such, let us return to our five key strategies of formative assessment starting with learning intentions and success criteria...

Chapter 10: Learning intentions and criteria for success

As I explained earlier, one of the five key strategies of formative assessment is clarifying and understanding learning intentions and criteria for success.

The notion here is simple: if pupils do not know what they are supposed to be learning and how their work will eventually be judged, then their ability to learn and make progress will be stymied. Obviously, we want pupils to know what we want them to learn and to understand what successful outcomes will look like.

This talks to the three processes that are central to formative assessment:

1. Establishing where pupils are in their learning
2. Establishing where they are going
3. Establishing how they're going to get there

As I explained in the previous chapter, learning intentions are also helpful in that they can provide a starting point – a foundation, if you like – for tracking pupil progress because they summarise what is taught in each lesson or unit. As long as learning intentions cover all the key concepts (end points) that must be learnt in a subject curriculum, then tracking and recording pupils' acquisition of these key concepts can provide a cumulative assessment log which will quantify their progress at any given point.

So far so good...

But here's an important caveat before we carry on: The use of learning intentions and success criteria does not mean that every lesson must start with a set of objectives scribed on the board which pupils have to copy down. First of all, lessons are artificial blocks of study not a complete learning sequence and not every lesson, therefore, needs to start with objectives. Secondly, there is rarely anything to be gained by getting pupils to copy verbatim from the board. Rather, the direction of travel should be shared with pupils when you begin a new topic or module.

A second caveat: learning intentions are not the same as activities. Setting out what pupils will *do* is therefore not particularly helpful; rather, we should focus on what pupils are expected to *think* about and *learn*. As Wiggins and McTighe (2010) said, we should start from what we want pupils to know and plan backwards. Wiggins and McTighe also advocate a two-stage process: first, we clarify the learning intentions, followed by the success criteria; second, we explore the activities that will lead to the required learning.

I would suggest that learning intentions are measurable statements which articulate what pupils should know and/or be able to do by the end of a lesson or sequence of lessons. The best learning intentions are pupil-centred rather than teacher-centred – they set out what pupils will learn, not what the teacher will teach and do so in language that pupils will understand.

The best learning intentions, I think, actually shape what pupils learn because when pupils know what they're expected to learn they can direct their attention towards those ideas or concepts. They help pupils to attend to the curriculum content they need to learn and avoid distractions, thus making efficient use of their limited working memory capacities.

Having clear learning intentions not only helps pupils to narrow their focus to the most important knowledge and skills, it can also help them to organise their notes, track their progress towards meeting the outcomes, and improve their ability to self-study.

Sharing learning intentions at the start of a sequence of lessons on a particular topic is an important element of direct instruction (which is proven to be a more effective strategy than less-structured approaches such as enquiry-based learning, particularly for novice learners) because knowing the intended outcomes in advance helps pupils to practice their metacognitive skills and to become more self-regulated.

Sharing learning intentions and success criteria helps pupils to understand how what they're learning today fits into the 'bigger picture' and how they will be assessed. Sharing the big picture is about connecting learning, too; and making explicit the purpose of learning - articulating why pupils need to achieve the learning goals we're setting for them and of what use their learning will be to them in the future. As such, it can increase pupils' levels of motivation and engagement.

Learning intentions and success criteria are often opaque. To avoid this, we can give pupils examples of annotated work by way of exemplification. It can also be very helpful to provide pupils with opportunities to design their own assessments.

Now let us move on to the next key strategy for formative assessment: classroom questioning and discussions...

Chapter 11: Classroom discussions and questioning

Once we know what we want our pupils to learn and how that learning will be assessed, we need to gather evidence about pupils' progress toward these goals. One 'low stakes' way we can do this is by planning effective classroom discussions and questions...

In many ways, the art of asking good questions is what good teaching's all about. Indeed, Socrates argued that "questioning is the only defensible form of teaching".

There are, to my mind, two particular reasons for asking a question in class: either to cause pupils to think, or to provide information to the teacher about what to do next.

The former involves *dialogic* questioning, which is to say questions that encourage discussion, questions that are open, philosophical, and challenging. And dialogic questions – such as Socratic questions – don't just cause thinking, they promote critical thinking. Open questions which cause pupils to think in this way are widely regarded in academia as effective teaching strategies.

But, for the purposes of this discussion, we will focus on questions that help achieve the latter...

Closed questions, when effectively formulated, can be great assessment tools to use in the classroom. They can provide valuable assessment information to the teacher about pupils' learning and progress, about who has "got it" and who has not, and about what needs re-teaching, recapping or developing further.

What's more, closed questions used as a form of assessment reduce the marking load on teachers and make assessment "live" and responsive.

Further, closed questions used as a form of assessment turn assessment into a means of learning, they are assessment *as* learning as well as assessment *for* learning.

One of the most effective forms of closed questions, I think, is the multiple-choice question used at a hinge point of a lesson when a teacher needs to check whether pupils have grasped a key concept and are ready to move on to study another. Usually, pupils' ability to understand the next concept being taught is contingent on their mastery of the concept that has just been taught. It is important, therefore, that the teacher assesses pupils' levels of mastery before moving on.

The trick to making multiple-choice questions effective is to create several wrong options which are nevertheless plausible and closely related to the right answer. The best "wrong" options also uncover common misconceptions or false assumptions. As such, the best way to create the wrong options is to mine a class's work – or look back to a previous year when the topic was last taught – for pupils' common misconceptions, misunderstandings and mistakes. If nothing else, trawling through pupils' work to discover what they tend to get wrong and what tends to stump them, helps inform the lesson planning process, allowing the teacher to dedicate more time to those elements with which pupils most often struggle.

This act of mining pupils' work for misconceptions and then applying the findings in a way that helps anticipate pupils' difficulties and questions, is the difference between content knowledge and pedagogical content knowledge, between knowing your subject and knowing how to teach your subject in a way which makes sense to pupils.

Analysing misconceptions also helps an expert teacher to view a topic through the lens of the novice pupil, to narrow the knowledge gap between them, and to improve the lesson planning process.

A hinge question, then, is a diagnostic tool which a teacher employs when their pupils reach the "hinge" point. Pupils' responses provide the teacher with valuable evidence about what their pupils know, don't know and need to do next. A class's response to a hinge question should inform the teacher whether to completely reteach the topic, recap the main points, or move on to the next topic.

To be effective, every pupil must respond to a hinge question within a set timeframe, ideally one to two minutes. All pupils must participate in the process. As such, it is best to avoid a 'hands up' approach and instead employ a tactic that ensures every pupil shows the teacher their answer at the same time. This enables the teacher to assess every pupil and prevents pupils from being unduly influenced by their peers.

Simultaneous, all-class responses can be achieved by using mini whiteboards on which pupils write their answers then hold them up when instructed. Alternatively, voting buttons could be used. Or, more simply, pupils could hold up lettered, numbered or coloured cards to indicate their answer, or even just their fingers.

The teacher must be able to interpret pupils' responses quickly, ideally within a minute, so that the flow of the lesson isn't stunted. Before pupils show their responses, the teacher – as I say above – needs to set a pass rate for what they consider to be an acceptable level of 'mastery'. For example, the teacher might decide that they will move on to the next topic if more than 80 per cent of pupils answer the hinge question correctly. They will then need to consider what to do to support the 20 per cent who got the question wrong. The teacher could set a task for the 80 per cent to do while working with the 20 per cent, scaffolding their learning, recapping on key points, and so on. Or perhaps the teacher could enlist some of the 80 per cent as peer-teachers to explain the topic to the 20 per cent. This notion of pupils acting as teachers is proven to be extremely effective.

The use of multiple-choice questions is what Wiliam calls the *pedagogy of engagement* because the teacher requires every pupil to engage in the process, to think about the question and give her some information. After all, it is immediately evident if a pupil does not respond. Multiple-choice questions are also what Wiliam calls the *pedagogy of contingency* because the teacher's actions depend on the learning that is evidenced by her questioning.
Now let us turn our attention to key strategies three and four: activating pupils as instructional resources for each other, and as owners of their own learning...

Chapter 12: Activating pupils as instructional resources

There are two elements to explore in this chapter: Activating pupils as instructional resources for each other; and activating pupils as owners of their own learning...

Activating pupils are instructional resources for each other

Slavin, Hurley, and Chamberlain (2003) argue that activating pupils as instructional resources for each other leads to large gains. But there are two important conditions that must be met: Firstly, pupils must work *as a* group not just *in a* group; secondly, every pupil must be responsible for his or her own contribution to the group.

A simple way of activating pupils as instructional resources for each other is to ensure that all work is peer-assessed before it is handed to the teacher. Before a pupil can submit an essay, for example, they must get a partner to complete a peer-assessment checklist which might include criteria such as whether the essay includes a date and title, if it is written in paragraphs and uses sentence markers, and so forth. Pupils cannot submit work until it has been peer-assessed and the onus is on the peer-assessor not the originator of the work because it is them who will be held accountable if they've missed any of the criteria. This helps ensure pupils take the role of peer-assessor seriously, but it also ensures pupils fully understand the criteria which, in turn, will help them to improve their own work.

Self- and peer-assessment of this kind can often be effective strategies – particularly because we want our pupils to become increasingly metacognitive in their approach to learning – because these strategies: give pupils greater responsibility for their learning; allow pupils to help and be helped by each other; encourage collaboration and reflection; enable pupils to see their progress; and help pupils to see for themselves how to improve.

However, such strategies come with health-warnings...

Firstly, pupils need to be helped to develop the necessary skills and knowledge to be able to assess and give feedback.

Secondly, we need to provide pupils with time in lessons to process, reflect upon and respond to peer-feedback.

This process of self-monitoring, self-assessing and self-adjusting work can be aided if we:

- Allocate five minutes in the middle and at the end of a lesson in order to consider 'What have we found out? What remains unresolved or unanswered?
- Ask pupils to attach a self-assessment form to every formal piece of work they hand in
- Include a one-minute essay at the end of an instruction-based lesson in which pupils summarise the two or three main points and the questions that still remain for them (and, thus, next time, for the teacher)
- Ask pupils to attach a note to any formal piece of work in which they are honest about what they do and do not understand
- Teach pupils to evaluate work in the same way that teachers do so that pupils become more accurate as peer reviewers and self-assessors, and more inclined to "think like teachers" in their work.
- Start lessons with a survey of the most burning questions pupils may have. Then, as part of the final plenary, judge how well the questions were addressed, which ones remain, and what new ones emerged.
- Leave the second half of a unit deliberately 'open' to allow pupils to frame and pursue the inquiry (rather than be directed by the teacher) based on the key questions that remain and clues that emerge at the end of the first half
- Get pupils to develop a self-profile of their strengths and weaknesses as learners at the start of the year whereby they consider how they learn best, what strategies work well for

them, what type of learning is most difficult, and what they wish to improve upon. Then, structure periodic opportunities for pupils to monitor their efforts and reflect on their struggles, and successes, and possible edits to their own profiles.

Activating pupils as owners of their own learning

According to Deci et al (1982), when teachers are told they are responsible for pupils' progress, the quality of their teaching deteriorates, as does their pupils' learning. However, when pupils are told to take a more active role in monitoring and regulating their own learning, the pace of their progress increases.

A simple method to help pupils take ownership of their own learning is to give each pupil a laminated card, green on one side and red on the other. At the start of the lesson, the card is placed on the pupil's desk with the green side facing upwards. Once the teacher has given an explanation, if the pupil doesn't understand it, they flip the card over to red.

As soon as one pupil flips the card to red, the teacher selects a pupil who is still showing green, and that pupil goes to the front of the class and answers a question that the pupil who's showing red wants to ask.

This approach encompasses both the *pedagogy of engagement* and the *pedagogy of contingency* I mentioned earlier because there is nowhere to hide – pupils are either saying they understand, or they want some help. This means pupils are constantly required to think about whether they understand or not. This approach activates pupils as owners of their own learning, but it also allows the teacher to be responsive, and quickly, to pupils' needs.

This is an example of metacognition.

Metacognition describes the processes involved when pupils plan, monitor, evaluate and make changes to their own learning behaviours. Metacognition is often considered to have two dimensions: Metacognitive knowledge *and* self-regulation.

Let us delve a little deeper into the twin-concepts of metacognition and self-regulation...

Metacognition

Metacognition and self-regulation take equal top-billing on the EEF toolkit and, like feedback, which we explored earlier, are said to add an extra eight months of learning per year.

However, also like feedback, metacognition can mean different things to different people. So, before we continue, let's be clear how the EEF define it...

What is metacognition?

The EEF say that metacognitive approaches aim to help pupils think about their own learning more explicitly, often by teaching them specific strategies for planning, monitoring and evaluating their learning.

Metacognition gifts pupils a repertoire of strategies to choose from and the skills to select the most suitable strategy for any given learning task.

Is metacognition effective?

The EEF say that metacognition and self-regulation approaches have consistently high levels of impact. These strategies are usually more effective when taught in collaborative groups so that pupils can support each other and make their thinking explicit through discussion.

The potential impact of these approaches is high but can be difficult to achieve in practice as they require pupils to take greater responsibility for their learning and develop their understanding of what is required to succeed. The evidence indicates that teaching these strategies can be particularly effective for low achieving and older pupils.

When seeking to develop pupils' metacognitive abilities, say the EEF, teachers should consider which explicit strategies they can teach pupils to help them plan, monitor, and evaluate specific aspects of their learning.

Teachers should also consider how to give pupils opportunities to use these strategies with support, and then independently, and ensure they set an appropriate level of challenge to develop pupils' self-regulation and metacognition in relation to specific learning tasks.

In the classroom, teachers should consider how they can promote and develop metacognitive talk related to lesson objectives, and what professional development is needed to develop teachers' knowledge and understanding of these approaches.

Metacognition in the classroom

Before we answer the all-important question 'What is metacognition in the classroom?' I think it helpful to state what it is not...

Firstly, metacognition is not simply 'thinking about thinking', despite the morphology of the word. Although metacognition does indeed involve thinking about one's thinking, it is much more complex than this; rather, metacognition is actively monitoring one's own learning and, based on this monitoring, making changes to one's own learning behaviours and strategies.

Secondly, not every strategy used whilst performing a cognitive task can be described as metacognitive. Indeed, Flavell (1981) made a useful distinction. He said that strategies used to <u>make</u> cognitive progress are 'cognitive strategies'; strategies used to <u>monitor</u> cognitive progress, meanwhile, are 'metacognitive strategies'.

Thirdly, metacognition is not solely in the domain of the learner and not solely for the benefit of older learners. Although it's true that a metacognitive approach typically focuses on allowing the learner rather than the teacher to take control of their own learning, this is not to say that the teacher has no role to play. Indeed, the teacher is integral to the development of their learners' metacognitive skills. For example, in order for pupils to become metacognitive, self-regulated learners, the teacher must first set clear learning objectives, then demonstrate and monitor pupils' metacognitive strategies, and prompt and encourage their learners along the way. And metacognitive skills can be developed from an early age, certainly whilst pupils are at primary school; it is not something to be reserved for secondary pupils.

What's the difference between metacognition and self-regulation?

Metacognition describes the processes involved when learners plan, monitor, evaluate and make changes to their own learning behaviours. As I said a moment ago, metacognition is often considered to have two dimensions:

- Metacognitive knowledge, and
- Self-regulation.

Metacognitive knowledge refers to what learners know about learning. This includes:

- The learner's knowledge of their own cognitive abilities (e.g., 'I have trouble remembering key dates in this period of history')
- The learner's knowledge of particular tasks (e.g., 'The politics in this period of history are complex')
- The learner's knowledge of the different strategies that are available to them and when they are appropriate to the task (e.g., 'If I create a timeline first it will help me to understand this period of history').

Self-regulation, meanwhile, refers to what learners do about learning. It describes how learners monitor and control their cognitive processes. For example, a learner might realise that a particular strategy is not yielding the results they expected so they decide to try a different strategy.

Put another way, self-regulated learners are aware of their strengths and weaknesses, and can motivate themselves to engage in, and improve, their learning.

According to the EEF, we approach any learning task or opportunity with some metacognitive knowledge about:

- Our own abilities and attitudes (knowledge of ourselves as a learner)
- What strategies are effective and available (knowledge of strategies)
- This particular type of activity (knowledge of the task)

When undertaking a learning task, we start with this knowledge, then apply and adapt it. This, the EEF say, is metacognitive regulation. It is about "planning how to undertake a task, working on it while monitoring the strategy to check progress, then evaluating the overall success".

A metacognitive cycle

Metacognition and self-regulation might take the following form:

1. *The planning stage:*

During the planning stage, learners think about the learning goal the teacher has set and consider how they will approach the task and which strategies they will use. At this stage, it is helpful for learners to ask themselves:

- 'What am I being asked to do?'
- 'Which strategies will I use?'
- 'Are there any strategies that I have used before that might be useful?'

2. *The monitoring stage:*

During the monitoring stage, learners implement their plan and monitor the progress they are making towards their learning goal. Pupils might decide to make changes to the strategies they are using if these are not working. As pupils work through the task, it is helpful to ask themselves:

- 'Is the strategy that I am using working?'
- 'Do I need to try something different?'

3. *The evaluation stage:*

During the evaluation stage, pupils determine how successful the strategy they've used has been in terms of helping them to achieve their learning goal. To promote evaluation, it is helpful for pupils to ask themselves:

- 'How well did I do?'
- 'What didn't go well?' 'What could I do differently next time?'
- 'What went well?' 'What other types of problem can I use this strategy for?'

4. The reflection stage:

Reflection is an integral part of the whole process. Encouraging learners to self-question throughout the process is therefore crucial.

The EEF offer a slightly different version of this process which they call the *metacognitive regulation cycle*. Helpfully, they posit some concrete examples. For instance, they introduce us to John who is set a maths question to answer. John starts with some knowledge of the task (word problems in maths are often solved by expressing them as equations) and of strategies (how to turn sentences into an equation). His knowledge of the task then develops as it emerges from being a word problem into a simultaneous equation. He would then continue through this cycle if he has the strategies for solving simultaneous equations. He could then evaluate his overall success by substituting his answers into the word problem and checking they are correct. If this was wrong, he could attempt other strategies and once more update his metacognitive knowledge.

Most learners, say the EEF, go through many of these thinking processes to some extent when trying to solve a problem or tackle a task in the classroom. The most effective learners, however, will have developed a repertoire of different cognitive and metacognitive strategies and be able to effectively use and apply these in a timely fashion. They will, in other words, self-regulate and find ways to motivate themselves when they get stuck. Over time, this can further increase their motivation as they become more confident in undertaking new tasks and challenges.

Teaching metacognition

The EEF argue that metacognition and self-regulation must be explicitly taught. This might look as follows:

1. *The planning stage:*

The teacher encourages pupils to think about the goal of their learning (set by the teacher, or themselves) and to consider how they will approach the task. This might include:

- Ensuring they understand the goal,
- Activating relevant prior knowledge about the task,
- Selecting appropriate strategies, and
- Considering how to allocate their effort.

2. *The monitoring stage:*

Here, the teacher emphasises the need for pupils to assess their own progress. This might include self-testing and self-questioning, as well as making changes to their chosen strategies. Teachers can explicitly teach these skills by prompting pupils with examples of the things they should be considering at each stage of a learning task.

The EEF use the example of pupils drawing or painting a self-portrait in art. Effective teacher questioning while modelling a self-portrait, they say, can aid the development of metacognitive reflection as follows:

Planning:

- 'What resources do I need to carry out a self-portrait?'
- 'Have I done a self-portrait before and was it successful?'
- 'What have I learned from the examples we looked at earlier?'
- 'Where do I start and what viewpoint will I use?'
- 'Do I need a line guide to keep my features in proportion?'

Monitoring:

- 'Am I doing well?'
- 'Do I need any different techniques to improve my self-portrait?
- 'Are all of my facial features in proportion?'
- 'Am I finding this challenging?'
- 'Is there anything I need to stop and change to improve my self-portrait?'

Evaluation:

- 'How did I do?'
- 'Did my line guide strategy work?'
- 'Was it the right viewpoint to choose?'
- 'How would I do a better self-portrait next time?'
- 'Are there other perspectives, viewpoints or techniques I would like to try?'

Some of the above 'planning' questions activate prior knowledge (resources, previous exemplars) whereas others model the use of the best cognitive strategies (viewpoint, line guides). The 'monitoring' questions, meanwhile, emphasise both general progress (proportion, editing) alongside checking general motivation (meeting goals and dealing with challenge). The 'evaluation' questions concentrate on assessing the relative success of the cognitive strategies used (line guide, viewpoint, comparison with other techniques) and on what can be learnt from the experience.

The EEF suggest that these prompts are accompanied by explicit instruction in the relevant cognitive strategies. In the self-portrait example, for instance, pupils will only be able to consider these questions and approaches if they understand the importance of perspective and the different techniques.

The EEF proffers a handy 7-step guide to teaching metacognitive strategies, as follows:

1. ***Activating prior knowledge*** – here, the teacher discusses with pupils the different causes that led to World War One while making notes on the whiteboard.

2. ***Explicit strategy instruction*** – here, the teacher explains how a 'fishbone' diagram will help organise their ideas, with the emphasis on the cognitive strategy of using a 'cause and effect model' in history that will help them to organise and plan a better written response.

3. ***Modelling of learned strategy*** – next, the teacher uses the initial notes on the causes of the war to model one part of the fishbone diagram.

4. ***Memorisation of learned strategy*** – here, the teacher tests if pupils have understood and memorised the key aspects of the fishbone strategy, and its main purpose, through questions and discussion.

5. ***Guided practice*** – next, the teacher models one further fishbone cause with the whole group, with pupils verbally contributing their ideas.

6. ***Independent practice*** follows whereby pupils complete their own fishbone diagram analysis.

7. Finally, in ***structured reflection*** the teacher encourages pupils to reflect on how appropriate the model was, how successfully they applied it, and how they might use it in the future.

For my part, I have found that metacognition and self-regulation are best developed in the classroom when we follow a 6-step process as follows:

1. Thinking aloud

One of the most effective teaching strategies to promote metacognition is 'thinking aloud' whereby the teacher makes explicit what they do implicitly and makes visible the expertise that is often invisible to the novice learner.

The best thinking aloud occurs when the teacher is modelling excellence. For example, a teacher may write a short paragraph of persuasive text to model how to use rhetorical devices. As she is writing, the teacher explains every decision she is taking, and articulates the drafting and re-drafting process that is essential to all good writing.

There is some evidence, at least in terms of metacognition, that modelling and thinking aloud should not be too specific as this may inhibit pupils' reflection. Indeed, as the EEF says, "some 'deliberate difficulty' is required so that pupils have gaps where they have to think for themselves and monitor their learning with increasing independence".

2. Thinking hard

Teachers need to set an appropriate level of challenge if they are to help develop pupils' metacognition and self-regulation because if pupils are not given hard work to do – if they do not face difficulty, struggle with it and overcome it - they will not develop new and useful strategies, they will not be afforded the opportunity to learn from their mistakes and they will not be able to reflect sufficiently on the content with which they are engaging. Moreover, if pupils are not made to think hard, they will not encode new information into long-term memory and so learning will not occur.

The EEF offers some useful questions for pupils to ask that gauge the difficulty level of the work they're doing:

Knowledge of task:
- Is this task too challenging for me?
- What are the most difficult aspects of this task?
- How much time should I devote to this task?
- Are there easy bits I can get 'done'?

Knowledge of self:
- Is this task asking for subject knowledge I can remember?
- Do I understand the concept(s) that underpins this task?
- Am I motivated to stick at this tricky task?
- What can I do to keep myself focused?

Knowledge of strategies:
- Are my notes effective for understanding this task?
- Do I need to ask the teacher for help?
- What strategies can I deploy if I am stuck?
- What can I do to ensure I remember what I've learned?

3. Thinking efficiently

As well as thinking hard, pupils need to think efficiently if they are to cheat the limitations of working memory. Yes, pupils must be challenged and must struggle with new concepts if they are attend to them actively and therefore encode them into long-term memory, but if the work's *too* hard, they're likely to hit cognitive overload whereby they try to hold too much information in working memory at one time and therefore thinking fails.

The trick, then, is to ensure the work is hard but achievable. The work must be beyond pupils' current capability but within their reach. They must struggle but must be able to overcome the challenge with time, effort and support.

The concept of cognitive load theory (which was first espoused by John Sweller) is crucial to metacognition and self-regulation because:

- When we draw on existing knowledge from long-term memory to support working memory, creating what's called 'schema', we increase working memory capacity and overcome its limited size. This explains why knowledge is important and why pupils must be encouraged to try and activate prior knowledge before asking for help.
- We understand new concepts within the context of what we already know. The more pupils know and can draw from their long-term memory, the more meaningful new knowledge will become and the more they will be able to process and apply it.
- To ensure that learning activities don't demand too much of working memory and cause cognitive overload, we need to teach pupils coping strategies such as using mind-maps, taking effective notes (perhaps using the Cornell method), thinking aloud to work through problems, and breaking tasks down into smaller steps. Teachers can support this process through the use of structured planning templates, teacher modelling, worked examples, and breaking down activities into their constituent parts, revealing one part at a time and in sequence. Teachers can also help by being mindful of the fact that metacognitive tasks – such as asking pupils to reflect on their learning – can, if not well-timed, distract pupils from the task at hand. In other words, teachers shouldn't expect pupils to develop new cognitive *and* metacognitive skills simultaneously, rather one must follow the other.

4. Thinking positively

Research suggests that an important factor in the effective use of metacognitive strategies is the ability to delay gratification. In other words, pupils who are better able to delay rewards in favour of studying are better at planning and regulating their learning, and vice versa. This is nothing new, of course. Walter Mischel began his now-famous 'marshmallow tests' back in 1960. He gave young children a challenge of delaying their gratification by offering them a choice of one small reward – a single marshmallow – or waiting 15 minutes and receiving two marshmallows instead. During the experiment, children used a number of metacognitive strategies such as not looking at the marshmallow and closing their eyes and thinking of something completely different. Pupils need to be taught strategies for delaying gratification and for motivating themselves if they are to master metacognition. There are two types of motivation: extrinsic and intrinsic.

Extrinsic motivation refers to the performance of an activity in order to attain a desired outcome. Extrinsic motivation comes from influences outside an individual's control; a rationale, a necessity, a need. Common forms of extrinsic motivation are rewards (for example, money or prizes), or - conversely - the threat of punishment.

To build extrinsic motivation, and therefore improve metacognition, we can provide pupils with a rationale for learning by sharing the 'big picture' with them. In other words, we can continually explain how their learning fits in to the module, the course, the qualification, their careers and to success in work and life. For example, we can explain how today's lesson connects with yesterday's lesson and how the learning will be extended or consolidated next lesson, as well as how it will be assessed at a later stage. We can explain how this learning will become useful in later life, too. And we can connect the learning in one subject with the learning in other subjects, making explicit the transferability of knowledge and skills and the interconnectedness of skills in everyday life.

Intrinsic motivation, meanwhile, is the self-desire to seek out new things and new challenges, in order to gain new knowledge. Often, intrinsic motivation is driven by an inherent interest or enjoyment in the task itself, and exists within an individual rather than relying on external pressures or necessity. Put simply, it's the desire to do something even though there is no reward except a sense of accomplishment at achieving that thing. Intrinsic motivation is a natural motivational tendency and is a critical element in cognitive, social, and physical development.

Pupils who are intrinsically motivated are more likely to engage in a task willingly as well as work to improve their skills through metacognition and self-regulation which – in turn – increase their capabilities. Pupils are likely to be intrinsically motivated if:

1. They attribute their educational results to factors under their own control, also known as autonomy.
2. They believe in their own ability to succeed in specific situations or to accomplish a task - also known as a sense of self-efficacy.
3. They are genuinely interested in accomplishing something to a high level of proficiency, knowledge and skill, not just in achieving good grades - also known as mastery.

5. Thinking together

Our job as teachers is to help pupils move from novice to expert. Part of this process is to ensure our pupils become increasingly independent over time. In short, we need to begin with lots of scaffolds in place but slowly remove those scaffolds as pupils develop their knowledge and skills. Asking challenging questions and guiding pupils with verbal feedback, prompting dialogue, and productive 'exploratory' talk is a great way to do this.

In practice, the teacher might achieve this by encouraging pupils to think in advance of a task about what could go wrong then, afterwards, to discuss what they found hard about the task.

Of course, it's not just about the teacher interacting with pupils; pupils must also interact with each other in order to test their metacognitive strategies and knowledge.

'Dialogic teaching' is a particularly effective method of managing these interactions because it emphasises classroom dialogue through which pupils learn to reason, discuss, argue, and explain. As the EEF explains, "A key element of [dialogic teaching] is to encourage a higher quality of teacher talk by going beyond the closed 'teacher question–pupil response–teacher feedback' sequence... [instead], dialogue needs to be purposeful and not just conversation, with teachers using questions to elicit further thought."

Dialogic teaching is the brainchild of Professor Robin Alexander whose most recent research identified six basic talk 'repertoires': talk settings, everyday talk, learning talk, teaching talk, questioning, and extending. The most relevant repertoires for developing metacognitive skills, so say the EEF, are learning talk and teaching talk. Learning talk includes narrating, questioning, and discussing; teaching talk, meanwhile, includes instruction, exposition, and dialogue.

6. Thinking alone

As pupils move from novice towards expertise, they become independent learners and, with a greater degree of autonomy, make active choices to manage and organise their own learning. But even as pupils become independent, they need their teachers to provide them with timely feedback and to help them to plan, monitor, and evaluate their progress.

According to Zimmerman, independent learners use a number of strategies to help them, including:

- Setting specific short-term goals
- Adopting powerful strategies for attaining the goals
- Monitoring performance for signs of progress
- Restructuring one's physical and social context to make it compatible with one's goals
- Managing time-use efficiently
- Self-evaluating one's methods
- Attributing causation to results and adapting future methods.

Russian psychologist Lev Vygotsky developed the idea of the *Zone of Proximal Development* which lies between what a learner can achieve alone and what a learner can achieve with expert guidance. The expert, in this case the teacher, initially takes responsibility for monitoring progress, setting goals, planning activities and allocating attention for example. Gradually, the responsibility for these cognitive processes is given over to the learner. The learner becomes increasingly capable of regulating his or her own cognitive activities.

- What do the students know already?
- What will they know with support from you?
- What remains to be known?

The four levels of metacognitive learners

David Perkins (1992) defined four levels of metacognitive learner which provide a useful framework for teachers when identifying where on the novice-expert continuum their pupils are and how much support is required:

1. ***Tacit learners*** are unaware of their metacognitive knowledge. They do not think about any particular strategies for learning and merely accept if they know something or not.
2. ***Aware learners*** recognise some of the thinking processes they use such as generating ideas, finding evidence, etc. However, thinking is not necessarily deliberate or planned.
3. ***Strategic learners*** organise their thinking by using problem-solving, grouping and classifying, evidence-seeking and decision-making, etc. They know and apply the strategies that help them learn.
4. ***Reflective learners*** are not only strategic about their own thinking, but they also reflect upon their learning whilst it is happening, considering the success or failure of their strategies and revising them as appropriate.

A useful checklist

To end this chapter, here is a useful checklist for teaching metacognition in the classroom in order to activate pupils as owners of their own learning...

1. ***Have I included clear learning objectives?*** Pupils need to understand what their learning objectives are so that they can plan how to achieve them. The process of planning should involve pupils identifying which strategies they already know that could be applied in a new situation.

2. ***How am I going to encourage my pupils to monitor their learning?*** Effective learners commonly use metacognitive strategies whenever they learn. However, they may fail to recognise which strategy is the most effective for a particular learning task. Teachers can ask questions to prompt pupils to monitor the strategies that they are using. For example, before pupils begin a task, the teacher can prompt them to identify where the task might go wrong and how they could prevent this from happening. During the task, the teacher could encourage pupils to focus on the learning objectives and encourage them to think about how they can maintain that focus. This will encourage pupils to think more actively about where they are now, where they are going and how to get there.

3. ***How can I create opportunities for pupils to practise new strategies?*** When teachers introduce pupils to a new strategy, it helps to give them the opportunity to use it first with support and then independently. It is important to monitor pupils' progress and provide them with feedback on the specific strategies they are using to help shape their learning process.

4. ***How can I allow time for pupil self-reflection?*** Personal reflection enables pupils to critically analyse their performance in relation to a particular task and consider what they might do differently to improve their performance in future tasks. It is important that teachers dedicate time for pupils to reflect and provide them with the tools to do so. One way of doing this is to use thinking journals.

5. ***Does the classroom environment support metacognitive practices?*** Teachers are instrumental in shaping the culture of learning in their classrooms. By establishing a supportive learning environment that fosters and anticipates metacognitive practices, these practices will become an integral part of the learning process. Teachers should ensure they model metacognitive practices effectively, affording pupils plenty of opportunities to work collaboratively with their peers, encouraging reflection and evaluating their progress.

Part Five: Ensuring equity

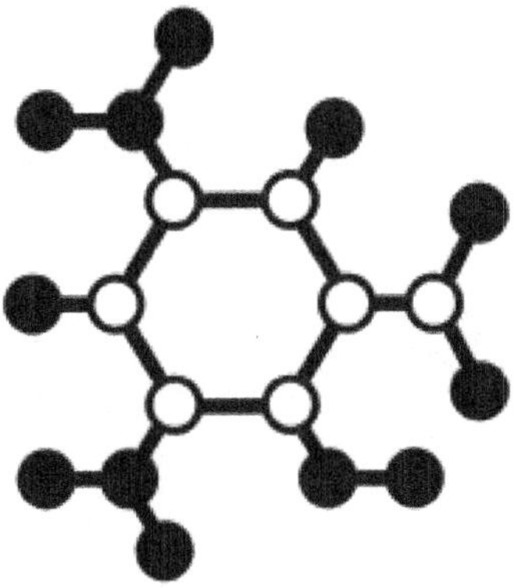

Chapter 13: The causes and consequences of disadvantage

Over the course of the next four chapters, we are going to explore ways to ensuring greater levels of equity in our schools – which is to say, we will discuss how we might provide fairer access to an ambitious curriculum and help every pupil, irrespective of their starting points and backgrounds, and their additional and different needs, to achieve in school and in life.

We will examine the various attainment gaps that commonly exist in our education system and consider ways of closing – or, at any rate, narrowing – those gaps. We will, in Chapter 14, examine the ethnicity gap. In Chapter 15, we will turn to the gender gap. In Chapter 16, we will discuss the poverty gap. And, in Chapter 17, we will consider the SEND gap.

But first, in this chapter, I would like to discuss attainment gaps in more general terms and share with you my three-point plan for addressing them.

Before I do so, a couple of important caveats...

Firstly, if we are honest, we have to accept that it's highly unlikely we will close some or all of these attainment gaps. Sadly, as much as I wish it were not so, we do not live in an egalitarian society and thus not all children are equal. They do not enter school equal and they will not leave school equal.

Whether we put this inequality down to nature or nurture, or perhaps, and as seems most likely to me, a nuanced combination of the two, we know that children start school with different levels of knowledge and skills and with different abilities and capabilities to know and do more.

No matter what we do to 'level the playing field', we are unlikely ever to do so. We can certainly improve awareness of the situation, and, above all, we can try to stop the gaps from widening as children travel through our education system. And we must truly believe in the transformative power of education and in our own capacities and – dare I say – duties, as educators, to improve the life chances of all those children in our charge including, perhaps especially, those who start their lives at a disadvantage.

To think otherwise is to accept that a child's birth will also be their destiny; that success or failure are preordained.

As I am often wont to say, teaching is a superpower because teachers make the world a better place one pupil at a time. Teachers really do change lives.

But, put simply, there are too many complex factors at play, and too many ingrained inequalities in society, for schools and colleges alone to close the gaps and achieve absolute equality.

Furthermore, the language of 'closing the gap' is not, to my mind, particularly helpful. For one, as I have just explained, it is often an unattainable goal. We may narrow some gaps, perhaps, or at least not perpetuate them further; but we are unlikely to close them. If we do close some gaps it is more likely to be a consequence of slowing the pace of progress and stunting the attainment of our non-disadvantaged cohort of pupils rather than of accelerating the pace of progress of all. Naturally, we do not want to close gaps by holding some pupils back; we want to set as our guiding star the notion that all pupils will be helped to improve. But if we want to help all pupils to achieve, then we must also accept that this means we cannot close attainment gaps because parallel lines never meet.

But that's not the only reason I think the phrase 'closing the gap' is unhelpful. As well as being an unattainable goal, the phrase 'closing the gap' is also, I think, the language of a deficit model. In other words, it focuses on what is missing and what is 'wrong' with some pupils, rather than on what differences exist and what we can do to help all pupils access and achieve within an ambitious curriculum.

It also encourages us to fall into the trap of assuming that there is such a thing as an 'average' pupil, a bell-curve against which we can plot ability and thus determine the 'more able' and the 'less able'. And yet 'ability', if that is the right term, is far more complex than this. Let's assume Pupil A is verbally articulate and yet struggles to commit their thoughts to paper whereas Pupil B struggles with oracy but is articulate when wielding the pen. Who is the more able and who is the less able of the two? Or imagine Pupil C is skilled at football but not so adept at cricket whereas Pupil D is a cricketing marvel but can't dribble a football for love nor money. Who is the more able sportsperson?

Not only does a deficit model focus on what's missing, it assumes that there are some more able, or higher-performing, pupils, and some less able, or lower performing, pupils. And yet ability – and indeed performance – is not binary. Some pupils will perform well in some subject disciplines but not others, and some pupils will perform better in some aspects of some subject disciplines but not others.

Every pupil is an individual and must be treated as such. We must not fall into the trap of thinking that Pupil A is disadvantaged and therefore is destined to fail. But nor should be assume that because Pupil A is deemed to be 'disadvantaged' and does indeed face some barriers to learning that they are uniformly less able to achieve in every unit and every subject they study in school and college and thus require additional interventions and support in order to 'catch up' with their peers.

Which brings me on to my next caveat...

Secondly, and related to this latter point, we are too obsessed, I think, with labels. Whether those labels pertain to socio-economic deprivation, such as Free Schools Meals (FSM) or Pupil Premium (PP), or to ethnicity and social status and gender, such as 'white working-class boys', or indeed to special educational needs and disabilities, such as 'speech, language and communication needs (SLCN), they can be problematic.

I am not suggesting that labels have no place in education. They can be a useful shorthand and thus help us report on generic attainment gaps at whole-school and national levels. They can help us to identify trends and to tackle endemic discrimination. And, in the case of medical diagnoses such as dyslexia or autism, they can explain why a child finds some aspects of school-life more challenging than their peers and they can open doors to specialist support, and not least to the money with which to buy that specialist support.

Yes, labels have a place in our system.

But the problem with labels arises when they are used by schools and teachers to determine expectations of what a child can achieve – or, more likely, cannot achieve – and to ascertain what additional support will be provided.

A further problem with labels, I would argue, is when those labels are used to describe a cohort of pupils and thus stereotype children.

Labels can mask significant individual differences within a cohort. There is no such thing, for example, as a typical 'Pupil Premium child' or a typical 'SEND child'. The mere notion is ridiculous. Every pupil is a human being, and every human being is different from every other human being in myriad ways. There may be some shared characteristics, of course; but labels lack nuance and lead us to assume that the problems faced by each child with the same label are exactly the same and that, as such, the solutions must also be the same.

Put simply, there is a difference between causes and consequences.

The *cause* is the label. The *consequence* is what this means in practical terms for each child in each situation. Let me explain...

The fact a pupil is eligible for the Pupil Premium – and thus is often labelled 'Pupil Premium child' – might tell you a little about their context. Perhaps they are eligible for free school meals (FSM – another label!). And thus, you may know that they are categorised as living in poverty (of which much more in Chapter 16). But that, in and of itself, tells you little about what, if anything, they may find difficult at school and thus what you can do to help them.

To help the child in school, we need to convert the cause, the label, into a consequence in order to better understand what the label means in practice.

And the first point to make loud and clear is that it might mean absolutely nothing! Just because a child is eligible for free school meals doesn't mean they are in any way academically disadvantaged at school. Likewise, just because a child is NOT eligible for free school meals does not mean that they are not academically disadvantaged.

And furthermore, a label does not mean that a pupil will be uniformly disadvantaged at school or college. Which is to say, that whilst a pupil may find some aspects of school more difficult than some of their peers, they are unlikely to find EVERY aspect of school difficult and may even find some aspects easier than most of their peers.

Labelling pupils leads to lazy decisions. It was common some years ago – and still happens in some schools today – to demand that teachers label pupils eligible for the Pupil Premium on their registers, to design 'strategic seating plans' (whatever they are!) and to provide evidence of what they do differently for these Pupil Premium children.

Why? Such a practice only serves to discriminate against pupils, and to define pupils – and publicly brand them – as being 'poor' and thus 'less able' and in need of help.

Being eligible for the Pupil Premium, as I have said, might mean absolutely nothing in terms of a pupil's abilities in a subject or indeed in every subject. And even if it did, the generic 'PP' label tells us nothing about what to do.

Let me exemplify this notion of causes and consequences using a somewhat simplistic – albeit accurate – example...

The example I will use will be that of a pupil eligible for the Pupil Premium, but the ideas relate equally to other labels including some of those I explore in the chapters that follow: Ethnicity, gender, poverty, and SEND.

Let us define our terms before we continue...

What is the Pupil Premium?

The Pupil Premium was introduced by the Coalition Government in 2011 and is money given to schools to help support disadvantaged pupils. 'Disadvantage' here being defined by three categories:

Firstly, the Pupil Premium is awarded to pupils who are categorised as 'Ever 6 FSM'. In other words, it is given to pupils who are recorded in the January school census who are known to have been eligible for free school meals (FSM) in any of the previous six years, as well as those first known to be eligible that month.

Secondly, Pupil Premium funding is awarded to pupils who are adopted from care or who have left care. In other words, the funding is given to pupils who are recorded in the January school census and alternative provision census who were looked after by an English or Welsh local authority immediately before being adopted, or who left local authority care on a special guardianship order or child arrangements order (previously known as a residence order).

Finally, Pupil Premium funding is awarded to pupils who are categorised as 'Ever 5 service child' which means a pupil recorded in the January school census who was eligible for the service child premium in any of the previous four years as well as those recorded as a service child for the first time in the January school census.

Since the Pupil Premium was introduced in 2011, I think it fair to say that its success has been variable...

The gap has closed fastest in schools with the highest concentration of disadvantaged pupils. In contrast, schools with the lowest proportions of disadvantaged pupils have seen the gap widen, particularly at key stages 2 and 4, suggesting that disadvantaged children are not prioritised when they are in the extreme minority.

What's more, the overall gap has widened.

One in three children in the UK now grows up in poverty and the attainment gap between rich and poor is detectable at an early age. White working-class pupils (particularly boys) are among the lowest performers and the link between poverty and attainment is multi-racial.

The limited impact of PP can, I believe, be attributed to several factors...

Firstly, as I explained above, the PP is awarded to pupils who are eligible for free school meals (as well as those in care and care-leavers, and children from service families) but FSM eligibility is a poor proxy for educational and social disadvantage. Indeed, as many as 50-75% of FSM children are not in the lowest income households. What's more, it's often the time-poor and the poorly educated who are less engaged and motivated at school, rather than those facing economic deprivation.

That's not to suggest that a majority of pupils from poorer households do not have difficulties at school and are not deserving of additional funds to help close the gap between them and their better-off peers, but it is important to note that other pupils not currently in scope for the PP are also academically disadvantaged and are equally deserving of our attention.

Secondly, PP children are not a homogenous group. Indeed, the group mean often masks significant differences amongst all those eligible for the PP. It is wrong to group together those eligible for PP and assume they all face the same challenges and must therefore be served the same diet of interventions.

Thirdly, closing the gap is more difficult for some schools than others because the size of the 'gap' is necessarily dependent on the non-PP demographic in a school. Put simply, the more advantaged the non-PP cohort, the harder it is to close the gap. And yet we too often focus on measuring the disadvantage and do not consider the make-up of those pupils in a school who are not eligible for PP funding.

Finally, PP data is often meaningless because assessments change and the PP cohort itself changes over time - not least as a result of recent benefits reforms which have taken a large number of pupils out of eligibility despite no discernible differences in their circumstances. In other words, pupils who were previously eligible for the PP are no longer so but are just as disadvantaged socio-economically. Further, in-school sample sizes are usually too small to make inferences, and this also means that a school's 'closing the gap' data is largely meaningless.

All of which is not to suggest that we should scrap the PP or indeed abandon all hope of ever narrowing the gap. If the government were to cease funding disadvantage and were to include the funds in school budgets then, I firmly believe, it would only be a matter of time before those funds were diminished or cut completely.

But we need to recognise the limitations of the current funding system and use common sense and pragmatism when analysing our data. Most importantly of all, we need to ensure that we focus on every child in a school not just those eligible for discrete funding, and work on a case-by-case basis to understand the barriers that some pupils face at school. Talking of which...

The three-point plan

I have developed a three-point plan for supporting pupils with additional and different needs, including those eligible for the Pupil Premium which is as follows:

1. Identify the barriers
2. Plan the solutions
3. Agree the success criteria

Let's take a closer look at this plan, again using the example of the Pupil Premium by way of illustration...

Step 1: Identify the barriers

Before you can put in place Pupil Premium intervention strategies aimed at supporting disadvantaged pupils, you must first understand why a gap exists between the attainment of disadvantaged pupils and non-disadvantaged pupils.

In short, you need to ask yourself: What are the consequences of disadvantage faced by my pupils? What barriers might their disadvantage pose in class? How does their disadvantage translate itself, if at all, in terms of their ability to access the ambitious curriculum I am teaching and to achieve in line with their peers?

This may sound obvious but it's a step often missed by schools and colleges who assume all pupils eligible for PP, or other sources of disadvantage funding, must be academically disadvantaged and similarly so. However, as I say above, when identifying the barriers to learning in your school or college, it is important to remember that not all the pupils who are eligible for PP will face all, or even some, of the barriers to learning that I will set out shortly, and that there is no such thing as a typical disadvantaged pupil. Rather, each pupil must be treated on an individual basis and the support given must be tailored to meet their needs, not the needs of a homogenous group.

As such, schools and colleges should identify, on a case-by-case basis, what, if any, consequences those pupils eligible for PP or other sources of funding face when it comes to accessing and achieving within an ambitious curriculum.

Let me emphasise this point once again: not all pupils who come from socio-economically deprived homes will struggle at school and do less well than their more affluent peers. A majority will, but it's not set in stone.

Likewise, not all pupils who come from affluent families will do well in school. It may be that some of these pupils have time-poor parents and spend their evenings plugged into a device rather than talking at the dinner table or reading books.

In short, avoid stereotypes and work hard to understand the truth for each of your pupils.

When seeking to identify *consequences* of disadvantage on a pupil's schooling, here are some possible answers to look out for...

- Pupils for whom English is an additional language having limited vocabulary
- Poor attendance and punctuality
- Mobility issues caused by a pupil moving between schools
- Issues within a pupil's family unit
- Medical issues, sometimes undiagnosed
- A lack of sleep or poor nutrition
- A lack of family engagement with learning
- Education not being valued within local community
- A lack of role models, especially male role models
- A lack of self-confidence and self-esteem.

Step 2: Plan the solutions

Once you have identified the barriers your disadvantaged pupils face towards learning, you need to plan the solutions.

In a moment, I will explore the logistics of step 2 of my three-point plan in more detail, but first I'd like to focus on the most common cause of disadvantage amongst our pupils: language and literacy skills...

Language and literacy

Currently, about 1 in 3 young people grows up in poverty in the UK – in the last year or two, this proportion has risen from 1 in 4. What's worse, a report by the Resolution Foundation in February 2019 predicted that by 2023 37% of children would live in poverty – the highest proportion since the early 1990s.

The academic achievement gap between rich and poor is detectable from an early age – as early as 22 months in fact – and the gap continues to widen as children travel through the education system.

Children from the lowest income homes are half as likely to get five good GCSEs and go on to higher education as the national average. And white working-class pupils (particularly boys) are amongst our lowest performers.

What's more, the link between poverty and attainment is multi-racial - whatever their ethnic background, pupils eligible for free school meals underperform compared to those who are not.

In short, if you're a high ability pupil from a low-income home (and, therefore, a low social class), you're not going to do as well in school and in later life as a low ability pupil from a higher income home and higher social class.

Interestingly, the gap does not grow at a consistent rate. If you were to divide the gap that exists by the age of sixteen into fifths, two would already be present by the age of five, one would have developed during primary school and two during secondary school. Two-thirds of the primary school component develops during reception and key stage 1.

In other words, educational disadvantage starts early, and these early gaps are particularly pronounced in early language and literacy.

By the age of 3, more disadvantaged children are – on average – already almost 18 months behind their more affluent peers in their early language development. Around two fifths of disadvantaged five-year-olds are not meeting the expected literacy standard for their age.

I would argue that the Pupil Premium should, therefore, be spent primarily on improving pupils' literacy and language skills.

Early intervention

Black and Wiliam (2018) argue that "Children from working class families, who are only familiar with the restricted code of their everyday language, may find it difficult to engage with the elaborated code that is required by the learning discourse of the classroom and which those from middle class families experience in their home lives."

Children born into families who read books, newspapers and magazines, visit museums, art galleries, zoos, and stately homes and gardens, take regular holidays, watch the nightly news and documentaries, and talk - around the dinner table, on weekend walks, in the car – about current affairs and about what they're reading or doing or watching – develop what is sometimes called *cultural capital.*

These children acquire, unknowingly perhaps, an awareness of the world around them, an understanding of how life works, and – crucially – a language with which to explain it all. And this cultural capital provides a solid foundation on which they can build further knowledge, skills and understanding.

The unlucky ones - those children not born and brought up in such knowledge-rich environments, and who therefore do not develop this foundation of cultural capital - don't do as well in school because new knowledge and skills have nothing to 'stick' to or build upon.

These children may come from broken or transitory homes, be in care, have impoverished parents who work two or more jobs and so spend little time at home or are too exhausted when they get home from work to read to or converse with their children.

These parents may not themselves be well educated and so possess very little cultural capital of their own to pass on to their children. Maybe these parents came from disadvantaged backgrounds and so books and current affairs never featured in their lives and remain alien to them. Maybe they did not do well at school or did not enjoy their schooling and so do not know how to – or do not wish to – help prepare their child for the world of education.

Let's be clear – educational disadvantage is an accident of birth. It is not about ability, innate or otherwise. But, unfortunately, a child's birth is often their destiny...

The Matthew Effect

The Matthew Effect is a term coined by Daniel Rigney in his book of the same name, using a title taken from a passage in the Bible (Matthew 13:12) that proclaims, 'The rich shall get richer and the poor shall get poorer".

In the context of academic disadvantage, the Matthew Effect posits that disadvantaged pupils shall get more disadvantaged because they do not possess the foundational knowledge that they need in order to access and understand the school curriculum.

It is not, as I said earlier, that these children are less able, but that they don't have the same amount of knowledge about the world as their more fortunate peers with which to make sense of new information and experiences.

Put simply, the more you know, the easier it is to know more and so the culturally rich will always stay ahead of the impoverished, and the gap between rich and poor will continue to grow as children travel through our education system.

The best use of Pupil Premium funding, therefore, is to help disadvantaged pupils to build their cultural capital.

Indeed, the Ofsted Education Inspection Framework also highlights the importance of cultural capital. It says that inspectors will judge the extent to which schools are equipping pupils with the knowledge and cultural capital they need to succeed in life. Ofsted says that its definition of this knowledge and cultural capital matches that found in the aims of the national curriculum: namely, that it is "the essential knowledge that pupils need to be educated citizens, introducing them to the best that has been thought and said and helping to engender an appreciation of human creativity and achievement".

Once you're clear that the best use of PP funding is to build cultural capital then all the hard work of action planning, implementing, monitoring and evaluating intervention strategies, and reporting the impact of your Pupil Premium activities becomes easier...

The next big question, then, is 'how?'

Cultural capital

Cultural capital is a somewhat contentious term that has taken on new meanings within the world of education since its inclusion in the national curriculum and Ofsted's inspection framework.

In the field of sociology, cultural capital comprises the social assets of a person (education, intellect, style of speech, style of dress, etc.) that promote social mobility in a class-driven society.

Cultural capital includes all the accumulated cultural knowledge that confers social status and power, and it comprises all the material and symbolic goods that society considers rare and worth seeking.

The concept was coined by Pierre Bourdieu and Jean-Claude Passeron in Cultural Reproduction and Social Reproduction (1977). It was expanded on by Bourdieu in his essay The Forms of Capital (1985) and his book The State Nobility: Élite Schools in the Field of Power (1996).

In the essay, Bourdieu describes cultural capital as a person's education (knowledge and intellectual skills) that provides advantage in achieving a higher social status.

Cultural capital, then, is a complex concept and takes many forms but it is, in part, concerned with using education to improve a pupil's social standing, to confer on them the knowledge they need in order to achieve a higher status.

One of the most impactful forms that cultural capital takes in practice, I think, is a child's word power because the size of a pupil's vocabulary in their early years of schooling (the number and variety of words that the young person knows) is a significant predictor of academic attainment in later schooling and therefore of success in life. In short, words are a means of achieving a higher social standing.

So, let us turn to the question of how we can build cultural capital...

How can we build cultural capital?

Most children are experienced speakers of the language when they begin school but reading the language requires more complex, abstract vocabulary than that used in everyday conversation.

More affluent young people who develop reading skills early in their lives by reading frequently add to their vocabularies exponentially over time.

In The Matthew Effect, Daniel Rigney explains: "While good readers gain new skills very rapidly, and quickly move from learning to read to reading to learn, poor readers become increasingly frustrated with the act of reading, and try to avoid reading where possible.

"Pupils who begin with high verbal aptitudes find themselves in verbally enriched social environments and have a double advantage."

Furthermore, E D Hirsch, in his book The Schools We Need, says that "The children who possess intellectual capital when they first arrive at school have the mental scaffolding and Velcro to catch hold of what is going on, and they can turn the new knowledge into still more Velcro to gain still more knowledge".

Department for Education data suggests that, by the age of seven, the gap in the vocabulary known by children in the top and bottom quartiles is something like 4,000 words (children in the top quartile know around 7,000 words).

For this reason, when seeking to build our vulnerable learners' cultural capital, we need to understand the importance of vocabulary and support its development so that children born into poverty who do not develop this foundational knowledge before they start school are helped to catch up.

So, what can we do to help the word poor become richer and, with it, to diminish the difference between the attainment of vulnerable learners and their peers?

One answer is to plan group work activities which provide an opportunity for the word poor to mingle with the word rich, to hear language being used by pupils of their own age and in ways that they might not otherwise encounter.

Another approach is to ensure that vulnerable learners have equal access to a knowledge-rich diet and provide cultural experiences in addition to, not in place of, the school curriculum. This might involve museum and gallery visits, or mentors who talk with pupils about what's happening in the world, perhaps reading a daily newspaper with them before school or at lunchtime.

Yet another solution is additional intervention classes (taking place outside the taught timetable to avoid withdrawing pupils from classes) in which we teach and model higher-order reading skills because, as the literate adults in the room, we use these skills subconsciously all the time, so we need to make the implicit explicit.

For example, we could use these intervention sessions to model:

- Moving quickly through and across texts
- Locating key pieces of information.
- Following the gist of articles
- Questioning a writer's facts or interpretation
- Linking one text with another
- Making judgments about whether one text is better than, more reliable than, or more interesting than another text

We can also promote the love of reading for the sake of reading; encouraging pupils to see reading as something other than a functional activity. It is the responsibility of every adult working in a school to show that reading because we like reading is one of the hallmarks of civilised adult life.

Finally, because we know that the socio-economic attainment gap – like many other vulnerabilities – emerges early in a child's life and that, therefore, the child's family is crucial in helping to close that gap, we might also support community projects such as reading mentor schemes, helping improve parents' literacy levels and encouraging parents and members of the community to engage with education.

Community outreach

Finally, it's worth remembering that, although Pupil Premium funding is for the purposes of the school it is awarded to, it can also be used for the benefit of pupils registered at other maintained schools or academies and on community facilities such as services whose provision furthers any charitable purpose for the benefit of pupils at the school or their families, or people who live or work in the locality in which the school is situated.

We know that the attainment gap emerges early in a child's life and that, therefore, the child's family is crucial in helping to close that gap.

We know, too, that reading books from an early age is a vital weapon in the battle for social mobility.

As such, Pupil Premium funding can legitimately - and wisely - be used to support community projects such as reading mentor schemes, helping improve parents' literacy levels and encouraging parents and members of the community to engage with education.

The Pupil Premium grant can be used, for example, to fund a community outreach officer who helps educate disadvantaged or hard-to-reach parents in the locality about the work of the school, how best to support young people with their education, and as an advocate for the use of community facilities such as libraries, museums and galleries.

They could lead cultural visits after school, at weekends and in the holidays for those children who would not otherwise enjoy such experiences.

If the impact of such activity can be linked to an increase in literacy levels and cultural capital, then it is money well spent and will help to close the gap in a sustainable way.

Admittedly, this will involve some bravery on the part of secondary schools will not know with absolute certainty which pre-school or primary-age pupils are likely to attend their school aged 11 but they can make an educated guess and, even if some Pupil Premium money is spent on young people who do not go on to attend that school, it is still money well spent within the school community and schools have a duty to look beyond their gates and be a force for good in society.

The logistics of step 2...

So far, I have underlined the importance of *identifying the barriers* because not all pupils who are eligible for the Pupil Premium or other sources of disadvantaged funding are academically disadvantaged and even those who are will not face the same barriers to learning as each other. As such, I said, it is crucial that schools treat each pupil as an individual and provide support on a case-by-case basis.

Once we have identified the barriers each pupil faces, we must decide what action we can take to help them overcome those barriers and afford each pupil an equal chance of success at school. This is step 2 – plan the solutions. And, under this heading, I have already tackled language and literacy but what else should we consider when planning the solutions...?

Some starting principles for intervention and support

There are, I believe, some common principles we need to consider when deciding which strategies to use...

Firstly, we should ensure our strategies promote an ethos of attainment for all pupils, rather than stereotyping disadvantaged pupils as a group with less potential to succeed.

Secondly, we should take an individualised approach to addressing barriers to learning and emotional support and do so at an early stage, rather than providing access to generic support as pupils near their end-of-key-stage assessments.

Thirdly, we should focus on outcomes for individual pupils rather than on providing generic strategies for whole cohorts.

Fourthly, we should deploy our best staff to support disadvantaged pupils; perhaps develop existing teachers' and TAs' skills rather than using additional staff who do not know the pupils well.

Fifthly, we should make decisions based on frequent assessment data, responding to changing evidence, rather than use a one-off decision point.

And finally, we should focus on high quality teaching first rather than on bolt-on strategies and activities outside school hours and outside the classroom.

I have already articulated one such strategy: the building of cultural capital by closing the vocabulary gap. Although context is all and you must make decisions based on what you know about your own pupils, in addition to building cultural capital, I believe that disadvantaged funding can usefully be focused on:

1. Improving pupils' transitions between the key stages and phases of education
2. Developing pupils' cross curricular literacy skills
3. Developing pupils' cross curricular numeracy skills

Why use disadvantage funding to improve transition?

According to Galton (1999), almost forty per cent of pupils fail to make expected progress during the year immediately following a change of schools or settings. Although the effect of transition is particularly felt as pupils transfer from primary school to secondary school at age 11 - DfE data shows that average progress drops between Key Stage 2 and Key Stage 3 for reading, writing and maths – this is by no means the only transition that needs improving. Students' transfer from secondary school to FE college is similarly crucial and often mismanaged with college leaders and teachers wrongly assuming their sixteen-year-old learners are much more independent and mature than they are.

Whatever stage a pupil is at, when they transfer from one setting to another, the effects of transition are amplified by risk factors such as poverty and ethnicity. Those pupils eligible for PP and other forms of disadvantage funding are, therefore, amongst those most likely to suffer when they change schools. Although schools cannot mitigate all of the social and emotional effects of transition, they can do more to help pupils make the academic leap more smoothly and successfully.

Why use disadvantage funding to improve literacy?

I've already talked about word power and teaching vocabulary, but language and literacy are much more than this of course...

Disadvantage funding can be used to run interventions in which teachers or mentors model higher-order reading skills because, as the literate adults in the room, teachers use these skills unconsciously all the time so they need to make the implicit explicit. For example, intervention sessions could be used to model:

- Moving quickly through and across texts
- Locating key pieces of information.
- Following the gist of articles
- Questioning a writer's facts or interpretation
- Linking one text with another
- Making judgments about whether one text is better than, more reliable than, or more interesting than another text

As I said earlier, disadvantage funding could also be used to promote the love of reading for the sake of reading, too; encouraging our pupils to see reading as something other than a functional activity.

Why use disadvantage funding to improve numeracy?

Numeracy skills, like literacy skills, are gateway skills that enables pupils to access and succeed in the whole school or college curriculum.

Numeracy skills are also vital for success in work and life and can help to mitigate the effects of socio-economic deprivation.

Numeracy can, I think, helpfully be divided into four categories:

1. Handling information
2. Space, shape and measurements
3. Operations and calculations
4. Numbers

'Handling information' is about graphs and charts, comparing sets of data and types of data, processing data, and probability.

'Space, shape and measurements' is about both space, shape and measure, and solving problems with space, shape and measure.

'Operations and calculations' is about addition and subtraction, multiplication and division, number operations, and the effective use of calculators.

'Numbers (and the use of the number system)' is about using numbers, whole numbers, size and order, place value, patterns and sequences, and numbers 'in between' whole numbers.

In addition to those four categories, numeracy encompasses three sets of skills:

1. Reasoning
2. Problem-solving
3. Decision-making

Reasoning might involve identifying structures, being systematic, searching for patterns, developing logical thinking, and predicting and checking. Problem-solving might involve identifying the information needed to carry out a task, breaking down a problem or task into smaller parts, interpreting solutions in context, and making mental estimates to check the reasonableness of an answer. And decision-making might involve choosing appropriate strategies, identifying relevant information and choosing the right tools and equipment.

Disadvantage funding can be used to fund teacher professional development to raise awareness of how to teach numeracy across the curriculum...

For example, in English, numeracy can be developed by using non-fiction texts which include mathematical vocabulary, graphs, charts and tables.

In science, pupils will order numbers including decimals, calculate means, and percentages, use negative numbers when taking temperatures, substitute into formulae, rearrange equations, decide which graph to use to represent data, and plot, interpret and predict from graphs.

In ICT, pupils will collect and classify data, enter it into data handling software to produce graphs and tables, and interpret and explain the results. When they use computer models and simulations, they will draw on their abilities to manipulate numbers and identify patterns and relationships.

In art and design and technology, pupils will use measurements and patterns, spatial ideas, the properties of shapes, and symmetry, and use multiplication and ratio to enlarge and reduce the size of objects.

In history, geography and RE, pupils will collect data and use measurements of different kinds. They will study maps and use coordinates and ideas of angles, direction, position, scale, and ratio. And they will use timelines similar to number lines.

Disadvantage funding can also be used for numeracy intervention strategies...

At the whole-school level, the PP and other forms of disadvantage funding may also be used to help create a positive environment that celebrates numeracy and provides pupils with role models by celebrating the numeracy successes of older pupils.

At subject level, PP funding may be used to help provide high quality exemplar materials and display examples of numeracy work within a subject context. Departments could highlight opportunities for the use of numeracy within their subject and ensure that the learning materials that are presented to pupils match both their capability in the subject and their numerical demands.

Step 3: Agree the success criteria

The third and final action on my three-point plan is to *agree the success criteria.*

Once you've identified the barriers to learning faced by your disadvantaged pupils and have planned the best solutions to help them overcome these barriers, you need to be clear about what success will look like. Ask yourself: what do I expect to see as an outcome? What is my aim here? For example, is it to:

- Raise attainment
- Expedite progress
- Improve attendance
- Improve behaviour
- Reduce exclusions
- Improve parental engagement
- Expand upon the number of opportunities afforded to disadvantaged pupils...?

Whatever your immediate goal is, ultimately you should be seeking to diminish the difference between the attainment of disadvantaged pupils in your school and non-disadvantaged pupils nationally, as well as narrowing your within-school gap. As such, if your initial aim is pastoral in nature, for example to improve behaviour and attendance, or reduce exclusions, then you must take it a step further and peg it to an academic outcome. Although pastoral outcomes are important, all our activity must ultimately lead to an academic success criterion - in other words, improving attainment. The PP and other forms of disadvantaged funding exist to close the attainment gap, after all.

Monitoring and evaluating

In terms of ensuring you meet your success criteria, it's crucial that any intervention strategy is monitored as it's happening and not just evaluated once it's finished. The monitoring may involve more anecdotal data such as pupil and teacher feedback, but evidence must be gathered throughout the lifespan of the intervention in order to ensure it is working – or working as well as it could – and so that timely decisions can be taken to stop or tweak an intervention if it is not having the desired effect on pupil progress. Waiting until the intervention has finished to evaluate its success is too late: if it did not work or did not work as well as it could have done, then time and money have been wasted.

When interventions work best

When setting the success criteria, it's important to consider the best individual approach. For example, evidence suggests that interventions work best when they are short term, intensive, focused, and tailored...

Short term

The best interventions help pupils to become increasingly independent over time. In other words, the scaffolds slowly fall away. Interventions should, therefore, be planned to run for a finite amount of time, ideally less than a term. Of course, if the evidence shows the intervention is working but that further improvement is needed, then the intervention can be extended, but to slate an intervention for a year, say, is often misguided.

Intensive

Similarly, interventions should be intensive, perhaps with three or more sessions a week rather than just one. And those sessions should also be intensive in the sense of being short, say 20 to 50 minutes in length rather than an hour or more.

Focused

Interventions should be keenly focused on a pupil's areas of development rather than be generic. For example, rather than setting a goal of, say, 'improving a pupil's literacy skills', an intervention strategy should be focused on a specific aspect of literacy such as their knowledge of the plot of Stone Cold or their ability to use embedded quotations in an essay.

Tailored

Interventions need to be tailored to meet the needs of those pupils accessing them. They must be as personalised as any classroom learning and not be 'off the peg' programmes. Assessment data should be used to inform the intervention and to ensure it is being pitched appropriately to fill gaps in the pupil's knowledge.

So, what works?

Many schools turn to the EEF when deciding which intervention strategies will work best for those pupils eligible for PP and other types of disadvantage funding. If you refer to their toolkit, here's a quick reminder of the health warnings I issued in Book Two of this series...

How does the EEF toolkit work?

The EEF teaching and learning toolkit is based on meta-analyses of other studies. A meta-analysis is a way of collating the outcomes of similar studies and converting the data into a common metric, then combining those in order to report an estimate which represents the impact or influence of interventions in that given area.

As I explained in Book Two, there are a number of advantages of meta-analyses when conducted as part of a systematic review. For example, they allow large amounts of information to be assimilated quickly. They also help reduce the delay between research 'discoveries' and the implementation of effective strategies. Meta-analyses enable the results of different studies to be compared, and in so doing highlight the reasons for any inconsistencies between similar studies.

However, meta-analyses are not without their problems. For example, it is a misconception that larger effect sizes are associated with greater educational significance, and it is a misconception that two or more different studies on the same interventions can have their effect sizes combined to give a meaningful estimate of the intervention's educational importance because studies that used different types of 'control group' cannot be accurately combined to create an effect size (not least because what constitutes 'business as usual' in each control group will be different to the others).

Likewise, unless the studies used the same range of pupils, the combined effect size is unlikely to be an accurate estimate of the 'true' effect size of a particular strategy. Also, the way in which researchers measure the effect can influence the effect size. What's more, increasing the number of test items can influence the effect size. If the number of questions used to measure the effectiveness of an intervention is increased, this may significantly increase the effect size.

This doesn't mean we shouldn't look to meta-analyses such as the EEF toolkit for advice on which interventions to use to support our disadvantaged pupils. But we should dig beneath the meta-analyses and analyse the original studies on which the effect sizes are based because the averages may hide huge variations depending on the nature of the intervention and the context in which it was used.

Chapter 14: The gender gap

Every year I have the privilege of addressing the National Pupil Premium Conference at the Birmingham NEC.

I usually focus on how to make best use of Pupil Premium funding in order to close achievement gaps between pupils from different socio-economic backgrounds.

But, whilst our focus on bridging the social and economic divide between pupils has sharpened as a result of the Pupil Premium, there are many more achievement gaps that I think require equal attention.

One such gap – that between the attainment of boys and girls – is a perennial issue for schools and often features in school improvement plans and inspection reports which, more often than not, state that schools need to address the issue of boys' underachievement in English and girls' underachievement in maths and the sciences.

As such, in this chapter, we will explore the reasons these gender gaps exist and share some proven strategies for addressing them.

A caveat: I recognise that every school is different, as indeed is every teacher and every pupil. It is a universal truth, therefore, that what works in one context might not work so well in another. I also recognise that there are myriad reasons why attainment gaps exist and, as ever, closing them in theory is always much easier than doing so in practice.

However, I firmly believe that a pupil's birth should not be their destiny and that we as teachers and school and college leaders assume a vital role in levelling the playing field; we must ensure every pupil is afforded an equal opportunity to succeed in school and college and in life.

What are the gender gaps?

The OECD says that there are five key 'gaps' in the educational outcomes of boys and girls – reading skills, reading for pleasure, maths performance, STEM uptake, and STEM careers.

Firstly, boys lag behind girls at the end of compulsory education in reading skills by the equivalent, on average, of a year's schooling.

Secondly, boys are far less likely to spend time reading for pleasure.

Thirdly, and in contrast, boys perform better than girls in maths, although the gender gap is narrower than in reading.

Fourthly, there remain significant disparities in the subjects that boys and girls choose to study, with girls less likely to choose scientific and technological fields of study than boys.

Finally, even when girls choose these subjects, they are less likely to take up careers in related fields. This widens the gap later in life in the career and earning prospects of women.

Furthermore, boys in OECD countries are eight percentage points more likely than girls to report that school is a waste of time. Meanwhile, in higher education and beyond, young women are under-represented in maths, science, and computing. In 2012, only 14 per cent of young women who entered university for the first time chose science-related fields of study, including engineering, manufacturing and construction. By contrast, 39 per cent of young men who entered university that year chose to pursue one of those fields of study.

Why do the gender gaps exist?

On the one hand, some people believe that the attainment gap between boys and girls is the result of biological differences. After all, there are more than a hundred genetic differences between the male and female brain.

For example, according to Blum (1997), boys' brains generally have more cortical areas dedicated to spatial-mechanical functioning, whereas girls' brains generally have greater cortical emphasis on verbal-emotive processing. As a result, girls tend to use more words than boys and girls tend to think more verbally.

According to Sax (2005), the male visual system (optical and neural) relies more heavily on type M ganglion cells which detect movement, whereas girls generally have more type P ganglion cells which are sensitive to colour variety and other sensory activity. As a result, boys tend to rely more on pictures and moving objects when they write, whereas girls tend to use words that refer to colour and other sensory information.

According to Rich (2000), a girl's prefrontal cortex is generally more active than a boy's, and her frontal lobe generally develops at an earlier age.

These are the decision-making areas of the brain (as well as the reading/writing/word production areas) and the difference can lead to girls being less impulsive than boys but better able to sit still and read, and to read and write earlier in life.

According to Gurian and Stevens (2005), boys' brains go into a "rest state" many times each day. For some boys – especially those with behavioural difficulties – self-stimulating and disruptive behaviours such as tapping a pencil (although it can be symptomatic of emotional or psychological problems in some boys) may reflect male brains trying to stay awake in a classroom that is not well-suited to their kind of learning.

Brain scans have shown that when the male's brain gets bored, some of his brain functioning shuts down (in other words, there is a drift into a brain state that negates learning and performance). When the female brain gets bored, however, more of her brain functioning stays active. As a result, even when she's bored, a girl is more likely to retain the ability to take notes and listen carefully.

According to Rich (2000), structural differences in girls' brains generate more "cross-talk" between hemispheres, leading to better multi-tasking. Boys' brains, in contrast, tend to lateralise and compartmentalise brain activity. Thus, girls can pay attention to more information on more subjects at any given time, whereas boys tend to pile a lot of information into a single-task focus. In other words, boys concentrate best, in general, when they follow steps A to Z without distraction.

What's more, Havers (1995) says that boys take more time than girls to transition between tasks. They tend to become more irritable, therefore, when teachers move them continually between activities.

Finally, Taylor (2002) argues that the bonding chemical oxytocin also contributes to the gender gap because, with less oxytocin in the male neural and physiological system, boys tend toward greater impulsivity and aggression. Gurian (1996) adds that boys are more naturally aggressive and competitive than girls, and boys generally gravitate more toward competitive learning and relationships characterised by "aggression nurturance".

The role of attitudes and society

On the other hand, some people believe that the gender gap can be explained by differences in attitude not biology; aptitude, they argue, knows no gender.

According to many international reports on the gender gap in education – most notably perhaps a 2012 OECD report called Closing the Gap: Act now – boys and girls, men and women, when given equal opportunities, have an equal chance of achieving at the highest levels.

In a 2015 paper called The ABC of Gender Equality, the OECD expands on this and argues that gender equality in education relies on addressing not biological differences but differences in "attitude, behaviour, and confidence".

In other words, gender disparities in performance do not stem from innate differences in aptitude, but rather learned, societal differences in students' attitudes towards learning and their behaviour in school, from how they choose to spend their leisure time, and from the confidence they have – or do not have – in their own abilities as students.

In fact, the OECD paper shows how the gender gap in literacy narrows considerably – and even disappears in some countries –

among young men and women in their late teens and early 20s when attitudes and behaviours mature and level.

In the final analysis, I'd suggest that it doesn't matter whether we believe gender gaps in education are the result of biology or attitude – or indeed, as seems most likely to me, a nuanced combination of the two. What matters most is that we teachers and education leaders believe that the gaps can and should be addressed.

The OECD cites evidence from the Programme for International Student Assessment (PISA) which shows that, in 2012, 14 per cent of the boys and nine per cent of the girls who were surveyed did not attain the PISA baseline level of proficiency in any of the three core subjects.

On the other hand, in the top-performing economies in PISA, such as Shanghai-China, Singapore, Hong Kong-China and Chinese Taipei, girls performed on a par with their male classmates in maths and attained higher scores in maths than boys in most other countries and economies around the world.

Hopefully this shows that the gap is not inevitable and can be addressed. The big question, therefore, should not be "why" but "how?".

How do we close the gender gaps?

In a moment, I will explore ways of closing the gap that exists between boys and girls in literacy (where boys lag behind), then I will focus my attention on the gap between girls and boys in STEM subjects (where girls lag behind). But firstly, I will explore some generic strategies for closing the gender gap and indeed other attainment gaps...

Parents

A pupil's home-life is vital to their academic success and so it seems logical to suggest, when looking at ways of closing the gap, that parents have a major role to play. We might assume that all parents give their sons and daughters equal support and encouragement for all of their schoolwork, and articulate equal aspirations for their futures, but PISA results show that this is not always the case. In every country that surveyed the parents of students who sat the

PISA test in 2012, parents were more likely to expect their sons, rather than their daughters, to work in a STEM-related field – even when boys and girls performed at the same level in maths. Giving boys and girls an equal opportunity to realise their potential, therefore, demands the involvement of parents who can encourage their sons and daughters.

According to a report by the Joseph Rowntree Foundation called Closing the Attainment Gap in Scottish Education (2014), to help this happen, schools should ensure they have in place effective parental involvement programmes that focus on helping parents to use appropriate strategies to support their children's learning at home rather than simply seeking to raise aspirations for their children's education.

Teachers

Teachers, too, have a vital role to play by becoming more aware of their own gender biases and how these might affect how they award marks to pupils. Teachers should encourage more independent problem-solving among their pupils – once they have explained and modelled a key concept – and should use teaching strategies that demand more of their pupils, since all pupils, but particularly girls, perform better in maths when their teachers ask them to try to solve mathematical problems independently.

The Joseph Rowntree report says that teachers should use carefully implemented nurture groups and programmes to increase social, emotional and behavioural competencies. Collaborative work in small groups can also be effective, as can peer-tutoring, meta-cognitive training and one-to-one tutoring using qualified teachers, trained teaching assistants, or trained volunteers.

Mentoring schemes work best when they adhere to particular characteristics associated with efficacy, and after-school activities – such as study support – work best when they are academically focused.

School leaders

The Joseph Rowntree report also says that school leaders can help close the gap by developing policies which better create, collect and share knowledge of:

- Interventions that improve the performance of different groups of pupils
- Ways to make curriculum design and planning (at school, class and individual level) more nuanced and effective for different groups of pupils
- Ways to deploy staff and resources to raise achievement in different groups
- Methods to monitor and evaluate pedagogies, resources and initiatives for impact on different groups as well as general average attainment

Funding, the report argues, should be targeted in order to avoid a situation where budget increases in one area are undermined by reduced budgets elsewhere.

Using research

In general, the most effective intervention strategies for closing the gap are those which are informed by research evidence and focus on improving attainment by using effective pedagogies, have a shared strategic plan that encompass academic, social and emotional learning, are supported by significant staff development, and are data-driven and consistently monitor impact on attainment.

Moreover, effective strategies involve an investment in high-quality, evidence-informed, context-specific, intensive and long-term professional development.

Boys' literacy

Let's now explore the gender gap in literacy proficiency and look at ways of raising boys' attainment in reading and writing.

An international PISA survey in 2012 found that 15-year-old boys were more likely than girls of the same age to be low-achievers in school; 14 per cent of boys and nine per cent of girls failed to attain the baseline level of proficiency in any of the three core subjects measured by PISA – namely, reading, maths and science. In fact, six out of 10 students who did not attain the baseline level in any of these subjects were boys.

In the UK, attainment data consistently shows girls outperforming boys in reading, with the gap remaining relatively stable from early years to GCSE over the past 10 years or so.

When the National Literacy Strategy was introduced in England in 1998, only 64 per cent of boys reached the level expected of their age group at the end of primary school compared with 79 per cent of girls, a gap of 15 percentage points. By 2000, the gap had narrowed to six percentage points, but since then it has remained relatively static, meaning 20 per cent of boys (and 12 per cent of girls) start secondary school unable to read at the expected level.

The evidence suggests that the gap is not simply a result of how schools teach pupils to read. Rather, the foundations are laid much earlier: in 2011, there was a gap of 11 percentage points between boys' and girls' achievement in reading at age five (71 per cent of boys working securely within the level expected for their age versus 82 per cent of girls).

Between ages five and seven the gap narrows significantly: in 2011, 89 per cent of girls achieved the expected level in reading in key stage tests compared with 82 per cent of boys. However, from then on it increased again: at age 14, girls outstripped boys in English by 12 percentage points. And at GCSE, only 59 per cent of boys achieved A* to C in English compared with 73 per cent of girls, a 14-percentage point difference.

In fact, just before the grading system changed in England to a 1-9 scale, the gap between the proportion of girls and boys receiving grades A* or A across all subjects was at its widest since the top grade was introduced in 1994: in English, 21 per cent of girls achieved A* or A compared with just 12 per cent of boys.

Improving boys' reading is important because reading and writing achievement are strongly linked. National Literacy Trust data from 2011 shows that 49 per cent of young people who read above the expected level for their age also write above the expected level (42 per cent write at the expected level; nine per cent write below their expected level).

Conversely, 59 per cent of young people who read below the expected level also write below the expected level (35 per cent write at the expected level; six per cent write above their expected level).

National Literacy Trust data also shows strong links between reading and writing in terms of enjoyment, behaviour and attitudes.

For example, 65 per cent of young people who enjoy reading "very much" or "quite a lot" also enjoy writing "very much" or "quite a lot". Young people who read frequently are also more likely to write frequently, with 38 per cent of young people who read daily also writing daily.

Therefore, if schools don't encourage boys to read more, it is likely that other literacy skills will be affected. What's more, poor literacy has a negative impact on a student's achievement in all their school subjects and limits their opportunities in later life.

Why do boys under-perform in reading and writing?

The Organisation for Economic Cooperation and Development (OECD), which runs the PISA tests, says there are many possible reasons for boys' poor performance in literacy and many of them are connected with differences in behaviour.

Firstly, boys don't enjoy reading as much as girls. Girls not only outperform boys in reading tests, they are also more engaged with reading than boys at many levels.

A 2011 National Literacy Trust survey of nearly 21,000 eight to 16-year-olds showed that boys are not only more likely than girls to struggle with reading, but they are also more likely to enjoy reading only "a little" or "not at all" (56 versus 43 per cent). The 2009 PISA survey found that across all OECD countries just 52 per cent of 15-year-old boys said they read for enjoyment compared with 73 per cent of girls.

Secondly, and as a consequence of the fact boys don't enjoy reading, boys read less than girls. In fact, boys spend one hour less per week on homework than girls – and each hour of homework per week translates into a four-point higher score in the PISA reading, maths and science tests.

National Literacy Trust research has found that 35 per cent of girls say they read outside of class every day compared with just 26 per cent of boys. Meanwhile, the OECD has found that – outside of school – boys spend more time playing video games than girls and less time reading for enjoyment, particularly complex texts like fiction.

The OECD states: "Reading proficiency is the foundation upon which all other learning is built; when boys don't read well, their performance in other school subjects suffers too."

According to a report by the Boys' Reading Commission (an All-Party Parliamentary Group), boys' underachievement in reading is a significant concern for schools across the UK. In a survey, 76 per cent of UK schools said boys in their school did not do as well in reading as girls; 82 per cent of schools said they had been compelled to develop their own strategies to tackle this.

The issue, so says the National Literacy Trust, is deep-seated. Test results consistently show this is a long-term and international trend.

Boys' attitudes towards reading and writing, the amount of time they spend reading, and their achievement in reading and writing are all poorer than those of girls. However, boys' underachievement in literacy is not inevitable. It is not simply a result of biological differences; the majority of boys can achieve in literacy and can become fluent readers.

What can we do to close the literacy gap for boys?

Rather than being biological, the Boys' Reading Commission found that boys' underachievement in reading was associated with the interplay of three factors...

Firstly, the home and family environment: at home, girls are more likely to be bought books and taken to the library than boys, and mothers are more likely to support and role-model reading for their children than fathers.

One obvious solution, therefore, is to ensure that boys are bought books and taken to the library, and that fathers become more active as role-models by reading to their children more often – and are seen to read for personal pleasure.

Secondly, the school environment: many teachers have a limited knowledge of contemporary and attractive texts for boys and boys are not always given the opportunity to develop their identity as a reader through experiencing reading for enjoyment.

One obvious solution, therefore, is to ensure that teachers are explicitly educated in what constitutes appropriate choices of texts for boys and also act as role-models in school by being seen to read and discuss books, particularly male teachers in subjects not usually associated with reading.

Thirdly, male gender identities: boys tend not to value learning and reading as a mark of success. One obvious solution, therefore, is to challenge the stereotype in the ways suggested above: ensure parents and teachers (particularly men) act as effective role-models and are explicit about the importance of reading and writing as a means of learning and explicit, in turn, about the importance of learning as a means of succeeding at school and in life.

A sustained approach

These solutions are useful starting points but, alone, will not turn underachieving and demotivated boys into readers; rather, a sustained approach is required.

Schools need to encourage positive gender identities that value reading, develop a supportive social context for boys' reading and counteract the possible negative triggers that can turn boys off.

For example, a refreshed commitment in schools to promoting reading for enjoyment would strongly benefit boys who want to read around their interests. To enable this to happen, reading for pleasure needs to be an integral part of a school's teaching and learning strategy (and built into the curriculum) and teachers need to be supported in their knowledge of relevant quality texts that will engage all students.

There is also the danger that a predominantly female workforce (particularly in the primary phase but also in secondary school English departments and libraries) might subconsciously privilege texts that are more attractive to girls. Schools need to ensure male teachers also act as effective role-models to boys.

Younger and Warrington's four-year research programme (Raising Boys' Achievement, DfES 2005), which examined the relative effectiveness of the strategies employed by schools to raise boys' achievement, suggested four different categories of school-based approaches:

1. *Pedagogic*: in other words, classroom-based approaches centred on teaching and learning
2. *Individual*: i.e., a focus on target-setting and mentoring
3. Organisational: i.e., whole-school curriculum design
4. *Socio-cultural*: i.e., approaches which attempt to create an environment for learning

It's good to talk

Younger and Warrington's analysis showed that pedagogic strategies to improve reading were most successful when combined with a holistic approach, which focused not on teaching reading but on helping boys to become "successful and satisfied readers".

When this happened and pupils were given space to talk and reflect on reading, share ideas and discuss why it was enjoyable, standards of reading improved.

Younger and Warrington's research is backed up by OECD data which shows the clear link between the motivation to read and reading skills.

They argued that for some boys the desire and motivation to read needs to be explicitly fostered through reading aloud, having a reading environment, having significant amounts of talk about texts, and having high levels of peer-to-peer book recommendations, and teacher-to-pupil and pupil-to-teacher, as well as quality time to read and then talk about what was read. The research stresses the importance of talk in supporting boys' literacy.

Responding to Younger and Warrington's paper, the National Literacy Trust made key recommendations.

Firstly, schools should promote reading for enjoyment and involve parents (particularly fathers) in their reading strategies. Schools should provide pupils with opportunities to read around their own interests and enjoy reading. Schools should have a reading strategy and should focus on the needs of groups of pupils who are more likely to fall behind – including boys – as well as the effectiveness of the school library in supporting these strategies.

Secondly, every teacher should have an up-to-date knowledge of reading materials that will appeal to disengaged boys. Schools should have a library at their heart and the school librarian should play an important role in enthusing teachers with the knowledge of reading materials. Schools should be encouraged to invest in their library provision.

Thirdly, school libraries should target pupils (particularly boys) who are least likely to be supported in their reading at home, perhaps by working in partnership with children's centres to target younger families who most need support. Libraries should also encourage pupils to take part in important initiatives, such as the annual Summer Reading Challenge initiative.

Finally, every boy should have weekly support from a male reading role-model. One boy in five thinks reading is more for girls than boys. This reflects the fact that mothers are more likely than fathers to support their children's reading, that mothers are more likely to read in front of their children, and that the teacher who teaches a student to read is more likely to be a woman.

Many boys will be supported in their reading by males within the home, but for those who aren't, the recruitment of male reading volunteers is a helpful strategy for schools to employ. Schools could make use of volunteering initiatives to engage young men in the support of boys' reading.

Younger and Warrington also recommended the following:

Pedagogic approaches:

- Teachers should use a variety of interactive classroom activities including both short, specific focused activities and more sustained, on-going activities, as and when appropriate.
- Teachers should acknowledge the central importance of talk – of speaking and listening as a means of supporting writing.
- Teachers should take advantage of the gains to be achieved through companionable writing with response partners and through group work.

- Teachers should be prepared to take risks to bring more creativity and variety to literacy.
- Teachers should make more integrated use of ICT so that quality presentations can be more easily achieved, and drafts can be amended with greater ease.
- Teachers should use a proactive and assertive approach in the classroom, which avoids the negative or confrontational, conveys high expectations and a sense of challenge, and uses praise regularly and consistently.

Mentoring approaches:

- Schools should have a coherent and integrated approach to target-setting and mentoring in which mentors prioritise their time to give credibility to the process.
- Schools should ensure there is a mutual understanding and shared commitment to all aspects of the mentoring process, as well as a common belief and conviction among teachers and students in the system.
- Mentors should be credible to students; collaborative and supportive on the one hand, offering strategies, advice and encouragement, but crucially they should be assertive and demanding on the other, so that disengaged students have the opportunity to protect their own image and use their mentor's pressure to "excuse" their own involvement in academic work.

Socio-cultural approaches:

- Schools should ensure boys are actively involved in whole-school activities, such as artists-in-residence schemes, poetry weeks, dance sessions run by professional dancers, and drama productions which allocate lead roles to disengaged boys.
- Schools should establish paired reading schemes between boys in different year groups with the explicit rationale of promoting self-esteem among the older "expert" boys.
- Teachers should be willing to take risks in order to engage individual students in roles where they are actively supported to make choices and to achieve success.
- Teachers and other staff should be fully committed to creating opportunities that afford students the space they need in order to articulate their feelings and emotions.

Of course, focusing on improving boys' proficiency in literacy is not without risk...

First, schools need to be careful not to disengage girls who struggle with reading by catering solely for boys. Many approaches that effectively support boys are also helpful to girls, but not all.

Second, it is tempting to treat underachieving boys as a homogenous group, but of course they are not. Not all boys are interested in the same things or have the same difficulties. Not all boys have difficulties because of the same circumstances, either. And, perhaps more importantly, not all boys struggle with reading and writing. In focusing on raising boys' attainment in English, there is a danger that schools will imply that all boys underachieve and are not expected to do well because literacy isn't for boys: this might become a self-fulfilling prophecy by reinforcing it as a social norm.

Now let's turn our attentions to the gap between boys and girls in STEM subjects (where girls lag behind) ...

Girls and STEM

As I explained earlier, boys perform better than girls in maths, although the gender gap is narrower than in reading (where girls outperform boys). Also, there remain significant disparities in the subjects that boys and girls choose to study, with girls less likely to choose scientific and technological fields of study than boys. And even when girls do choose these subjects, they are less likely to take up careers in related fields. This widens the gap later in life in the career and earning prospects of women.

In 2012, only 14 per cent of young women who entered university for the first time chose science-related fields of study, including engineering, manufacturing and construction. By contrast, 39 per cent of young men who entered university that year chose to pursue one of those fields of study.

One reason for this gap is the perpetuation of gender stereotypes and attitudes. Educational aspirations are formed at a young age and gender stereotyping frequently takes place in subtle ways at home, in schools, and in wider society. For example, primary school teachers and secondary English and languages teachers are predominantly women, while secondary maths and science teachers are predominantly men. What messages are boys and girls getting about adult life choices? Also, textbooks are often guilty – even today – of referring to female nurses and male engineers, for example.

One solution, therefore, would be to encourage more men into primary teaching and more women into secondary maths and sciences, and to ensure more examples are given of female mathematicians and scientists, both in textbooks and in verbal examples given by teachers. Schools should also explicitly raise students' awareness of the likely consequences of stereotypical male and female choices of subjects on their later careers and earnings.

Addressing the stereotype in this way may also increase girls' confidence, because evidence suggests that at present, in general, girls are not as confident as boys in their ability to solve maths and science problems.

And girls' lack of confidence leads to lower levels of attainment. On average across OECD countries, the point score difference in maths performance between high-achieving girls and boys is 19. However, when comparing boys and girls who reported similar levels of self-confidence in maths or of anxiety towards maths, the gender gap in performance disappears.

Changing gender stereotypes in school is, however, only part of the answer: attitudes are also crucially determined by what happens at home. Schools need to educate parents, as well as students, in gender equality matters.

In a paper pithily entitled Research-Informed Practices for Inclusive Science, Technology, Engineering, and Math (STEM) Classrooms: Strategies for educators to close the gender gap, the authors – an equally tongue-twisting line-up of Scutt, Gilmartin, Sheppard, and Brunhaver from Stanford University – articulate seven key practices which, they argue, can create more gender-inclusive STEM classrooms. The seven practices – which I have related to the English school system – are as follows.

1. Study maths

The paper's authors argue that it is hard to overstate the importance of a solid foundation in mathematics for all potential STEM students, but more specifically they argue that "calculus (is) an especially important step in increasing the likelihood of girls to pursue STEM".

Sadler and Tai's study, Two High School Pillars Supporting College Science, found that the best foundation for studying science at an advanced level was to study advanced mathematics. They found that studying maths for longer increased the average grade in biology and chemistry more than studying biology and chemistry.

2. Develop spatial skills

Spatial awareness is the ability to recognise or solve problems associated with the relationships between objects or figures, including position, direction, size, form, and distance. Although it is stereotypical to say that women have poor spatial awareness – and a claim without scientific evidence of genetic or hormonal differences between the genders – spatial skills are malleable through practice and improving spatial skills has proven, in the US, to improve the retention of engineering students and therefore it is a strategy worth exploring for schools wishing to narrow the gender gap in STEM subjects.

Among undergraduate women who failed a spatial skills initial assessment test in the US, 77 per cent of those who took a spatial-visualisation course were still enrolled in or had graduated from the school of engineering. In contrast, only 48 per cent of those women who failed the test and did not take the spatial-visualisation course were still enrolled in or had graduated from the school of engineering.

While the spatial-visualisation course did not raise women's scores above those of men, the intervention did close the gender gap in the scores achieved by men and women.

Early training in spatial skills is beneficial because spatial skills help students interpret diagrams in maths and science tests and textbooks. In fact, in one study quoted in the Stanford paper, "when mental rotation ability was statistically adjusted for, the significant gender difference in (key stage 3 maths) was eliminated ... this suggests that spatial ability may be responsible in part for mediating gender differences in (maths ability)". Spatial skills, the authors argue, may be a keystone in closing the gender gap in maths as well as the broader STEM gender gap.

3. Develop communication skills

The Stanford paper also suggests that, to help girls succeed in STEM subjects, teachers should emphasise the importance of communication skills in the practice of science and engineering, thereby changing the perception that individuals cannot be gifted or skilled in both maths and languages.

The vast majority of STEM jobs involve teamwork, which necessitates communication. According to labour market information here in the UK, effective communication skills play a major role in career advancement in STEM fields. A study that observed formal and informal teaching of communication found that there were five important features of speaking in engineering: simplicity, persuasiveness, results-oriented, numerically rich, and visually sophisticated.

Despite the importance of communication to engineering, interpersonal communication and collaboration skills are generally portrayed as the opposite of maths and science skills, implying that people are almost always more skilled in one than the other. However, research provides compelling evidence that communication skills are essential in engineering and suggests that integrating maths and communication skills in engineering would be of particular benefit to female students.

4. Encourage resilience

Developing students' resilience is about helping them to embrace challenges and setbacks by teaching them that academic skills are malleable. In addition to combatting the negative stereotypes that girls and women face about their technical abilities, the practice of developing resilience is also an important life lesson for all students.

Girls may feel apprehensive about performing on a spatial skills task because they fear that performing poorly will confirm the existing negative stereotype. This so-called "stereotype threat" may actually cause girls to perform worse than they would otherwise do and therefore the danger lies in this phenomenon's nature as a self-fulfilling prophecy. However, a mindset shift – whereby girls are presented with experiential accounts of the origins of stereotypes – can have measurable positive consequences to combat this downward spiral.

Several popular studies by Professor Carol Dweck have found that focusing on the power of practice rather than innate talent can be a key motivator for students and teaching the power of a growth mindset (as opposed to a fixed mindset) allows girls to perform better, even when they understand the stereotypes against them.

5. Give students an active expert role

Enabling students to adopt an 'active expert role' – whereby they answer questions, make comments, teach others and express their own voice through presentation – can make students feel like they belong to the expert group. Since this feeling of belonging is what girls often lack in STEM fields, active expert roles can help girls in particular to enhance their sense of belonging to their classmates and to the learning material.

6. Have a clear marking policy

The Stanford report says that "girls may underestimate their performance in math classes in part due to gendered expectations of their competencies". Thus, having a clear marking policy and giving constructive feedback should help girls to properly gauge their success based on their performance alone.

A study by sociologist Shelley Correll found that girls rely more on performance feedback in making self-assessments of their mathematical competency because, Correll argues, "they must contend with lower societal expectations of their mathematical competency". This implies, therefore, that when girls cannot form a firm sense of their ability, they fill in the gap with societal expectations.

In short, girls need a better picture of where they stand in maths and science classes than do boys because otherwise, they will use their biased self-assessment. The implications of these studies are that marks and test scores in maths and science must be better explained to students and feedback must be clearer and more constructive.

7. Re-evaluate group work

While group work has often been encouraged as an exercise to build teamwork and communication skills, research cited in the Stanford report suggests that there may be subtle, unintended consequences which may cause us to reconsider the way group work is approached in the classroom.

One study on interpersonal communication which focused on gender and engineers versus non- engineers, for example, found that "engineering males were more likely than other groups to draw negative conclusions about speakers who engaged in self-belittlement by admitting to difficulties or mistakes – particularly with technological issues". According to a study by Wolfe and Powell, this tendency towards self-belittlement in spoken language is more commonly exhibited by women.

It is likely that self-belittlement takes place during group work activities. While the original study suggests women try to eliminate their use of self-effacing speech, the Stanford report poses a better strategy: it recommends teachers reconsider how they structure group work.

Debbie Chachra, in an editorial entitled The Perils of Teamwork, which is cited in the Stanford report, argues that asking students in STEM classes to work in teams does not have the desired supportive effect.

Since school students have various levels of experience, they tend to divide based on skill sets and self-efficacy. As such, girls are often given less technical and more managerial tasks. This can perpetuate a vicious cycle, says Chachra, to make girls feel that they do not belong in the maths and science fields.

Biased marking

One other solution – from left field – was mooted in a BBC News article in April 2015. The article outlined the results of a study in France which analysed the records of almost 4,500 11-year-olds at

35 secondary schools and found that girls benefited from a marking bias by maths teachers.

The girls in the study – which was jointly carried out by the London School of Economics (LSE) and the Paris School of Economics – were given six per cent higher marks than boys for similar work. According to the researchers, as well as motivating them at the time, the assessment boost also encouraged the girls to take science subjects later in their school careers.

Camille Terrier of the LSE told the BBC that: "Altogether, these results show that positively rewarding pupils has the potential to affect their progress and course choice. Since we note that marks in maths influence the progress of students, they could be a way to reduce the inequalities in achievement between boys and girls."

Be wise

A research review commissioned by the WISE campaign (Women into Science and Engineering) made eight recommendations to attract more girls into studying STEM, and to help improve girls' attainment in these subjects.

The eight recommendations, with which I will conclude this chapter, are as follows.

1. Use information about the demand for STEM skills and qualifications, particularly the commercial value of mathematics and science qualifications, so that young people and their parents understand that taking these subjects will improve future job prospects. For example, not everyone understands that you can go from taking science at school to an exciting career in broadcast engineering, advanced manufacturing, covert surveillance, robotics, or computer gaming.
2. Use role-models from diverse backgrounds to appeal to the whole spectrum of the student population. Show women working with diverse groups of colleagues, rather than a single talking head, because most girls do not want to be the odd one out.
3. Girls respond to female role-models plus an explanation of the range of different careers available, using real jobs and current job titles. Role-models should be promoted from primary school

age and at key decision points such as in year 9 when they chose GCSE subjects and year 11 when they choose whether to continue with STEM education.

4. Show that there are vocational routes leading to technician and Apprenticeship jobs as a positive alternative or steppingstone into higher education.
5. Use social media such as YouTube, Facebook and online forums to promote role-models to girls, their parents, relatives and carers, making use of blogs, podcasts and Twitter.
6. Focus on sectors where there are fewer job profiles and case studies available: technology, computer programming, chemistry, energy and power, food, materials, advanced manufacturing, and the built environment.
7. Actively promote examples of how employers are making real changes to the working environment, supply chain and partnerships in order to ensure that women, men and women with families, and other under-represented groups are welcome and will progress on merit.
8. Collaborate with other organisations in order to have a bigger impact.

In the next chapter, we will explore the ethnicity gap.

Chapter 15: The ethnicity gap

As well as the gender gap, I'd suggest that schools be mindful of any ethnicity gaps that might exist, that is to say any differences in the attainment of pupils from different ethnic groups.

One ethnic group that has made the headlines in the UK in recent years is, perhaps surprisingly, white British boys, although, as I will argue in a moment, the attainment gap between white working-class boys and their peers may be less to do with ethnicity and more to do with gender – which we have already explored – and their socio-economic context – which we will explore in Chapter 16.

White working-class boys – an underperforming ethnic group?

Data suggests that white working-class boys are amongst the lowest performers in UK schools.

In 2019, the average Attainment 8 score for pupils in England who were not eligible for free school meals (FSM) was 45.6. Currently, around 10% of white pupils, 20% of black pupils and 45% of Bangladeshi pupils receive FSM. In total, there were 33697 boys on FSM who sat their GCSEs in 2019. Of these:

- 1093 Bangladeshi boys achieved an average score of 42.8
- 2880 Black boys achieved an average score of 34.5
- 22720 White boys achieved an average score of 28.5

This data shows that white boys in receipt of FSM (who we might term 'white working-class boys' though, of course, FSM eligibility is not synonymous with 'working-class') underperform compared to all other groups.

Of course, it's true that white British pupils perform slightly better, on average, than BAME children. But, because girls perform significantly better, on average, than boys, and pupils who are not eligible for FSM perform significantly better, on average, than pupils who are eligible for FSM, then white boys eligible for FSM perform markedly worse than pupils from every other category, including FSM pupils from every other ethnicity.

The Conservative MP Ben Bradley, speaking in a House of Commons debate in February 2020, said that, "We know that on average boys consistently underperform against girls, and white boys from disadvantaged backgrounds underperform against boys of all other races and ethnicities.

"Only around a third of white working-class boys pass their maths and English GCSEs," he said, "[and] disadvantaged white working-class boys are 40% less likely to go into higher education than disadvantaged black boys." Furthermore, "according to UCAS, only 9% of these boys will go to university, compared with around half of the general population."

This issue is not new, of course. Back in September 2013, the *Daily Express* warned that "White working-class boys could become an educational underclass". And in 2014, Impetus, the Private Equity Foundation, published a report called Digging Deeper in which it claimed that "white working-class boys have been left to underperform academically for decades".

Impetus believe part of the problem is a lack of aspirations: "Many of our charities identified parents who had had miserable educational experiences of their own as barriers to their children's own attainment," the report said. "This is a challenge to schools, who may be up against multiple generations who have no faith in schooling's ability to equip their children with qualification or skills."

Bradley also believes one of the causes of white working-class boys' underachievement is a lack of ambition: "We need to understand the communities that these boys grow up in. In former coalfield areas such as Mansfield, not so long ago boys generally left school before they were 16, and they went to work down the pit or in a factory. There was a simplistic kind of certainty to that, in that regardless of what happened at school, they would have a job and a career. [But] that certainty of career does not exist anymore [...] Many parents in the poorest communities do not have qualifications and therefore are not able to extol the virtues of school—indeed, they do not necessarily see the point of that education—and they cannot help their children to study because they do not have that level of attainment themselves."

Impetus recommended that, in order to address this issue, "there must be a strong link between education and employment [...] Better careers advice and guidance, alumni networks in every school, and school engagement with local employers are crucial here."

Who are white working-class boys?

For my part, I think it might be helpful to deconstruct the moniker of 'white working-class boys' – which is in danger of masking the true issues at play – and consider each element of this group's dynamic in turn, asking whether it is class, colour or gender that provides the main barrier to school success...

Class

Let's consider the 'working-class' element first of all...

Whilst 'working-class' is not synonymous with FSM or Pupil Premium eligibility (as I will explain in the next chapter), it is a helpful starting point.

I will explore socio-economic deprivation in Chapter 16 and I will explain that pupils from poorer backgrounds tend to do less well in school, not because they are 'less able' than their more affluent peers, but simply because they were born into poverty.

I will also explain that, although poverty may be the primary *cause* of a child's disadvantage, it is often the *consequences* of poverty that create barriers to learning – and idea I mooted earlier. For example, poverty may mean that a child's attendance and punctuality is poor because they do not have an alarm clock. Poverty may mean a child suffers from a lack of sleep or poor nutrition which affects their concentration and energy levels in school and thus hampers their achievement.

As such, and as I recommended in Chapter 14, when deciding how to support learners from poorer homes, we need to identify, on a case-by-case basis, the tangible *consequences* of their socio-economic deprivation on their education.

Because we know that the poverty gap emerges early in a child's life and that, by the age of 3, socio-economically disadvantaged children are – on average – already almost 18 months behind their more affluent peers in their early language development, it surely follows that we can help overcome some of their disadvantage by improving their literacy and language skills.

Now let us turn to ethnicity...

Colour

So far we've explored how being working-class can affect the attainment of 'white working-class boys'. But to what extent does being 'white' place them at an added disadvantage...?

Actually, we might better ask: *Does* being white disadvantage them? Or might this be an unhelpful misnomer?

Certainly, Kenan Malik, writing in the Guardian in 2018, believes ethnicity is not, as widely claimed, a primary cause of academic disadvantage. Rather, ethnicity masks the true issue: class.

"So fixated [are] academics and policymakers by ethnic categories, that they largely ignored [social class]. The 2000 Ofsted report, for instance, demonstrated that the impact of social class on school performance was more than twice as great as that of ethnicity. Yet, it disregarded its own data and focused on the problems posed by ethnic differences."

Malik went on: "The debate about the white working-class [...] poses the problem as a zero-sum game. It pitches the interests of working-class whites against those of minority ethnic groups and imagines that too great a focus on black and Asian children has undermined white working-class culture."

I think he might be right. I suspect the focus on *white* working-class boys is misguided and we should instead focus instead on socio-economic deprivation – and thus social class – as well as gender, and not concern ourselves too much with ethnicity as a cause of disadvantage. After all, the attainment gap caused by poverty is multi-racial.

Let us now look at the gender issue...

Gender

We know that being working class has a demonstrable impact on a pupil's performance in school, whilst ethnicity – it seems – is less of a determining factor. So, to what extent does being a boy impact on a pupil's attainment or is gender, like ethnicity, a misnomer...?

I tackled the gender gap in the previous chapter, of course, so will not repeat myself here. But, to add to what I said earlier, I would note that boys perform markedly worse than girls in every ethnic group.

Indeed, the difference between the attainment of girls and boys is now much greater than that between white and BAME pupils.

In 2016, the Higher Education Policy Institute calculated that, if current trends continue, a boy born in that year will be 75% less likely to attend university than a girl.

But why? Well, as I explained in the previous chapter, on the one hand the attainment gap between boys and girls may be the result of biological differences. After all, as I noted, there are more than a hundred genetic differences between the male and female brain. But, on the other hand, as I also explained earlier, the gender gap might be explained by differences in attitude *not* biology.

Ofsted's advice

To conclude this discussion about the ethnicity gap, although it is at the time of writing over 12 years old, I think the recommendations contained in Ofsted's 2008 good practice report on white working-class boys are worth considering. Ofsted found that schools that were successful in raising the attainment of this group shared the following features:

- an ethos which demonstrates commitment to every individual, and which treats staff and pupils with fairness, trust and respect
- consistent support to develop boys' organisation skills and instil the importance of perseverance; any anti-school subculture 'left at the gates'
- rigorous monitoring systems which track individual pupils' performance against expectations; realistic but challenging targets; tailored, flexible intervention programmes and frequent reviews of performance against targets
- a highly structured step-by-step framework for teaching, starting with considerable guidance by the teacher and leading gradually to more independent work by the pupils when it is clear that this will enhance rather than detract from achievement
- a curriculum which is tightly structured around individual needs and linked to support programmes that seek to raise aspirations
- creative and flexible strategies to engage parents and carers, make them feel valued, enable them to give greater support to their sons' education and help them make informed decisions about the future
- a strong emphasis on seeking and listening to the views of these pupils
- genuine engagement of boys in setting individual targets, reviewing progress, shaping curricular and extra-curricular activities and making choices about the future
- key adults, including support staff and learning mentors, who are flexible and committed, know the boys well and are sensitive to any difficulties which might arise in their home
- a good range of emotional support for boys to enable them to manage anxieties and develop the skills to express their feelings constructively
- strong partnership with a wide range of agencies to provide social, emotional, educational and practical support for boys and their families in order to raise their aspirations.

Before we move on to the socio-economic gap, I'd like to tarry a while longer on the subject of ethnicity and take a moment to reflect on the Black Lives Matter movement and consider its implications on education...

Black Lives Matter

I firmly believe that the best schools reflect their local communities; they bring the community into their school and take pupils out into that community.

The best schools also look *beyond* their local communities and regard themselves as part of the national and international conversation.

These schools teach pupils how to be active members of their communities *and* how to be good citizens of the world.

A school's success can, I think, be measured by the extent to which it prepares all the young people it serves for their next steps in life - do pupils leave the school as well-rounded, cultured, inquisitive, caring, kind, resilient, knowledgeable human beings ready to make their own way in the world? And do schools, as a consequence, make the world a better place?

And, surely, a part of this mission to prepare pupils for their place in the world is ensuring that pupils are taught about issues such as the Black Lives Matter movement and that schools do more to actively tackle racism, and promote equality, diversity and inclusion?

Before we explore how schools might do this, let's be clear what the Black Lives Matter movement is...

A brief history of the Black Lives Matter movement

Black Lives Matter (BLM) is a political and social movement that advocates non-violent civil disobedience in protest against incidents of police brutality and all other racially motivated violence against black people.

The BLM movement began in July 2013 after George Zimmerman was acquitted in the shooting death of the African American teenager Trayvon Martin.

The movement gathered momentum following the deaths in 2014 of two African Americans, Michael Brown and Eric Garner.

But it was, perhaps, in May 2020 when BLM rose to international prominence in the aftermath of George Floyd's death. Floyd, a 46-year-old black man, was killed in Minneapolis, Minnesota, whilst being arrested for allegedly using counterfeit money.

During the arrest, Derek Chauvin, a white police officer, knelt on Floyd's neck for several minutes after Floyd had already been handcuffed and was lying face down. Two police officers, J. Alexander Kueng and Thomas Lane, assisted Chauvin in restraining Floyd, whilst another officer, Tou Thao, prevented bystanders from intervening.

Immediately before he died, Floyd complained about being unable to breathe, and expressed his fear that he was about to die and called for his mother.

It is estimated that between 15 and 26 million people participated in the subsequent BLM protests in the United States, making Black Lives Matter one of the largest movements in United States history.

In the UK, BLM held protests in various London locations including Trafalgar Square, whilst similar protests took place in Manchester, Bristol, and Cardiff.

The UK protests not only showed solidarity with US protesters, but also commemorated black people who had died in the UK.

On 7 June 2020, during a BLM protest in Bristol, a statue of the slave trader Edward Colston was pulled down by protesters and rolled into the harbour.

The part schools can play

To support BLM, schools need, I think, to ensure their staff are trained in tackling discrimination and that their systems and structures, and policies and procedures, promote equality and diversity and tackle racism; and schools need to ensure that their recruitment processes are not discriminatory and that their staff body is representative of the pupils and communities they serve.

Teacher training and recruitment

On the latter point about recruitment, recent research from the race equality think-tank, Runnymede, found a chronic under-representation of BAME teachers in the UK.

There was unanimous agreement amongst BAME participants that there should be more BAME staff in the school workforce generally (and within their schools specifically) and most agreed that role models for pupils were desirable, and some went further to argue that representation was a necessity to protect pupils from being stereotyped or misunderstood.

But schools can only recruit more BAME teachers if those teachers are entering the profession, and this may necessitate changes to initial teacher training (ITT).

Talking of ITT, changes may also be needed to better prepare all teachers to teach BAME students...

In a paper entitled 'Race, culture and all that: an exploration of the perspectives of White secondary student teachers about race equality issues in their initial teacher education', the author Vini Lander, who is Professor of Race and Education at Leeds Beckett University, argues that "teacher education in England is set largely within a White majority context".

The existence of the Teachers' Standards, Lander says, "does not guarantee that student teachers [will] understand the associated rationale or concepts underpinning them. In fact, the Teacher Development Agency's (TDA) own survey of newly qualified teachers [spanning the years 2003–7] shows that approximately one third of NQTs felt well or better prepared to teach pupils from minority ethnic backgrounds (30% in 2003 and 37% in 2007) and pupils who have English as an additional language (EAL) (20% in 2003 to 34% in 2007)."

This, Lander says, "is by no means an indication of how NQTs felt about issues of race equality but the survey is the only national benchmark on NQTs' preparation regarding race-related issues."

The TDA (2007) noted that: "...the Sector continues to make progress in both these areas, although ratings were still lower than for other aspects of initial teacher training".

The Runnymede survey also found that, whilst there were many teachers who were positive and felt supported by the senior leadership teams in their school, there were also many BAME teachers who reported feeling isolated and lacking in management support with regards to incidences of racism and career progression.

Structural barriers such as racism, including assumptions about capabilities based on racial/ethnic stereotypes, were everyday experiences for the BAME teachers involved in the Runnymede survey. In particular, BAME teachers spoke about an invisible glass-ceiling and widespread perception among senior leader that BAME teachers have, to quote the report, "a certain level and don't go beyond it".

Educating pupils about racism

As well as working to recruit and train staff, schools also need to ensure they educate their pupils about racism – and other forms of discrimination – and challenge their prejudices; but they also need to ensure that pupils are treated fairly. Here, it's worth noting that the government's Timpson review into school exclusions in 2019 found that black Caribbean pupils were round 1.7 times more likely to be permanently excluded compared to white British children.

Nicola Harvey, writing on the Optimus Education website in June 2020, said that "It is everyone's responsibility, particularly decision makers in schools, to come together and stand for equality, diversity and inclusion."

In other words, school leaders must not only promote diversity and inclusion, but must take affirmative action, too.

Raising awareness

School leaders, Harvey says, should be visible and show support. They could, for example, "have open discussions and ask for feedback from BAME colleagues, students and parents to understand their experiences – even if it feels uncomfortable –

[because] just listening with a sense of compassion is the first step to change."

They could also "familiarise staff with the Anti-Racism Resource List and use the subject areas in the reports to educate senior leaders, school staff and students on appropriate subjects covered within the reports". Similarly, they could "help parents talk about racial equality [by sharing] the Parents Guide to Black Lives Matter which has a range of age-related resources, activities and tips".

Further, school leaders could "start a committee to review policies, staff meeting subjects and school events ensuring BAME staff, parents and students feel included and are represented". In consultation with BAME colleagues and parents and governors, they could "write to [the] school community sharing [their] commitment to promoting diversity".

The curriculum

Harvey suggests that school leaders should also seek to "decolonise the curriculum". Indeed, there has been much talk of revisiting the national curriculum to ensure it is representative of black voices.

The Black Curriculum is a social enterprise group that campaigns for black history to be taught in schools all year round. Its aims are to: 1. To provide a sense of belonging and identity to young people across the UK; 2. To teach an accessible educational Black British history curriculum that raises attainment for young people; and 3. To improve social cohesion between young people in the UK.

The Black Curriculum, responding to Covid-19, now offers up to 12 hours of teaching material on Black British history, designed to prepare pupils for success in a diverse landscape. Their material is divided into four 3-hour workshops (Politics and the Legal system, Land and the Environment, Art History and Migration).

They also offer 30-minute virtual assemblies covering a range of themes from their syllabus, as well as interactive, immersive and challenging teacher training which covers racial literacy, decolonising pedagogy and curriculum, and teaching intersectionality.

Also in terms of the curriculum, Harvey suggests making sure "the school library is stocked with books showing ethnically diverse content from BAME authors." Creating "a curriculum map with positive and successful BAME inventors and role models to inspire students in their learning all year round: may also help and she provides the following examples:

- In science, students could learn about **Charles Drew**, the African American man who created the first large-scale blood bank in the 1900s, an invention still being used in hospitals today.
- In English, write about **Gandhi** and his aim to lead India peacefully in a non-violent movement against British rule.
- In business studies, students may be inspired by **Madam C. J. Walker** – one of the first female black self-made millionaires.
- In PE, students could play STOP, PAUSE and GO movement games to learn about **Garrett Morgan**, the black man who invented the traffic light system.

The BookTrust has also published a Black Lives Matter reading list which may be of use to schools.

Harvey concludes that, although her list of actions may seem extensive, it is merely the tip of the iceberg: "The cultural, systemic and unconscious biases need to change. To get started, you may want to choose two or three activities from above, create a plan of action and then build upon this over time. Either way, it is everyone's responsibility, particularly decision makers in schools, to come together and stand for equality, diversity and inclusion. Do something today to make a difference."

Chapter 16: The poverty gap

I explored many aspects of socio-economic deprivation in my discussion about the Pupil Premium in Chapter 13 and so will not do so again here at any great length. However, I do wish to discuss the poverty gap in more detail before we explore the SEND gap and then conclude our discussions about ensuring equity...

Here's an important point with which to start: Pupils from poorer backgrounds tend to do less well in school, not because they are 'less able' than their more affluent peers, but simply because they were born into poverty. Their birth proves to be their destiny, both at school and in later life.

Before I explore this point further, it's important to remember – as I explained in Chapter 13 – that not all pupils from socio-economically deprived homes are at an academic disadvantage in school or college.

As I also explained in Chapter 13, there is no such thing as a typical 'Pupil Premium child', just as there is no such thing as a typical 'SEND child', and we must treat each pupil as an individual.

Where children from poorer homes are indeed academically disadvantaged and therefore considered to be vulnerable at school, although the causes may be broadly similar (i.e. their socio-economic deprivation), the barriers they face towards learning may manifest themselves in very different ways and, as such, the solutions we put in place to help them must also be different.

In short, 'one size does not fit all'.

So, accepting that an individual approach is essential, let us now look at the issue of poverty in more detail...

According to the Joseph Rowntree Foundation (JRF), “Poverty means not being able to heat your home, pay your rent, or buy essentials for your children. It means waking up every day facing insecurity, uncertainty, and impossible decisions about money. It means facing marginalisation – and even discrimination – because of your financial circumstances. The constant stress it causes can lead to problems that deprive people of the chance to play a full part in society.”

If that’s what poverty is, then how is it measured?

Well, this is complicated because there are numerous ways to define poverty and those definitions tend to change over time, for example as a result of reforms of the welfare system. But, broadly speaking, the most common measures of poverty in the UK at the time of writing are:

- **Relative income poverty**, whereby households have less than 60% of contemporary median income
- **Absolute income poverty**, whereby households have less than 60% of the median income in 2010/11, uprated by inflation
- **Material deprivation**, whereby you can’t afford certain essential items and to partake in certain activities
- **Destitution**, whereby you can’t afford basics such as shelter, heating and clothing.

What causes poverty?

The causes of poverty, by whichever measure you wish to choose, are factors that reduce your resources *or* increase your needs and the costs of meeting them.

Some of these causes – like a poor education, as will see shortly – can also be consequences, creating a cycle that traps young people.

Life events and moments of transition – getting sick, suffering a bereavement, being made redundant or the breakdown of a relationship – are common triggers for poverty.

According to the JRF, some of the most common causes of poverty in the UK today are:

- Unemployment and low-paid jobs lacking prospects and security
- An ineffective benefits system
- High costs of living
- Discrimination
- Weak relationships
- Abuse, trauma or chaotic lives

Another cause of poverty, pertinent to our discussion here, is low levels of skills and/or education. Why? Well, young people and adults without the skills and qualifications they need tend to find it difficult to get a job, especially one with security, prospects and decent pay.

The consequences of poverty, meanwhile, are myriad but include:

- Health problems
- Housing problems
- Being a victim or perpetrator of crime
- Drug or alcohol problems
- Homelessness
- Teenage parenthood
- Relationship and family problems

Another consequence of poverty, and crucial to our current purposes, is lower educational achievement... in other words, not only can poor education cause poverty, but it can also be caused by it, suggesting it can become a vicious cycle. For example, experiencing poverty early in a child's life can have a harmful effect on their brain development and this impacts on their educational achievement.

So, why should this be? Why should poverty make children vulnerable at school...?

How does poverty impact on pupils' education?

As I explained in Chapter 13, about 1 in 3 young people in the UK currently grows up in poverty. What's more, a report by the Resolution Foundation in February 2019 predicted that, by 2023,

37% of children would live in poverty. The highest proportion since the early 1990s.

The academic achievement gap between rich and poor is detectable from an early age - as early as 22 months in fact - and the gap continues to widen as children travel through the education system.

Children from the lowest income homes are half as likely to get five good GCSEs and go on to higher education as the national average. And white working-class pupils (particularly boys) are amongst our lowest performers.

What's more, the link between poverty and attainment is multi-racial - whatever their ethnic background, pupils eligible for free school meals underperform compared to those who are not.

In short, if you're a high ability pupil from a low-income home (and, therefore, a low social class), you're not going to do as well in school and in later life as a low ability pupil from a higher income home and higher social class.

In other words, it is social class and wealth - not ability - that defines a pupil's educational outcomes and their future life chances.

One of the ways we identify pupils from socio-economically deprived homes is through their eligibility for free school meals (FSM). Indeed, FSM eligibility is one of the main factors determining Pupil Premium (PP) eligibility because the PP is awarded to pupils who are recorded in the January school census if they are known to have been eligible for free school meals (FSM) in any of the previous six years, as well as those first known to be eligible that month.

But FSM eligibility is a poor proxy for educational and social disadvantage. Indeed, as many as 50-75% of FSM children are not in the lowest income households.

What's more, it's often the time-poor and the less educated who are less engaged and motivated at school, rather than those facing economic deprivation.

So, we need not only to be wary of assuming that every child from a socio-economically deprived home will be academically disadvantaged, although many will, but we also need to be cognisant of the fact that some of our means of identifying deprivation are not without fault. As ever, and as I said earlier, the best way forward is to regard each pupil as an individual and to better understand what barriers to learning each child might face in school and how their vulnerability manifests itself.

Poverty may be the primary cause of a child's vulnerability in school, but it is often the consequences of poverty that create barriers to learning. For example, poverty may mean that a child's attendance and punctuality is poor because they do not have an alarm clock, or their parents work several jobs including a night shift and are not available to wake their child up and ensure they get ready for school on time. Poverty may mean a child suffers from a lack of sleep or poor nutrition, too, which affects their concentration and energy levels in school and thus hampers their achievement.

As such, and again as I said in Chapter 13 (apologies for repeating myself), I recommend that your first action when deciding how to support vulnerable learners from poorer homes is to identify, on a case-by-case basis, the *consequences* of their poverty on their education and go from there.

In short, you need to ask yourself: What are the barriers to learning faced by your vulnerable pupils? This may sound obvious but it's a step often missed by schools who assume all pupils identified as being vulnerable (say, because they are eligible for FSM) must be disadvantaged and similarly disadvantaged.

How does the poverty gap emerge?

Notwithstanding the problems I have outlined above, and as I explained in Chapter 13 when I used the example of the Pupil Premium to exemplify my three-point plan, we know with some certainty that the socio-economic attainment gap emerges early in a child's life - certainly before that child enters formal education aged 5. In fact, two fifths of the attainment gap that exists at age 16 is present before the child starts school. And these early gaps are particularly pronounced in early language and literacy.

By the age of 3, more disadvantaged children are – on average – already almost 18 months behind their more affluent peers in their early language development. Around two fifths of disadvantaged five-year-olds are not meeting the expected literacy standard for their age.

It would surely follow, then, that one of our primary tasks when tackling the vulnerability caused by poverty should be improving these children's literacy and language skills?

Children born into more affluent families who can afford to have books, newspapers and magazines in the home, and who can afford to visit museums, art galleries, zoos, and stately homes and gardens, and to take regular holidays, and have the time to talk – around the dinner table, on weekend walks, in the car – about current affairs and about what they're reading or doing or watching – develop an awareness of the world around them, an understanding of how life works, and – crucially – a language with which to explain it all.

And this world knowledge and its attendant language provide a solid foundation on which they can build further such knowledge and language capabilities.

The unlucky ones - those children born into poverty and not therefore brought up in such knowledge-rich environments, and who therefore do not develop this foundation - don't do as well in school because new knowledge and skills have nothing to 'stick' to or build upon.

It is not, as I said earlier, that socio-economically deprived children are in any way less able, but that they don't have the same amount of knowledge about the world as their more affluent peers with which to make sense of new information and experiences.

Put simply, the more you know, the easier it is to know more and so the culturally – and indeed materially – rich will always stay ahead of the impoverished, and the gap between rich and poor will continue to grow as children travel through our education system.

One of the best things to do to help children born into poverty, therefore, is to build their world knowledge and language capabilities – what, as I said earlier, we might call 'cultural capital'.

Children born into more affluent families acquire, unknowingly perhaps, an awareness of the world around them, an understanding of how life works, and – crucially – a language with which to explain it all – which, in turn, provides a solid foundation on which they can build further knowledge, skills and understanding.

Those children born into poverty, however, do not develop this foundation and therefore don't do as well in school because new knowledge and skills have nothing to 'stick' to or build upon.

Of course, it's not just being born into poverty that has this effect. And that's what I'd like to explore this in this chapter... the other, albeit related, social causes of academic disadvantage...

As well as children born into poverty, children who come from broken or transitory homes, who are in care, who have impoverished parents who work two or more jobs and so spend little time at home or are too exhausted when they get home from work to read to or converse with their children, are academically disadvantaged.

These parents may not themselves be well educated and so possess very little 'cultural capital' of their own to pass on to their children.

Maybe these parents came from impoverished backgrounds and so books and current affairs never featured in their lives and remain alien to them. Maybe they did not do well at school or did not enjoy their schooling and so do not know how to - or do not wish to - help prepare their child for the world of education.

In other words, children can be vulnerable in school for many reasons including, though not limited to, poverty. We need to look at the time-poor, too, as well as working class children, particularly boys. We need to look at children with high levels of mobility, and so on.

But, as I said above, the crucial point in every case is that educational disadvantage is an accident of birth; it is not about ability, innate or otherwise.

Let's briefly take a look at the potential academic disadvantage caused by high levels of mobility...

Mobility

As I have said, children born into poverty are not alone in being academically disadvantaged. Children who have high mobility – in the sense that they move schools a lot – are also vulnerable.

Service children, for example, tend to move schools more than average as they follow their parents from military posting to military posting. This is, after all, why service children are eligible for the Service Pupil Premium (SPP), a stream of the Pupil Premium Grant...

The SPP is awarded to pupils who are categorised as 'Ever 5 service child' which means a pupil recorded in the January school census who was eligible for the service child premium in any of the previous four years as well as those recorded as a service child for the first time in the January school census.

Although each service child, as indeed each child with high levels of mobility, is an individual and the consequences of their mobility on their education will be different, meaning of course that the solutions must also be different, one way of helping pupils with high levels of mobility is to improve our transition arrangements to support pupils immediately before and after they move schools.

According to Galton (1999), almost forty per cent of children fail to make expected progress during the year immediately following a change of schools. We tend to focus on the primary-to-secondary transition but pupils change schools all the time and so we should be ready to support their transfer.

Although schools cannot mitigate all of the social and emotional effects of transferring between schools, we can do more to help pupils make the move more smoothly.

There are five aspects of school transfer that we might wish to focus on...

1. **Administration**: here, we could improve the general management of the transition process such as the formal liaison between schools. In practice, this might take the form of the transfer of pupil records and achievement data, meetings with

pupils and parents, and visits from headteachers, senior leaders and teachers.

2. **Social and emotional**: here, we might forge better links between pupils/parents and their previous/next school prior to and immediately after transfer.

3. **Curriculum**: here, we might try to improve curriculum continuity between schools by funding teachers to share plans that show what content is taught on either side of the transition. We could also fund cross-phase teaching, the teaching of bridging units, summer schools, joint CPD networks and INSET days, the sharing of good practice and shared planning, and teacher exchanges, and so on.

4. **Pedagogy**: here, we could establish a shared understanding of how pupils are taught - as well as how they learn - in order to achieve a greater continuity in classroom practice and teaching. This might be achieved by understanding differing teaching styles and skills, by engaging in shared CPD and teacher exchanges, and by primary and secondary teachers observing each other in practice.

5. **Management of learning**: here, we could ensure that pupils are active participants, rather than passive observers, in the transition process. This might be achieved by empowering pupils and their parents with information about achievement and empowering them with the confidence to articulate their learning needs in a new environment. This might take the form of giving information to parents/pupils, providing pupils with learning portfolios and samples of achievements, and raising pupils' awareness of their needs and talents by sharing and explaining data.

Chapter 17: The SEND gap

In Book Two of this series on School and College Curriculum Design, I explained that differentiation was – fundamentally – about enabling every pupil, no matter their background and starting point, to access an ambitious curriculum and achieve. I said that we can do this best by building routines into our teaching and learning practices. In particular, I advocated a 4-step teaching sequence.

I'd now like to offer some health-warnings about using some traditional forms of differentiation for pupils with SEND...

When we talk about differentiation, we often have in mind ways of scaffolding learning for our SEND pupils. But pupils – like learning – are complex and no pupil is uniformly 'less able' than another. Rather, some pupils have acquired more knowledge and skills in one area than another pupil or have practised a task more often. Of course, some pupils have additional and different needs – such as those young people with learning difficulties or disabilities – and they require a different approach. But to say they are 'less able' because they have SEND is, I think, an unhelpful misnomer.

To suggest a pupil is 'less able' implies there is an average pupil against which we are comparing all others. But there is no such thing as 'average'; rather, we are all made up of myriad individual characteristics. If you take an average of each of us (height, weight, IQ, shoe size, etc), you won't find any individual who is average in all respects. This is known as the Jaggedness Principle...

Readers of the first two books in this series on School and College Curriculum Design will be familiar with what follows – and are therefore welcome to skip ahead – but for the benefit of new readers and to refresh the memories of those who read the earlier books some time ago, here is a brief summary...

The Jaggedness Principle posits that 'average' doesn't exist and that, therefore, we'd be wise not to compare pupils to the average, deeming some to be 'less able' and others 'more able'. What's more, the term "less able" infers an immovable position – if you are 'less able' you are destined to remain so ad infinitum, living life languishing in the left-hand shadow of the bell-curve.

I'm not suggesting that every pupil performs the same – or has the same capacity to do so. We are not all born equal. But defining someone as less able as a result of a test means we are in danger of arbitrarily writing off some pupils by means of a snapshot taken through a pinhole lens.

When approaching differentiation for pupils with SEND, therefore, we would – I think – be wise to remember that all pupils – like all human beings – are different, unique, individual. Differentiation, therefore, should not be about pupils with SEND as a homogenous group. Rather, we should treat each pupil on an individual basis. Nor should we assume that what works with one pupil will work with all and that what was proven to work with SEND pupils in another school, in another county, in another country, (according to research evidence and meta-analyses) will work in our classroom.

All this rather begs the question: 'What does work?'

Differentiation in the guise of teaching to the middle and scaffolding for SEND pupils while stretching and challenging higher-performing ones (and therefore expecting less of lower-performing pupils), carries with it an inherent danger: it is, by any another name, 'dumbing down'.

Differentiation of this kind is delivered by means of placing limits on learning, lowering a glass ceiling on top of pupils' ambitions. Differentiation of this kind might take the form of differentiated questions using Bloom's Taxonomy. For example, the teacher might start a classroom discussion by asking a question from the bottom of the taxonomy – a knowledge-based question which requires a recall of facts – to a lower-performing pupil before moving up the taxonomy with higher-performing pupils.

But sticking to the bottom of Bloom's Taxonomy does not allow SEND pupils to deepen their understanding; rather, it leads to surface learning. What's more, this approach is guilty of assuming that because the taxonomy grows in difficulty, the bottom end isn't as important and that higher-performing pupils don't need to waste their time down there. It's true that Bloom is a spectrum of task difficulty: it goes from easy – such as recalling knowledge – to harder – such as evaluating an argument. But it is a spectrum because it explores the full range of cognitive learning. Knowledge is just as important as evaluation. Without knowledge, pupils can't access the higher bits. In other words, without the bottom layers of the pyramid – the foundations – the whole structure crumbles.

To demonstrate their complete mastery of a topic, every pupil (no matter their current level of performance) should be able to answer a combination of recall-type questions (these are questions which can be answered in a short period regardless of prior learning) and developmental-type questions (these are questions which stretch pupils and develop the skills required for academic success). Every pupil at every level of their academic development needs to answer questions on the full spectrum of Bloom's Taxonomy; every pupil needs access to both mastery and developmental questions.

Rather than expecting different outcomes of different pupils, we should have high expectations that all our pupils will reach the same destination, albeit some will take a different route and need more time to do so.

This notion that all pupils achieve the same outcome forms the basis of 'mastery learning' which I explored in Book Two of this series so will not do so in any detail here.

Briefly, though, mastery learning, as I explained in Book Two, is founded on the belief that all pupils are capable of learning anything if that learning is presented in the right way. Mastery learning works on the basis that understanding is the result of intention and effort, and that difficulty is enjoyable.

In practical terms, mastery learning is about pupils demonstrating they have mastered something before being able to move on to the next thing. The teacher decides the level of mastery required – 80 or 90 per cent, say – and pupils are given opportunities to learn through a variety of instructional methods before taking a test. If pupils do not attain the right level of mastery in the test, they are given additional instructional activities to complete before retaking the test (which is usually in a different form or uses different questions).

One benefit of the mastery approach is that it avoids the negative effects of differentiation which can translate as lower expectations of what SEND or the so-called 'less able' pupils are able to achieve. With differentiation, activities can also be oversimplified. Mastery, however, allows teachers to genuinely challenge pupils.

Mastery learning also meshes perfectly with the 'progression model' of curriculum planning and sequencing I advocated in Book One of this series as a means of identifying the waypoints of our curriculum.

In short, then, differentiation should be about ensuring every pupil is headed toward the same destination. We should not 'dumb down' or expect less of SEND pupils; rather, we should articulate the same high expectations of all – expectations regularly reinforced through our language and our actions – but accept that some pupils, some of the time, will need different levels of support, different kinds of support, and to be afforded different timescales to reach that destination.

Of course, some pupils fear challenge. We need to eliminate – or at least mitigate – their feelings of fear and hesitation by creating a classroom environment which encourages the making of mistakes as an integral part of the learning process, and a pedagogical culture which explicitly says (through our choice of language, our modelling and thinking aloud, and the routines in which we engage) that there is nothing to fear by trying your best and pushing yourself to do hard work. After all, challenge is innate. Pupils love challenge when it is private because, in the safety of their own homes or when with trusted friends, there isn't the fear of humiliation or peer pressure.

To promote challenge in the classroom, therefore, we need to reduce the threat level, we need to ensure no-one feels humiliated if they fall short of a challenge. Rather, they need to know that they will learn from the experience and perform better next time. They will learn by increments.

I offered some practical ways of reducing the threat level in Book Two of this series and, specifically, I explained that, to my mind, a positive learning environment is one in which all pupils:

- Feel welcomed
- Feel valued
- Are enthusiastic about learning
- Are engaged in their learning
- Are eager to experiment
- Feel rewarded for their hard work

Behind all of these characteristics and any more we care to mention, I said, there is a simple, albeit oxymoronic, aim: to ensure pupils are comfortable with discomfort. In other words, we want our pupils to know that the work they'll be asked to do in our classrooms will be tough, that they will be challenged with hard work and made to think. We want our pupils to know that there will be no hiding place in our classrooms; they must ask and answer questions and attempt everything we ask of them.

However, in so doing, we want them to feel safe and protected, we want them to be eager for challenge, and to willingly attempt hard work because they know that we've strung a safety net beneath them: yes, they might falter but we will catch them if they fall.

We also want our pupils to know that taking risks and making mistakes is not just accepted in our classrooms but is positively and proactively welcomed as an essential part of the learning process. Indeed, the only people who don't make mistakes either never get any better at anything or have reached the point of automaticity - they have fully mastered something and so can now do it through habit. Our pupils are not at the point of automaticity and so must make mistakes if they are to get better in our subject. If they don't make mistakes, they cannot receive feedback; if they don't receive feedback, they will not know how to improve; if they don't know how to improve, then they are unlikely to do so.

Of course, in order to set the right level of challenge for our pupils – hard but achievable with time, effort and support – we need to locate, perhaps through the use of exit tickets or hinge questions, pupils' 'struggle zones', the point just beyond their current capability but within their reach, something they cannot yet do but will be able to with time, effort and support.

In Book Two, I set out two methods of 'finding the sweet spot' whereby work will be hard but achievable: exit tickets and hinge questions.

I also exhorted the importance of high expectations by means of the Pygmalion Effect – research that claims reality can be positively or negatively influenced by other people's expectations. The higher the expectations you have of somebody, the better they perform. In other words, when teachers have high expectations of their pupils, their pupils perform well.

To take our discussion about differentiating for SEND pupils forward, I will review eight of the most common forms of differentiation in use in our classrooms today and analyse their respective advantages and disadvantages, then I'll examine the role that teaching assistants (TAs) or additional learning support (ALS) can play in ensuring that learning is differentiated, before using the example of pupils with speech, language and communication needs (SLCN) to illustrate the three-wave method of supporting pupils with SEND.

Different forms of differentiation

Differentiation wears many guises. I'd like to review eight of the most common forms of differentiation in use in our classrooms today and analyse, as I see them, their relative advantages and disadvantages. I do so not to imply that I know what works best for you and your pupils, but simply to provide you with the space and opportunity to step back and consider each of these approaches afresh. I would not profess to know what works for you and I would never presume to teach grandma how to suck eggs. All I ask is that you keep an open mind to what might and might not be the most effective strategies...

Differentiation by task

What is it? The teacher gives different pupils different tasks, the level of difficulty of which is determined by the pupil's 'ability'.

What are the advantages? It allows the task to be set to test the mastery of skills of different groups of pupils dependent on their needs.

What are the disadvantages? It can be time-consuming, and it can lead to difficulties comparing pupils' achievements because we can't assess the same things. It also places a limit on what some pupils can achieve.

Differentiation by resource

What is it? The teacher gives different pupils different resources to support their learning, such as scaffolded worksheets or texts at differing word levels.

What are the advantages? It allows pupils of different abilities to access the curriculum but in a manner appropriate to them.

What are the disadvantages? It can be very time-consuming and promote learned helplessness.

Differentiation by assessment

What is it? The teacher gives different pupils different assessment tasks based on what they need them to demonstrate.

What are the advantages? It allows an assessment task to be set to test the mastery of skills of different groups of pupils dependent on their needs. It can be quick to prepare because it can simply consist of different questions

What are the disadvantages? It can be time-consuming and can lead to difficulties in comparing pupil achievements because different assessments may not be testing the same thing. What's more, it runs counter to current examination practice in most subjects whereby papers are no longer tiered, and every pupil is assessed in the same manner.

Differentiation by pace

What is it? The teacher allows pupils differing timescales to read the end goal, accepting that every pupil learns at a different pace.

What are the advantages? It allows pupils to work at their own pace whilst striving towards the same destination.

What are the disadvantages? It may mean that some pupils do not reach their destination and therefore do not cover all the curriculum content. It may mean the teacher loses the integrity of their carefully planned and sequenced curriculum and that whole-class instruction becomes difficult.

Differentiation by support

What is it? The teacher offers different levels of support to different pupils.

What are the advantages? Pupils receive personalized support from the teacher, teaching assistant or other pupils.

What are the disadvantages? It is difficult for the teacher to manage whole class progress and know exactly what has been taught and learnt so they can assess pupil progress and move through the curriculum.

Differentiation by extension

What is it? The teacher provides additional tasks to pupils who finish soonest, enabling them to move on to more difficult content whilst the rest of the class catches up.

What are the advantages? It allows the teacher to set a task that tests pupils' mastery of skills. It can be quick to prepare if it takes the form of questions of differing difficulty.

What are the disadvantages? It can be time-consuming if it takes the form of different detailed activities. It can lead to difficulties in comparing achievement because different tasks may not be testing the same thing.

Differentiation by dialogue

What is it? The teacher uses one-to-one or small group discussions – such as verbal feedback – to provide assessment information and support which enables pupils to make progress.

What are the advantages? It is an integral part of the lesson, builds rapport, enables the teacher to gain crucial assessment information and personalise the learning, and can be applied to all.

What are the disadvantages? It is sometimes difficult to carve out sufficient time in a lesson to talk to pupils on an individual basis without slowing the flow of the curriculum. Some pupils may receive a lot of feedback information whilst others – whom the teacher deems to be making sufficient progress – are largely ignored.

Differentiation by grouping

What is it? The teacher places pupils into different groups depending on their current progress and their strengths and weaknesses, in order to carry out different tasks, use different resources, undertake different assessments, work at a different pace, access a different level of support, work on extension tasks, and so on.

What are the advantages? Differentiated grouping allows different groups to be tracked differently, it encourages collaborative learning and allows pupils to support each other. Sometimes, pupils are placed in groups of similar 'ability'; other times, 'less able' pupils are placed with their 'more able' peers who offer support, perhaps in the form of peer-teaching.

What are the disadvantages? It can lead to stigmatisation if some groups are deemed 'less able'. Like all group work, it can lead to off-task learning or to some pupils doing all the work whilst others 'coast' if it is not tightly controlled and if the teacher doesn't explicitly teach group work skills or behaviours first.

Providing an inclusive learning environment

The SEND Code of Practice says that 'Special educational provision is underpinned by high quality teaching and is compromised by anything less.' Providing an inclusive learning environment whereby pupils' needs are met without drawing attention to their difficulties, therefore, is crucial because this will maximise their learning potential but limit any feelings they may have of embarrassment and frustration.

Here are some practical tips for:

- Supporting pupils with memory difficulties
- Teaching spelling
- Teaching reading
- Teaching writing
- Teaching through intervention

Supporting SEND pupils with memory difficulties

When supporting pupils with memory difficulties, the teacher could:

- Revisit previous learning at the beginning of the lesson, allowing pupils to recall and make associations with new learning.
- Give an overview of the lesson so the pupils can see the outcome and make sense of the content.
- Revisit learning at regular intervals throughout the lesson.
- 'Chunk' new information and regularly check understanding.
- Use a step-by-step approach to completing any task with regular checkpoints for monitoring progress and giving feedback.
- When giving instructions, limit the number, repeat them and provide notes and a checklist.
- Use simple, concise sentences when giving direct instruction.
- Consider the pace of delivery – speak more slowly if necessary.
- Use songs, rhyme and rap to aid memorisation.
- Allow 'wait time' for pupils to process information before articulating an answer.
- Allow pupils to work collaboratively.
- Ensure that the tasks are relevant to the learning and eliminate those that will interfere with that learning, such as copying from the board or writing the date and title.
- When pupils are on task, avoid interrupting their learning.
- At the end of the lesson, summarise the learning and say what the next lesson will be about. Paint the big picture for pupils, showing how each lesson fits in and builds upon the last.

Supporting SEND pupils with spelling

When teaching spelling, the teacher could:

- Provide subject-specific key words in handouts.
- Encourage pupils to take risks with their spelling, suggesting that they underline these words.
- Encourage a metacognitive approach by asking pupils to analyse their spelling mistakes and identify the learning required.

Supporting SEND pupils with reading

When teaching reading, the teacher could:

- Only ask a pupil to read aloud if you know they want to.
- Ensure that books are at the right level of difficulty for pupils.
- Use audiobooks when appropriate.
- Teach reading skills, such as skimming, scanning and close reading.
- Encourage pupils to condense and make sense of what they read, for example by making mind maps and drawing diagrams and flow charts.
- Explicitly teach key vocabulary pupils will encounter in the text before they start reading.
- Encourage the pupils to take question the writer's techniques and intentions and consider their own views and experiences in relation to the text.
- Instil in pupils a desire to read by providing reading materials that are of interest to them.

Supporting SEND pupils with writing

When teaching writing, the teacher could:

- Check pupils' understanding of the task before they begin writing.
- Use ICT to improve written outcomes, for example voice recognition software or mind mapping software.
- Provide examples and model good practice.
- Break down a writing task into manageable chunks.
- Teach, model and encourage pupils to plan.
- Give specific feedback at each stage so pupils know what to repeat or improve.

- Provide a mix of written and verbal feedback.
- Improve proofreading by building in proofreading time in lessons, using a 'buddying' system, teaching and modelling strategies, providing proofreading checklists, encouraging pupils to read work aloud, and leaving 'thinking time' between writing and proofreading.

Supporting SEND pupils through intervention

When teaching through additional interventions, the teacher could:

- Ensure the lessons are structured, cumulative and multi-sensory.
- Ensure the pupil governs the pace of delivery
- Ensure the specific needs of the pupil are met
- Ensure the knowledge and skills taught in the intervention session are transferred back to the classroom
- Ensure progress is reviewed at regular intervals and is tracked
- Ensure the pupil enjoys the learning and feels motivated, confident and self-empowered.

Now, by way of illustration and as I promised earlier, I'll home in on ways to support pupils with a particular – and commonplace – learning difficulty...

A case study: supporting pupils with SLCN

We are going to explore ways of supporting pupils with a particular form of SEND called SLCN. We'll do this in order to exemplify a wider point. In other words, the advice contained within the remainder of this chapter can be adapted and applied to support pupils with many other forms of SEND and indeed some disadvantaged pupils.

What is SLCN?

SLCN is a major cause of SEND in school pupils and college learners and prevents many pupils from accessing the curriculum and fulfilling their potential.

SLCN stands for speech, language and communication needs.

All children and young people need good speech, language and communication skills in order to access the school curriculum, make good progress and achieve good outcomes from school and from life. After all, speech, language and communication underpin basic literacy.

But, as well as being integral to literacy and therefore academic success, speech, language and communication skills are also closely linked to pupil behaviour and to their social, emotional and mental health and wellbeing. After all, if pupils cannot communicate effectively, they cannot interact with their peers or express their feelings. Let's call this *emotional* literacy.

Speech, language and communication may sound tautologous but there are important differences between the three elements of SLCN. Let's deconstruct the acronym...

S stands for <u>speech</u>: Pupils need to be able to speak fluently - which is to say with a clear voice, using appropriate pitch, volume and intonation, and without too much hesitation - in order to express themselves and demonstrate their understanding in every school subject. Being able to speak enables pupils to clearly convey their learning.

L stands for <u>language</u>: Pupils need to command a range of appropriate vocabulary in order to facilitate and further their learning across the curriculum. For example, they need to understand instructions from teachers and others. Pupils also need to be able to use verbal reasoning in order to acquire, process, analyse and understand the new information they encounter every day at school.

C stands for <u>communication</u>: Pupils need to know how to adapt their communication style in order to suit the purpose and audience. They need to be able to use and follow the non-verbal rules of communication such as active listening and taking conversational turns, and they need to be able to use language to explain, describe, persuade and so on.

Language development is something generally associated with early years education. However, language and communication skills continue to develop throughout pupils' teenage years. Pupils continue learning new vocabulary and complex language structures to enhance their learning and interaction with others. It is therefore important for secondary teachers and FE college teachers, not just their primary school colleagues whom we tend to think are more crucial to pupils' language acquisition and development, to be able to encourage and extend this development. Put simply, language and communication between teachers and pupils enables learning.

Furthermore, pupils need the ability to use language for negotiation, compromise, resolving conflict, developing relationships and for managing and regulating their emotions. All pupils need the skills required to be proficient communicators – for attainment, behaviour, emotional and social development and their readiness for the workplace.

However, there are many pupils who struggle to develop these skills. For some pupils this may mean specialist support is needed and/or access to alternative and augmentative means of communication such as signs, symbols and communication aids. For others, however, tailored support from within school can make a considerable difference. Without this support, pupils with SLCN will struggle to understand instructions, access the curriculum, manage their behaviour and reach targets that could otherwise be well within their grasp.

It is therefore vital that secondary school teachers and FE college teachers, not just primary school teachers, understand how to support and guide pupils, students and learners with SLCN.

The first action I recommend schools and colleges take is to ensure they are correctly identifying pupils with SLCN. It's an action that holds water for all pupils with SEND because the first step towards supporting these pupils is to identify the learning difficulties that may hinder them in accessing our ambitious curriculum.

Identification of need

UK Department for Education census data from January 2018 shows that the percentage of pupils with special educational needs increased from 14.4% in 2017 to 14.6% and that the percentage of pupils with a statement or education health and care plan (EHCP) increased from 2.8% in 2017 to 2.9%. A further 1,022,535 pupils were on SEN support in January 2018, this equates to 11.7% of the total pupil population, an increase from 11.6% in 2017.

The 2018 data shows that SLCN remains one of the most significant causes of SEN with 22.8% of pupils with SEN support and 14.6% of pupils with a statement or EHCP being identified as having SLCN as their primary need.

So why, if SLCN is so prevalent, with most statistics suggesting an average 7% of young people have some form of SLCN, that's an average of two pupils in every class, are many secondary school teachers seemingly unaware of it?

One reason, I think, is the fact that pupils' needs are often being wrongly identified and coded when they move from primary school to secondary school and, as a consequence, from secondary school to FE college. This has legal implications because, according to the SEND Code of Practice (2014), schools have a statutory duty to publish information on their website about how they implement their policy for SEN (known as the SEN Information Report) and this must include information on 'policies for identifying children and young people with SEN and assessing their needs'. If SLCN is not being correctly identified, those policies are clearly ineffective, and pupils may suffer the consequences.

The charity The Communication Trust believes that an average of 40% of children with SLCN are not being identified as such and, they say, the most difficult to spot are older pupils, particularly those who have difficulties with vocabulary (45% not identified), those who struggle with formulating sentences (52% not identified) and children with difficulties understanding (48% not identified). That's not to say that primary school pupils are always identified correctly and supported – they're not – but it is to argue that a far greater proportion of pupils go unidentified or wrongly coded when they transfer to secondary school. Take, for example, that last statistic: 48% of pupils with difficulties understanding are not identified in secondary schools. In primary, it's only 29% which is still clearly a concern but nevertheless highlights the discrepancy.

Ofsted has reported on this problem of identification. The inspectorate said that inspection evidence suggests some children and young people have been "allocated support for their behaviour when, in fact, they had specific communication needs."

The Communications Trust says that, because "SLCN is often under-identified, [...] it's important to think about how many pupils you might typically expect to have SLCN in your school. This way you can see if your current data suggests there could be pupils who have not been identified or who have been misidentified."

Identification is key across all phases of education, from early years through primary, secondary and beyond. SLCN can be complex and difficult to identify, so an ongoing focus on identification is absolutely imperative. If an average 7% of young people have SLCN, and your school has a close-to-average SEN population of 14-15% overall, you can expect your school population to mirror this. In other words, you can expect two in every class of thirty pupils to have some form of SLCN.

In May 2010, the government published a report called 'The transitions between categories of special educational needs of pupils with Speech, Language and Communication Needs (SLCN) and Autism Spectrum Disorder (ASD) as they progress through the education system,' in which it argued that pupils who initially had SLCN and who changed their category of primary need when they transferred from primary school to secondary school, were most likely to be identified as having moderate learning difficulties (MLD) or specific learning difficulties (SLD).

The report went on to argue that "the decline in the proportion of pupils identified as having SLCN as the pupils progress through secondary school needs close monitoring to ensure that [...] pupils are being properly identified in terms of their special needs in the first instance [and that] pupils who do have SLCN receive adequate support as they progress through secondary school."

The report also found that, although the main problem was that many pupils were not identified as SLCN, some who were identified as such were in fact pupils for whom English was an additional language.

The report concluded that further investigation was needed in order to determine whether there was systematic misidentification of children's needs and specifically if those with EAL often have their needs mistakenly identified as SLCN.

So how can schools, colleges and teachers identify pupils with SLCN...?

There are several common risk factors to look out for. For example, boys are more likely (at a ratio of 2.5:1) to have SLCN than girls. Summer-born pupils are 1.65 times more likely to have SLCN than those born in the autumn. And pupils eligible for free school meals are 2.3 times more likely to have SLCN than those not eligible.

SLCN may manifest itself in pupils' limited social interactions, poor literacy skills, poor behaviour, low self-esteem and poor levels of achievement.

Here are some more tips for identifying pupils with SLCN:

A pupil who is experiencing <u>difficulties with receptive language</u> may do some of the following:

- They may have a limited vocabulary knowledge compared with other children of their age.
- They may not volunteer answers in class.
- They may parrot what you've said but without understanding it.
- When you ask them a question, they may appear to be answering a different question.
- They may have difficulty following instructions. They may appear forgetful or may take time to decipher/process more complex and/or longer sentences.
- They may show disruptive behaviour or become quiet and withdrawn. This may be because they are unable to understand what is being asked of them, are frustrated, or are frightened of failing.
- They may appear to stop concentrating when you are talking to them in a group. They may not be able to understand what you are saying, and so switch off.
- After an instruction to the group, they may look around the room at what the other pupils are doing before they start the activity. They may not have understood the instruction and are using their peers' actions as clues to help them carry out the activity.
- In activities that involve a lot of talking, like class discussions, they may be quiet and not join in, or they may join in but give inappropriate answers.

A pupil who is experiencing difficulties with expressive language may do some of the following:

- They may use the wrong words for things or use a word that sounds similar
- They may use very general words where a more specific word would be better.
- Their language may sound immature compared with other children of their age.
- They may omit the endings of words.
- They may miss out the small parts of a sentence like determiners such as 'the' and 'a'.
- They may wrongly order the words in a sentence, and/or miss important information in a sentence.
- They may seem to be struggling to express themselves, for example they may know a word but appear not be able to access it, resulting in lots of fillers or gesticulation.

A pupil who is experiencing difficulties with social communication/pragmatic language, may do some of the following:

- They may find it difficult to take turns in conversation.
- They may find it difficult to follow social conventions and may have difficulties initiating and maintaining conversations.
- They may find it difficult to understand non-literal language such as metaphors and sarcasm, which they take literally.
- They may have poor eye contact - not appearing to look at you or at peers when talking with them.
- They may show some disruptive or difficult behaviour due to difficulties understanding how to use language flexibly for a range of purposes.
- They may not use much expression in their face or tone of voice.
- They may talk about the same topic of conversation over and over and/or change topic frequently.

A pupil who is experiencing difficulties with speech sounds may do some of the following:

- They may be unintelligible to unfamiliar listeners.

- They may omit parts of words and/or have difficulties making some specific sounds in speech.
- During phonics work, they may not be able to produce - or discern the difference between - some of the sounds.

One form of SLCN is stammering although this does not always manifest itself as you might expect. A pupil with a stammer may do some of the following:

- They may prolong sounds (e.g., Sssssssorry)
- They may 'block', meaning that, when they are attempting a word, they make no sound at all or make a strangled sound.
- They may repeat sounds or parts of a word (e.g S s si sir, or p p please)

Understandably, some pupils become tense because of their stammer. They may have some tension in their face – particularly in the muscles around the eyes, lips or neck, and/or make extra movements when they speak, as though they are trying to force words out. They may blink or tap their hands or feet. Some pupils also try to mask their stammer. They may, for example, avoid speaking in certain situations or to certain people. They may also change the word they were going to use mid-sentence.

What can teachers do to help?

A small number of pupils with the most severe SLCN will require specialist support such as speech and language therapy. Some will require some targeted interventions outside of the classroom. Most will require some tailored support in the classroom. And all will benefit from quality first teaching and from a learning environment that supports their development.

Before I proffer my own advice on how to support pupils with SLCN, let us hear what the pupils themselves say...

According to the charity, I CAN, pupils with SLCN say that to help them access the curriculum and make better progress they want:

- Opportunities to ask questions and seek clarifications
- Teachers to use drawings and diagrams such as mind-maps to support verbal instructions

- Teachers to explain what they need to include in their answers to questions
- The use of bullet points instead of writing on the whiteboard and in handouts
- To learn the vocabulary that they need to know *before* a lesson
- Lessons where the teacher talks briefly and then they work in groups
- Thinking time after a question is asked
- Opportunities to work with a partner

I will now share some proven strategies for supporting pupils with additional and different needs such as SLCN. I will do so under the following headings:

- Quality first teaching
- In-class differentiation and additional interventions

I'll stress again that the advice I offer in relation to pupils with SLCN can, in most cases, be applied to other pupils who may be at some disadvantage in terms of accessing our ambitious curriculum and of achieving long-term learning.

Quality first teaching

The best way to improve outcomes for pupils with additional and different needs including those with SLCN, is through quality first teaching because, if we improve the quality of timetabled teaching in the classroom, all pupils – including those with SEND – will make better progress.

A study by Hanushek and Rivkin (2006) found that teacher effectiveness had more impact on outcomes than anything else - pupils in the classroom of the most effective teacher out of a group of fifty teachers took just six months to make the same amount of progress that pupils taught by the least effective teacher out of fifty took two years to achieve – in other words, between the most and least effective teacher out of fifty, there was eighteen months' wasted time.

What's more, Hamre and Pianta's research (2005) showed that, in the classrooms of the most effective teachers, socio-economic differences were null and void - in other words, pupils from the most disadvantaged backgrounds made the same progress as the least disadvantaged.

Since the National Strategies were launched in England in the late-1990s, it has been common practice to talk of three waves of intervention for pupils with SEND. The 3-wave model is often expressed as a pyramid similar to Bloom's taxonomy whereby Wave 1 sits at the bottom and thus provides the foundations on which all other forms of SEND support are built. According to the National Strategies, Wave 1 is "quality inclusive teaching which takes into account the learning needs of all the pupils in the classroom". As such, if we do not first provide pupils with quality classroom teaching, then no amount of additional intervention and support will help them to catch up.

A 2008 government paper defined the key characteristics of quality first teaching as follows:

- Highly focused lesson design with sharp objectives
- High demands of pupil involvement and engagement with their learning
- High levels of interaction for all pupils
- Appropriate use of teacher questioning, modelling and explaining
- An emphasis on learning through dialogue, with regular opportunities for pupils to talk both individually and in groups
- An expectation that pupils will accept responsibility for their own learning and work independently
- Regular use of encouragement and authentic praise to engage and motivate pupils.

National Strategy guidance also said that quality first teaching includes a balance between the following approaches:

- Directing and telling
- Demonstrating
- Explaining and illustrating
- Questioning and discussing
- Exploring and investigating
- Consolidating and embedding
- Reflecting on and talking through a process

- Reflecting and evaluating
- Summarising and reminding
- Guided learning

In Book Two of this series, I argued that quality first teaching occurs when we introduce pupils to new curriculum content in four distinct stages:

1. Telling
2. Showing
3. Doing
4. Practising

I won't repeat that advice again here, but I would like to add some further tips to consider when using direct instruction ('telling') with pupils with additional and different needs such as SLCN...

Because pupils with SLCN:

- Find it difficult to listen to and understand lots of spoken language,
- Need more time to process spoken language,
- Can find it hard to separate out sounds, words, phrases,
- ...and yet can have visual strengths...

They will benefit from direct instruction in which their teachers:

- Cut down the amount of language used,
- Repeat important information several times,
- Build in time for processing answers to questions,
- Slow down and repeat instructions,
- Think aloud,
- Use visuals,
- Display key words on the board,
- Use sentence stems, mnemonics and other 'schema'.

Increasingly independent

Ultimately, whatever form it takes, 'quality first teaching' should ensure that all pupils, including those with SEND:

- Are engaged - in the sense of being active participants in the process of learning not passive recipients of information
- Are highly motivated to learn and enthusiastic about learning
- Are challenged by hard work and know that making mistakes is an essential part of learning
- Receive effective feedback about where they are now, where they need to go next and how they will get there
- As a result of feedback, make progress over time and become increasingly independent and resilient learners.

One way to enable pupils to become increasingly independent and resilient is to employ the popular '3B4ME' method which encourages pupils to persevere when they get stuck and overcome challenges by themselves. It works like this:

When a pupil experiences difficulty, before they ask for help, they must first use:

1. Brain (think for themselves)
2. Buddy (ask a peer)
3. Book or board (use classroom resources including wall displays and textbooks).

It's good to [teach] talk

It is also helpful to teach pupils with SEND (including those with SLCN) how to engage in classroom discussions, and for the teacher to consider the way in which they and other adults speak to pupils...

Pupil talk

In order to help pupils with SEND including SLCN to engage in classroom discussions and question-and-answer sessions, teachers need to teach pupils how to talk and work in groups. They need to provide plenty of opportunities for pupils to talk in class, to a partner, to a small group, to adults, and to the whole class. Teachers should also scaffold the questions they ask in order to build pupil confidence. They should give pupils time to process questions and instructions, building in 'thinking time'. And they should make pupils aware of the range of resources available to support them.

Teacher talk

It is important that teachers and other adults working with pupils with SEND including SLCN carefully consider the way in which they talk. For example, they should be cognisant of the length and complexity of the language they use with pupils and consider the range and level of questions pupils understand. They should encourage pupils to engage in discussions with peers. They should model and scaffold if needed and teach pupils how to recognise when they need help and how to ask for it. They should frequently check for understanding, perhaps involving other adults in the class where relevant.

The importance of literacy

The Educational Endowment Foundation report entitled 'Preparing for Literacy: Improving Communication, Language and Literacy in the Early Years' (2018), argues that approaches that emphasise spoken language and verbal interaction can support the development of communication and language [and], in turn, communication and language [can] provide the foundations for learning and thinking and underpin the development of later literacy skills." Their advice, though aimed at early years' teaching, could prove helpful for key stage 3 teachers of pupils with SEND including SLCN...

"Focusing on language and communication," the EEF say, "is especially important for young children and will support the development of a range of early literacy skills as well as their wider knowledge and understanding. In addition, developing communication and language is linked to other important outcomes including children's self-regulation, socio-emotional development, and reasoning."

A wide range of activities can be used to develop communication and language including:

- Shared reading,
- Storytelling, and
- Explicitly extending children's vocabulary.

These activities should be embedded within a curriculum of rich and varied experiences. Developing vocabulary is important for later literacy development, but it should not – the EEF warn – be seen as a silver bullet; "it should form part of a broad approach to improving communication, language, and literacy."

In terms of shared reading, the EEF recommend using the PEER framework and this might be a useful tool to help pupils with SLCN to read aloud. It is a simple sequence that can be used to support shared, or 'dialogic', reading. When reading together, adults can pause and:

- Prompt the pupil to say something about the book
- Evaluate their response
- Expand their response either by rephrasing it or adding information to it
- Repeat the prompt to help them learn from the expansion

There are five main types of prompts that can be used as part of the PEER sequence. The prompts can be remembered using the acronym CROWD:

- Completion—leave a blank at the end of a sentence for pupils to complete (this works particularly well with books with rhymes or repetitive phrases)
- Recall—ask pupils about something they have already read (these prompts support pupils to understand the story plot)
- Open-ended—often with a focus on pictures in books (this works well with illustrations and encourages pupils to express their ideas)
- Wh—prompts that begin with 'who', 'what', 'where', 'why', and 'when' ('what' questions can be used to develop vocabulary)
- Distancing—connects the book to pupils' own life experiences and provides an opportunity for high quality discussion

More strategies

Here are some more 'quality first teaching' strategies that work particularly well for pupils with SLCN – and indeed for all pupils:

- KWL charts
- Dual coding, including the use of mind-maps

- Thinking time
- Explicit vocabulary instruction

KWL charts

One common diagnostic technique is asking pupils at the beginning of a lesson or new topic to identify what they already know (or think they know) about what they are about to study. Their responses can then be listed in a table or on a graphic organiser. The contents of the first column provide us with a sense of pupils' prior knowledge, while also unmasking any misconceptions that may exist and therefore may need to be addressed.

Next, we should ask pupils to identify "what I want to learn" about the topic and ask them to raise any questions they may have at this early stage. These responses can be recorded in the second column to serve as indicators of areas of interest.

As the unit unfolds, the knowledge and skills that pupils begin to acquire should be recorded in the third column of the table, providing a record for pupils of "what I have learned".

An alternative to this is to begin a lesson or topic with an initial assessment, perhaps a low-stakes multiple-choice quiz. The results of these pre-tests can yield invaluable evidence about pupils' prior knowledge and misconceptions and, when repeated at various stages of the teaching sequence, can provide evidence of pupils' growing knowledge and understanding.

Regardless of the approach taken, information from diagnostic assessments can guide us in our planning so that lessons are more responsive to pupils' needs and their existing knowledge-base - surely the very definition of differentiation.

An important practical implication, of course, is that we must remember to plan opportunities for assessments and allow sufficient 'wriggle room' to make adjustments based on the feedback garnered by the assessments.

In-built flexibility like this is not just advisable, it is a key aspect of effective lesson-planning and differentiation because it enables learning to be personalised to match the needs and pace of pupils' learning - which is essential if we are to support pupils with SLCN. It also ensures that gaps in pupils' learning are identified and filled, which in turn will avoid an off-the-peg, one-size-fits-all approach to lesson-planning and enable good progress to be made by all pupils, irrespective of their additional and different needs.

Dual coding

Dual coding is the combination of words and images. We have two specific-yet-connected cognitive subsystems: one specialises in representing and processing non-verbal objects or events; the other specialises in language. In other words, we process verbal and visual information separately and so can double the capacity of our working memory if we utilise both verbal and visual processing at the same time.

What's more, dual coding allows us to boost the information traces in our long-term memory (as two connected traces are stronger than one single trace) and it enables us to recall - or recognise - the information in two different ways.

By combining an image with a complementary word (written or preferably spoken), we're utilising both a verbal/semantic process (deciphering spoken/written words) and an iconic process (deciphering images).

Dual coding works particularly well for pupils with SLCN because, as we have already seen, these pupils tend to have strong visual processing capabilities and benefit from the use of diagrams such as mind-maps and from short bullet-points rather than lots of dense text.

However, as with all teaching strategies, dual coding only works when it's done well. Reading a text aloud in parallel with the same written text onscreen (such as reading text verbatim from a PowerPoint slide) – even if this is short bullet points - is a bad combination because pupils are required to conduct one and the same verbal/semantic decoding process in two different ways - rather than splitting and therefore doubling working memory capacity, it requires pupils to process twice the information using one process, thus halving working memory capacity! As a result, working memory becomes overloaded in what's known as 'the redundancy effect'.

The best way to make use of dual coding is to, for example, explain a visual (a diagram, graph, mind-map, etc) verbally, not through text on the visual. If there is writing on the visual, it's best not to explain it. Furthermore, we should present visuals and text at the same time so that pupils don't have to remember one part while processing the other.

Thinking time

One important feature of effective classroom questioning is 'thinking time', sometimes referred to as 'wait time'...

In 1974, Mary Budd Rowe conducted research into the way in which teachers asked pupils questions in the classroom. Her findings on 'thinking time' – the amount of time, once a question has been asked, that a teacher allows to elapse before asking someone else or providing an answer themselves – were quite astonishing.

Rowe found that, on average, teachers left less than one second before answering their own question or before asking someone else to answer it.

Rowe also found that thinking time of less than one second prevented most pupils taking part in classroom discussions because such a short interval did not allow enough time for pupils to think through the question and then formulate an answer. This is particularly pronounced for pupils with SEND including SLCN who often struggle to process information, formulate their thoughts and articulate an answer clearly and concisely.

Rowe's research concluded that teachers, acknowledging their wait time was insufficient, compromised by asking more simple, closed questions where straightforward recall – as opposed to higher-order thinking – was enough for pupils to be able to provide an answer. As a further consequence of this, classroom talk was superficial.

The teachers involved in Rowe's research were encouraged to increase the amount of time they gave pupils to answer their questions. Teachers achieved this by allowing a period of time to elapse before pupils were allowed to put their hands up and answer. This extra time was used for one of the following purposes:

Thinking time – allowing pupils time to process the question and think through their answers before anyone was allowed to volunteer a response aloud.

Paired discussion time – allowing pupils to think about the question with a partner for a certain amount of time before giving an answer.

Writing time – allowing pupils to draft their thoughts on paper first before giving their responses.

Most of the above involves pupils working together to discuss their thoughts before sharing them with the whole class. In this way, effective questioning involves pupils taking group responsibility – if pupils have time to discuss the answer in pairs or groups before anyone responds verbally, pupils are more ready to offer answers and to attempt more difficult thinking, because they know that others will help them.

Having 'talking partners' as a regular feature of lessons is more democratic, too, because it allows every pupil in the room to think, to articulate and therefore to extend their learning. This has two advantages: firstly, pupils with SEND including SLCN, and those who are reluctant to volunteer answers, get to find their voice; secondly, the garrulous, over-confident pupils get to learn to listen to others. In short, it creates a spirit or ethos of cooperation which is at the heart of formative assessment.

Once the teachers in Rowe's study had had the opportunity to get used to increasing their wait time, Rowe went back to look at the effect it had had. She found:

- Pupils' answers were longer
- Pupils' failure to respond had decreased
- Responses were more confident
- Pupils challenged and/or improved other pupils' answers
- More alternative explanations were being offered

Teachers involved in the King's Medway Oxfordshire Formative Assessment (or KMOFA for short) project which began in 1999 and was undertaken by Professors Paul Black and Dylan Wiliam as part of their initial research into the effects of formative assessment, found that "increasing waiting time after asking questions proved difficult to start with...the pause after asking the question was sometimes painful [and] unnatural... [but] given more thinking time, students seemed to realise that a more thoughtful answer was required [and that they now] give an answer and an explanation without additional prompting."

For obvious reasons, pupils with SEND including SLCN particularly benefit from being afforded more thinking time to process what has been asked and to articulate a response. To ensure thinking time is especially effective for pupils with SLCN, the teacher and/or teaching assistant can warn pupils they're going to ask a question, explicitly teach clarification questions, model asking questions, use strategies such as 'snow-balling', flag up questions at the beginning of the lesson, provide a list of key questions in advance, and ask pupils to draw and/or write down an answer before they put their hand up.

Explicit vocabulary instruction

UK Department for Education research suggests that, by the age of seven, the gap in the vocabulary known by children in the top and bottom quartiles is something like 4,000 words (children in the top quartile know around 7,000 words). For this reason, when teaching pupils with SEND including SLCN, teachers need to be mindful of the importance of vocabulary and support its development so that pupils who, because of a specific need, did not develop this foundational knowledge before they started school and through primary school are now helped to access the curriculum.

One way to do this is to plan group work activities which provide an opportunity for pupils with SEND including SLCN to mingle with pupils with a more developed vocabulary, to hear language being used by pupils of their own age and in ways that they might not otherwise encounter.

Another solution is to model the clear and correct use of spoken language. In other words, we should give unambiguous instructions, use accurate descriptive and positional language, utilise precise terminology where appropriate, and give clear feedback.

Next, teachers can use simple, direct language and place verbs at the beginning of instructions. "Teacher talk" is not necessarily better than the language that pupils access in other environments but it is different. As a result, pupils' language proficiency might be different from that required to access the curriculum, or even to understand simple classroom instructions. Confusion and disobedience can result from the fact that pupils are unfamiliar with the language structures and "lexical density" of the more formal teacherly language of the classroom. This does not mean that teachers should use the same language as their pupils, but that they might sometimes need to use simpler language and emphasise important words.

Furthermore, teachers can teach active listening skills. Most pupils can hear but are not naturally active listeners. Active listening requires selective and sustained attention, working memory, cognitive processing, and information storage and recall mechanisms. Teachers can help pupils develop these skills by giving them tasks such as listening for specific or key information, listening to answer specific questions, and listening to follow instructions.

Teachers can also teach note-taking skills whereby pupils have to write down the key points ascertained from a piece of spoken language. What's more, they can develop communication skills such as turn-taking and the use of eye contact.

And teachers can build on pupils' language by elaborating on their answers to questions, adding new information, extending the conversation through further questioning, or reinforcing the language through repetition.

To help pupils build their vocabularies, teachers can also:

- Use fewer "what?" questions and use more "why?" and "how?" questions.
- Give pupils time to rehearse answers to questions, perhaps by discussing their answers in pairs before sharing them more widely.
- After each question has been asked, give pupils thinking time before they are expected to share their answers.
- Enforce a "no-hands-up" policy as often as possible.

- Model the kind of language they expect pupils to use in group discussions and answers.
- Build pupils' vocabularies by explicitly teaching the key words in their subject and by repeating key words as often as possible; give key words as homework and test pupils on their spelling and meaning so that they become the expected discourse of all pupils.

In addition to the above, teachers of pupils with SLCN should make sure that the development of spoken language permeates the school day. After all, spoken language is used all day, every day so we should take advantage and build spoken language activities into daily routines, such as during tutor time (e.g., ask a question of each pupil that must be answered in a sentence), when handing out materials, when pupils enter and leave the classroom, and when giving instructions.

Teachers can also make sure that pupils have a regular opportunity to speak. The teacher tends to dominate classroom discussion – and it is right that teachers talk a lot because they are the experts in the room in possession of the knowledge and experience that pupils need. But it is also important that pupils get a chance to interact with the teacher and with each other and to do so beyond responding to closed questions.

What's more, teachers can plan opportunities for one-to-one discussion. Spoken language develops best through paired conversation and when one of the people in the pair has a better developed vocabulary. Therefore, it is worth investigating ways of pairing up pupils with people with more sophisticated language skills, perhaps an older pupil or a parent or volunteer. This could be a case of volunteers reading a book with a pupil or simply engaging in conversation. One-to-one conversation also enables young people with SLCN to develop conversational skills such as turn-taking, intonation and eye contact.

The Educational Endowment Foundation report, 'Preparing for Literacy: Improving Communication, Language and Literacy in the Early Years' (2018), which I mentioned earlier, also claims that there is relatively limited evidence about how best to improve vocabulary, but the existing evidence suggests that the following should be considered:

- Providing pupils with a rich language environment (implicit approaches) as well as directly extending pupils' vocabulary (explicit approaches)
- Carefully selecting high-frequency words for explicit teaching
- Developing the number of words pupils know (breadth) and their understanding of relationships between words and the contexts in which words can be used (depth)
- Providing multiple opportunities to hear and use new vocabulary.

In terms of selecting high-frequency words for explicit instruction, it may be wise to begin by teaching the 'Tier 2' words identified by Isobel Beck. Tier 2 words are those words which appear commonly in written texts but not in spoken language. They are not subject-specific terminology nor necessarily complex words but are words that are vital to pupils' ability to access the school curriculum and to them being able to demonstrate their understanding.

Once these words have been identified, they need to be taught on a number of occasions and in different contexts. Beck offers this possible teaching sequence:

- Read a sentence in which the word appears
- Show pupils the word and get them to say it out loud
- Discuss possible meanings of the word
- Identify any parts of the word that may be familiar (e.g., Greek or Latinate roots, common prefixes and suffixes)
- Re-read the sentence with the word in it to detect any contextual clues
- Explicitly explain the meaning of the word through definition and the use of synonyms
- Provide several other examples of the word being used in context
- Ask pupils to use the word in sentences of their own.

The EEF also say that prioritising high-quality interactions with children will help to develop their communication and language. A distinction is sometimes drawn between talking with children and simply talking to children; talking to children tends to be more passive, while talking with children is based on their immediate experiences and activities and is likely to be more effective: "When done well, high quality interactions often look effortless, but they are not easy to do well, and professional development is likely to be beneficial."

Multiple frameworks exist to help structure high quality interactions. Guided interaction occurs when a teacher and pupil collaborate on a task and the teacher's strategies are highly tuned to the pupil's capabilities and motivations. The teacher is responsive to the pupil's intentions, focuses on spontaneous learning, and provides opportunities for the pupil's feedback. Discussion is a key feature of this approach and the use of a variety of questions helps to develop and extend pupil's thinking.

Sustained shared thinking involves two or more people working together to solve a problem, clarify an issue, evaluate activities, or extend a narrative. Key features include all parties contributing to the interaction—one aimed at extending and developing pupils' thinking.

According to the EEF, techniques that teachers might use include:

- ***tuning in***: listening carefully to what is being said and observing what the pupil is doing
- ***showing genuine interest***: giving whole attention, eye contact, and smiling and nodding
- ***asking pupils to elaborate***: 'I really want to know more about this'
- ***re-capping***: 'so you think that...'
- ***giving their own experience***: 'I like to listen to music when cooking at home'
- ***clarifying ideas***: 'so you think we should wear coats in case it rains?'
- ***using encouragement to extend thinking***: 'you have thought really hard about your tower, but what can you do next?'
- ***suggesting***: 'you might want to try doing it like this'
- ***reminding***: 'don't forget that you said we should wear coats in case it rains'
- ***asking open questions***: 'how did you?', 'Why does this...?', 'What happens next?'

Waves 2 and 3: In-class differentiation and additional interventions

Even with the provision of 'quality first teaching' as outlined above, some pupils will require more – and more tailored – support in the guise of Wave 2 in-class differentiations and Wave 3 additional interventions which take place outside the classroom and off the taught timetable.

Such intervention strategies may take the form of one-to-one support from a teaching assistant (TA) or additional learning support (ALS), small group targeted teaching by a SEND or High Needs specialist, or support from external agencies such as speech and language therapists.

Before we explore some proven strategies for making Wave 2 and 3 interventions work, let us first be clear that the ultimate aim of such additional support, in most cases, is for it to become redundant over time. In other words, we want pupils with SEND to become increasingly independent and for the scaffolds to fall away. Indeed, this is the stated aim of Education Health and Care Plans (EHCPs) and High Needs funding: over time, discrete SEN funding should be reduced as its impact is felt and pupils require less and less support.

With this aim in mind, it is important to ensure that all strategic interventions aimed at pupils with SEND are monitored whilst they are happening. Often, schools review an intervention once it's ended - perhaps at the end of the term or year - to see whether or not pupils made expected progress and if the strategy was successful. This review data is also often used to evidence the impact of said strategies and, where applicable, to prove that SEND monies have been used effectively and have provided value for the public purse.

But an end-of-strategy review is not enough; rather, interventions for pupils with SEND must be monitored whilst they are still taking place in order to ascertain whether or not they are working or working as well as they should be. If the monitoring data suggests a strategy is not having the desired effect, or not working for some pupils, then it must be stopped or changed before more time and money is wasted.

Another point worth making before we continue concerns the role of teaching assistants because it is often TAs not teachers who lead Wave 2 and 3 interventions for pupils with SEND.

When the Educational Endowment Foundation published the first iteration of its Teaching and Learning Toolkit, it claimed that TAs were 'not worth it'. However, if you look behind the headlines, you'll find an altogether more nuanced story... As with everything, the use of TAs only works if it's done well. In other words, it's not what you do but how you do it that matters.

Since it first published its toolkit, the EEF has commissioned evaluations of six TA-led interventions, involving more than 2,000 children in around 150 schools. In each case, the TAs were trained to deliver structured sessions to small groups or individual pupils and all six trials showed TAs had a positive impact on learning.

So, the big question is this: what is the best way to utilise TAs? Here are some tips inspired by the EEF research:

- TAs should not be used as an informal teaching resource for pupils with SEND.
- TAs should be used to add value to what teachers do, rather than replace teachers – pupils with SEND need as much, if not more, exposure to the teacher as all other pupils.
- TAs should be used to help pupils with SEND to develop independent learning skills and manage their own learning. To achieve this, TAs need to be trained to avoid prioritising task completion and instead concentrate on helping pupils with SEND to develop personal ownership of tasks.
- TAs should be fully prepared for their role in the classroom and need access to sufficient training and time to meet the teacher outside of class.

Furthermore, when supporting pupils with SEND in one-on-one or small group settings, TAs should use structured interventions.

The most effective intervention strategies are:

- Brief (20– 50mins)
- Regular (3–5 times per week)
- Sustained (running for 8–20 weeks)

- Carefully timetabled
- Staffed by well-trained TAs (5–30 hours' training per intervention)
- Well-planned with structured resources and clear objectives,
- Assessed to identify appropriate pupils, guide areas for focus and track pupil progress
- Linked to classroom teachin

Intervention strategies that work

Above I share some logistical features of effective intervention strategies, but the question remains, exactly what kind of support should be given to pupils with SEND during differentiated teaching and intervention sessions? Below, by way of illustration, are some suggestions specific to pupils with speech, language and communication needs (SLCN)...

In terms of in-class differentiation, pupils with SLCN are often helped by:

- The use of modified language
- The use of visual prompts
- The pre-teaching of subject specific vocabulary, as appropriate
- Access to a social skills group

In terms of additional interventions, pupils with SLCN are often helped by:

- Small group or one-to-one support for language to address specifically identified pupil targets
- Access to explicit social skills teaching
- Access to additional ICT teaching such as touch typing, dictaphone, tablet and so on
- A referral to and advice from the speech and language therapy service and the Learning Language Service (LLS)
- Ongoing advice from specialist teachers
- Advice from an educational psychologist

A graduated approach to SEN support

The provision of SEN support including for pupils with SLCN – as articulated in the SEND Code of Practice – often takes the form of a 4-part cycle of assess, plan, do, review. The cycle recommended by the SEND Code of Practice posits a 'graduated approach' whereby actions are reviewed and refined as our understanding of a pupil's needs – and indeed the support they require – increases.

The first part of the cycle is: ***assess***. At this stage, information is gathered from on-going, day-to-day assessments and this helps to form judgments about the progress an individual pupil with SEND is making, as well as to highlight any barriers that pupils may face. Where concerns about a pupil's progress persist, further discussions with the pupil, their parents and the SENCo may be necessary. It may also be necessary to conduct further specialist tests, or to request advice from a specialist such as, in the case of pupils with SLCN, a speech and language therapist.

The second part of the cycle is: ***plan***. At this stage, everyone needs to agree what additional and different support will be put in place as a result of the data gathered at the 'assess' stage. The planning stage should involve the pupil, their parents, and relevant school staff who know the pupil well.

The first step of the planning process is to agree some targets for the pupil in order to focus attention on what needs to improve first, and to give the pupil a clear idea of what they need to do to accelerate the pace of their progress.

To help the pupil achieve their targets, additional tailored support needs to be put in place, and this may include deploying specific teaching strategies, approaches or resources both in class and out of class such as those outlined above and in the previous article in this series.

Once targets are set and additional support agreed, clear and realistic timescales need to be set for monitoring and reviewing the plan. As I say above, it is crucial that additional interventions are subject to ongoing monitoring rather than just reviewed at their end-point.

The third part of the cycle is: ***do***. At this stage, as the SEND Code of Practice makes clear, it is the responsibility of every staff member who comes into contact with the pupil with SEND - including, of course, their teachers - to implement the plan on a day-to-day basis. It is not the sole domain of the SENCo. In practice, this might involve:

- Delivering quality first teaching to the pupil in every lesson.
- Enacting any specific adjustments, strategies or approaches to classroom teaching as identified in the ISP.
- Liaising with teaching assistants who are providing in-class support to pupils with SEND.
- Implementing any targeted additional, out-of-class interventions as identified in the plan.
- Engaging in ongoing monitoring of pupil progress and responding to the data by making any necessary adjustments to planning and teaching.
- Communicating regularly with the pupil, their parents, the SENCo and any other staff and external agents who are involved.

The final stage of the cycle is ***review***. At this stage, the school needs to formally evaluate how successfully the interventions and support they have offered have met the pupil's needs. At the review meeting, it is helpful to consider the following questions:

- What progress has the pupil made with regards addressing their speech, language and communication needs? Have they achieved their agreed targets and what is the evidence for this?
- What impact has the support/intervention had on the pupil being able to access the curriculum, make progress and communicate their learning? What are the pupil's, parents' and professionals' views on the effectiveness and impact of additional support/intervention?
- What changes need to be made to the pupil's targets and the specialist provision next term/year?

The SEND Code of Practice makes clear that the 4-step cycle of assess, plan, do, review is a process and is therefore continual. Even if a review shows a pupil has made good progress and no longer requires additional support in order to mitigate their speech, language and communication needs, they should still be monitored in order to ensure that their progress is sustained through inclusive quality first teaching.

Part Six: The golden triangle

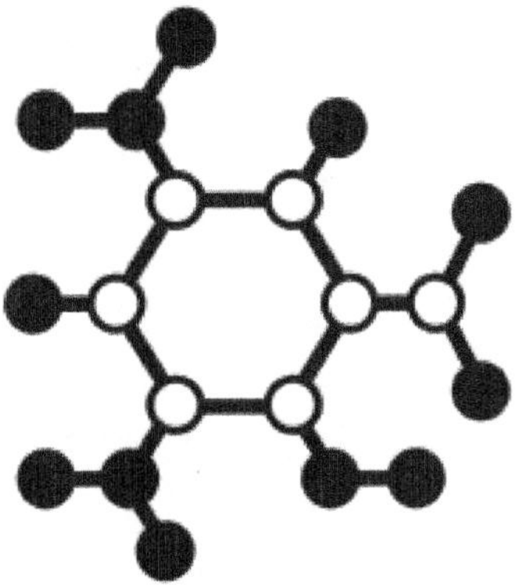

Chapter 18: Quality assurance

In Books One and Two of this series, I explained that we need to create both the **culture** *and* the **systems** within which a curriculum can flourish. Here's a reminder...

Creating a <u>culture</u> within which the curriculum can flourish

In terms of the culture, in Book One in this series I said that, to my mind, there were five core duties for senior leaders to perform:

1. Agree the curriculum vision
2. Determine the breadth and balance of the curriculum
3. Articulate the purpose of education
4. Create the learning environment
5. Protect staff time and skills

Firstly, then, it is the responsibility of senior leaders to **agree the vision** for their whole school or college curriculum. This, as we have already explored in Book One, involves defining what is meant by the term 'curriculum' and making decisions about the national, basic, local and hidden curriculums.

Secondly, senior leaders are key to determining how broad and balanced the whole school or college curriculum will be and why. They must make decisions about **which subject disciplines and vocations matter most** and **which subjects are afforded the most time** on the timetable. For example, senior leaders must be attuned to their community and learner needs and if their school population predominantly has English as an additional language (EAL), they may decide to timetable more English lessons.

Thirdly, senior leaders **articulate the purpose of education** in their school or college – and therefore guide middle leaders in determining the broad 'end-points' (schools) or 'body of knowledge' (FE) to be taught. For example, senior leaders must have an overview of what qualification types and levels are offered in their school or college and must ensure that their offer meets local needs (including learner needs, employer needs, community needs, etc) and that each entry-point to their curriculum leads to a higher level of study and/or into meaningful employment rather than to a series of dead-ends. Only senior leaders have the necessary oversight of the whole school or college curriculum to be able to make these decisions.

Fourthly, senior leaders **create the learning environment** in which a curriculum can flourish and in which middle leaders and teachers are encouraged to honestly self-reflect and admit to mistakes. Middle leaders must be allowed to regularly review the effectiveness of their curriculum and make changes to it without fear. A curriculum must be a living, breathing thing – constantly under review and constantly evolving in response to the shifting landscape and to assessment data. If the initial draft of the curriculum doesn't work as well as anticipated, middle leaders must be given the oxygen of a no-blame culture to learn from their mistakes and to improve their curriculum.

Finally, senior leaders should be the gatekeepers and defenders of staff skills and time. They have a duty to **provide appropriate training** to staff to ensure they are skilled at curriculum thinking, and they have a duty to **provide protected time** for staff to engage in the time-consuming task of designing, delivering and reviewing the curriculum in their subjects.

Building autonomy, mastery and purpose

In addition to these five aspects of curriculum culture, I believe that senior leaders should consider the impact of their demands on staff's autonomy, mastery, and purpose...

In terms of **autonomy**, school and college leaders need to better understand what motivates staff, and accept that teachers need to feel valued, rewarded, and professionally developed.

In practice, rather than telling staff what to do or presenting them with a school improvement plan of actions, school leaders might be advised to invite staff to identify a problem that exists in their department or in the wider school. Then they might be afforded the time – and resources – to solve it in their own way, perhaps during twilight INSET or in staff meeting time. It is important to end this process by implementing staff's innovations in order to make it clear that their contributions are valued.

Autonomy should certainly be afforded in the way subject specialists design their disciplinary curriculums.

In terms of **mastery**, school and college leaders might wish to improve their system of performance management. In particular, they may wish to sharpen the focus on performance *improvement* and personal *development* rather than on compliance with a set of norms. They may also want to ensure that performance feedback derives from a wide range of sources, not just from observation and not just from the line manager.

School and college leaders might also introduce a means by which teachers can be recognised and rewarded for their contributions beyond exam results. This means being clear and transparent about what being a high value member of staff means, having clear and transparent processes for identifying such members of staff, and ensuring that staff know that their potential has been recognised. This might mean developing a no-blame culture of openness, offering high quality feedback that allows teachers to learn from their mistakes without fear or favour.

In terms of **purpose**, school and college leaders need to understand and articulate what their institution has to offer teachers and what makes it unique. They should talk to existing staff and pupils about why it's a good place to be then communicate this clearly and frequently. They should also be clear about the school's direction of travel - about where it is headed and how it intends to get there – and this includes sharing their curriculum vision and explaining the purpose of education in their school.

That, then, is culture. So, what of the systems?

Creating the systems within which the curriculum can flourish

In Book Two in this series, I said that, in terms of developing systems to support the curriculum, senior leaders need to ensure that the way they manage staff performance helps rather than hinders the curriculum design and delivery process.

In short, I said, management systems need to be supportive and developmental, and they need to recognise hard work and accomplishment. They also need to be low-stakes, encouraging risk-taking and mistake-making when that's required in the pursuit of excellence; and there needs to be an ethos of 'no blame'.

The golden triangle

In this book I wish to expand upon the above ideas about cultures and systems and explore in greater depth what they might look like in practice...

I advocate forming a 'golden triangle' which connects the following aspects of school management:

1. Quality assurance
2. Performance management
3. Professional development

Although, if I'm honest, I actually dislike two of those commonplace terms...

Rather than 'quality assurance', I favour the term 'quality improvement'. And in place of 'performance management', I'd suggest 'performance development' is more apt and helpful.

In Chapter 19 I will home in on performance management and then, in Chapter 20, I will focus on professional development. Later in this chapter we will explore quality assurance in more depth but first an introduction to those three apexes of the 'golden triangle'...

Apex 1: Quality assurance

When it comes to quality assurance – or quality *improvement*, as I say – I believe that we should measure the quality of education (note: not the quality of *teachers* or *teaching* necessarily) in a holistic rather than an isolated way.

So, how can we quality assure – or quality *improve* – the education we provide in our schools and colleges?

Well, first of all, we need to ensure that we look beyond the classroom, important though this is, and ensure that our quality assurance activities take account of curriculum planning, too. As I have argued repeatedly throughout this series of books, the curriculum provides the foundations on which a quality education is built. Without an effective curriculum, no matter the quality of our teachers and their classroom practice, we will not achieve good outcomes and fully prepare our pupils for the next stage of their education, employment and lives. I have tackled the curriculum aspects before so, for our current purposes, I will focus on quality improving teaching, learning and assessment...

The Measures of Effective Teaching (MET) project by the Bill and Melinda Gates Foundation was a three-year study which sought to determine how best to identify and promote great teaching. The project concluded that it was possible to identify – and therefore measure – great teaching by combining three types of measures, namely:

1. Classroom observations,
2. Pupil surveys, and
3. Pupil achievement gains (or outcomes).

The project report said that "Teaching is complex, and great practice takes time, passion, high-quality materials, and tailored feedback designed to help each teacher continuously grow and improve."

The project's report shows that a more balanced approach – one which incorporates multiple measures such as the pupil survey data and classroom observations – has two important advantages: teacher ratings are less likely to fluctuate from year to year, and the combination is more likely to identify teachers with better outcomes on pupil assessments.

The report also offered advice on how to improve the validity of lesson observations. It recommended averaging observations from more than one observer: "If we want students to learn more, teachers must become students of their own teaching. They need to see their own teaching in a new light. This is not about accountability. It's about providing the feedback every professional needs to strive towards excellence."

The project claimed we had to learn four lessons if we were to improve our systems of quality assurance:

Firstly, teachers generally appear to be managing their classrooms well, but are struggling with fundamental instructional skills.

Secondly, classroom observations can give teachers valuable feedback, but are of limited value for predicting future performance.

Thirdly, value-added analysis is more powerful than any other single measure in predicting a teacher's long-term contributions to pupil success.

And finally, evaluations that combine several strong performance measures will produce the most accurate results.

The solutions to these problems are as follows:

Firstly, we should base teacher evaluations on multiple measures of performance, including data on pupil academic progress.

Secondly, we should improve classroom observations by making them more frequent and robust.

Thirdly, we should use or modify an existing observation rubric instead of trying to reinvent the wheel.

Fourthly, we should give evaluators the training and ongoing support they need to be successful.

And finally, we should consider using pupil surveys as a component of teacher evaluation.

In terms of using multiple measures of effectiveness, the project found that using lesson observations alone had a positive correlation with pupil outcomes of just 0.24. Using pupil surveys alone had a correlation of 0.37. Using value added data was the most accurate with a correlation of 0.69. But combining all three of these measures had a correlation of 0.72, proving yet again that using multiple measures of performance – measuring the effectiveness of teaching holistically – is the best solution.

So, if we accept that teaching is a highly complex job and it cannot easily be measured, what aspects of it should we measure in order to provide a more holistic judgment, albeit accepting that, even then, the outcomes will be limited? In other words, what elements of teaching matter most to us and lead to the most significant academic gains for pupils and, perhaps more pertinently, what elements of teaching can actually be observed and measured?

We will return to these questions later in this chapter when we home in on quality assurance in more detail. But let us first explore the second apex in our golden triangle...

Apex 2: Performance management

When it comes to performance management – or performance *development,* as I say – my philosophy is simple: it is no one's vocation to fail. In other words, no one wakes up in the morning determined to do the worst job they possibly can; no one opens their eyes, stretches and yawns, looks themselves up and down in the mirror and vows to fail as many pupils as they can before nightfall. But, despite the best of intentions, sometimes some people don't perform as well as they can or as well as we'd like.

When teachers under-perform, they need to be given time and support – including appropriate training – in order to improve. Many will. But those who don't, once they have been given sufficient time and opportunity to address their development needs, need to leave the classroom, ideally of their own volition and with our best wishes as they embark upon a new career, but sometimes, perhaps, more forcibly. Retaining people who cannot perform the duties for which they are paid (from tax-payers' limited coffers) serves no one well, least of all our pupils.

Accountability – when managed fairly and accurately, honestly and transparently – is a force for good. It ensures that the best people do the best jobs they can; it ensures that the teaching profession – and our next generation – is kept safe. Arguing against ineffective systems of performance management (such as one-off, high-takes lesson observations) is not – therefore – akin to arguing against the need for accountability. Indeed, performance management matters and it is important that school and college leaders get it right in order to help teachers improve, to reward hard work and challenge persistent underperformance.

A system of accountability based on lesson observations alone – or indeed any other single measure – is a broken one because lesson observations do not accurately or reliably measure the quality of teaching nor the effectiveness of our teachers. What they do, however, is create a climate of fear; they straitjacket teachers. As a result of one-off, high-stakes lesson observations, teachers tend to do one of two things:

1. They over-plan, over-teach and proffer showcase lessons which bear no relation to their everyday practice.

2. They become stressed by the experience of being watched and so under-perform.

In short, one-off, high-stakes lesson observations – and any other single-source evaluation tool – do not allow observers to see the teacher as they would normally teach. But even if a teacher is brave enough to teach a 'normal' lesson (whatever that means) and does not succumb to the natural stress of observation, the very presence of an observer in the room inevitably alters the classroom dynamics. This is called the Hawthorne Effect.

So, what's the answer?

First of all, let me be clear: I'm not suggesting we stop observing lessons altogether. In fact, I think walking into lessons to see what's happening is important. There is much to be gained by senior leaders, middle leaders and peers observing each other in the classroom, which is, after all, the engine-room of any school. By observing the classroom environment, for example, we can see the rapport the teacher has established with pupils, we can see how well the teacher manages behaviour and utilises resources. Lesson observations also allow us to see the ways in which transitions are handled and tasks are organised. And observations in the classroom can show senior and middle leaders how their policies and procedures, and systems and structures are translated into practice, and whether they are workable or onerous, helpful or a hindrance. A senior leader who becomes divorced from the classroom tends to make bad decisions that may seem sensible from their vantage point in an ivory tower but prove anything but sensible when put to the stress-test.

So, yes, observations certainly have value. But observations alone do not enable us to accurately judge the quality of teaching. For that we need to triangulate what we see and hear in classrooms with other sources of information, not least teachers' – much maligned but absolutely vital – professional judgment.

I will return to this discussion in the next chapter. But now let us explore the third and final apex in our golden triangle...

Apex 3: Professional development

Professional development works best, I find, when it is worthwhile, sustained and evaluated. But what might this mean in practice...?

The Standard for Teacher Professional Development (2016) – together with the ETF Professional Standards for teachers in FE settings and the DfE Teachers' Standards for teachers in schools – may hold the key...

The five strands of the Standard are as follows:

- Professional development should have a focus on improving and evaluating student outcomes.
- Professional development should be underpinned by robust evidence and expertise.
- Professional development should include collaboration and expert challenge.
- Professional development programmes should be sustained over time.
- Professional development must be prioritised by senior leadership.

As the Standard suggests, the most effective professional development is collaborative and driven by teachers. Professional development, therefore, should involve responding to advice and feedback from colleagues, and reflecting systematically on the effectiveness of lessons and approaches to teaching. This might take the form of peer-observations and feedback, of peer-coaching, or of more formal lesson study activities. It might also take the form of peer-to-peer work scrutiny, both of students' marked work and assessment records, and of medium- and long-term planning documentation.

Whatever form it takes, the best professional development gives ownership to staff and creates the time and space needed for them to work together, sharing best practice and learning from each other's mistakes.

Another way to ensure that professional development is effective is to make it an unmissable event, tailored to meet the differing needs of departments and teachers. Every member of staff should recognise the importance of professional development as a mandatory part of their jobs – not as a voluntary extra. But they'll only do that when professional development is worth engaging with and it will only be worth engaging with when it is relevant, timely, keenly focused on real classroom practice, and genuinely and tangibly impactful.

In order to ensure relevance and focus, professional development should be influenced by research evidence but informed by context. In other words, it should take its lead from what research indicates works best (for example, John Hattie's meta-analyses as articulated in his book Visible Learning or the EEF's toolkit, as well as individual academic research studies) but be mindful of the unique circumstances of each school and college, each subject, each teacher and each cohort of pupils.

As well as being unmissable, professional development should be regular, embedded and joined-up. Professional development should be seen as a collaborative enterprise involving all staff working together, rather than something that is 'done to' them by senior leaders.

Professional development also works best when it performs the twin functions of innovation and mastery. In other words, professional development should not just be about learning new ways of working – professional development for innovation – although this is undoubtedly important. Rather, it should also be about helping teachers to get better at something they already do – professional development for mastery. Professional development for mastery is about recognising what already works well and what should therefore be embedded, consolidated, built upon, and shared.

We will return to this discussion in Chapter 20. But now let us return to the first apex in our golden triangle – quality assurance – and delve a little deeper into the detail...

From quality *assurance* to quality *improvement*

In addition to what I say above, in practical terms, I'd suggest that one useful starting point when designing a new effective quality assurance process that converts quality *assurance* into quality *improvement* is to consult upon, agree and communicate a vision for the quality of education in your school or college. This vision is unique because it reflects your local context.

This vision creation stage of the process comes first because the vision informs all your future decisions, and all your subsequent actions will be sense-checked against this vision. The vision's job is to set out what you want the education you provide to look like – what will success look like? How will you know when you're providing the best possible quality of education you can, and when you are genuinely preparing all your pupils for the next stage of their education, employment and lives?

The next stage in the process of designing an effective quality improvement system, I would suggest, is to write a mission statement which articulates *how* your vision will be realised. The mission sets out what your school or college will do in practice – the collective actions you will take – in order to achieve your goal.

The third stage, once the vision and mission have been agreed, is to set the priorities for the next one to three years. These priorities should help focus the school or college on the actions it needs to take most urgently in order to achieve both its vision and mission. The priorities are the step-goals, if you like, on the journey towards the vision.

Before we explore the fourth stage – which is to agree a set of 'quality standards' – let us tarry a while longer on the subject of vision and mission...

In my book How to Lead (2012, second edition 2017), I explored the importance of vision and mission to effective school leadership. Here are some relevant highlights...

What's the difference between a vision statement and a mission statement?

I find it useful to think of the two terms, vision and mission, which are often used interchangeably, in the following way: vision is your destination; mission is your means of transport.

In other words, a vision statement sets out what you want your school or college to be like whereas a mission statement articulates the behaviours and values, systems and processes, you expect your school or college to adopt in order to get there.

What makes a good vision statement?

One of the five dimensions of what Vivianne Robinson calls 'student-centred leadership' (in her book of the same name) is establishing goals and expectations. "In a world where everything seems important, or at least important to someone," she says, "goal setting enable leaders to sort through the multiple demands to establish the relative importance of these various demands and thus provide a clear steer for an otherwise rudderless ship".

Goal setting in education, Robinson argues, is not about deciding what is and is not important. Goal setting works because it forces decisions about relative importance – about what is more important in this context, at this time, than all the other important things.

Establishing and articulating clear goals – what we might call our 'vision' – is crucial for any organisation but particularly important for schools which – you might say – sail on such troubled waters, tugged – as they are – back and forth on a tide of policy from successive governments and their quangos.

A vision makes explicit what an organisation stands for and what its people want it to achieve; it binds people (staff, students, governors, the community, employers, and so on) together in the pursuit of a common goal and reminds them why they do what they do every day. A vision provides a focus for decision-making and conveys a picture of what the future will look like.

According to John Kotter in his book, Leading Change, an effective vision is desirable in that it appeals to the long-term interests of employees, customers, stockholders, and others who have a stake in the enterprise. It is feasible in that it comprises realistic, attainable goals and is focused in that it is clear enough to provide guidance in decision making. An effective vision is also flexible in that it is general enough to allow individual initiative and alternative responses in light of changing conditions. It is also communicable. In other words, it is easy to communicate and can be successfully explained within five minutes.

The most effective vision statements, Kotter says, are ambitious enough to force people out of comfortable routines.

For my part, I believe an effective vision is one which is shared – not just in the sense that it is communicated but that it is understood and owned by most (if not all) of the people in the organisation. It is all well and good for a leader to have a clear vision of what he or she wants to achieve but it will forever remain an aspiration and will never be achieved if it is not understood and shared by everyone else in the organisation.

In schools and colleges, a vision will only be realised if every teacher, every teaching assistant, every member of support staff, and every middle and senior leader makes it happen through their everyday behaviours and actions. It is no use having a vision which many staff disagree with or misunderstand, or which does not suit the organisation's context. It has to make sense, be achievable and be meaningful. It has to take the organisation forward in the right direction. It has to be something that everyone wants to see take shape. In other words, it has to benefit everyone.

Ideally, a vision statement should express what is unique about an organisation and not be an 'off-the-peg' statement which could easily be applied to any school in any part of the country or indeed the world. What are the unique challenges the organisation needs to overcome? What will success look like for that particular institution? What makes its stakeholders different?

Writing the vision statement

A good starting point when writing a vision statement, therefore, is the organisation's existing vision or, if it does not have one, its motto or values. Why? Because although a vision statement is about the future, it should have solid foundations in the past, in the organisation's history, in what the organisation stands for and in the very reason it exists. Continuity is important to all those with a stake in the place. No one likes change; it is uncomfortable. People like to know that what they have built, what they have worked hard for, what they believe in, is to be retained and protected. A vision which refers to what the organisation already does well as well as articulates what it hopes to do better in the future keeps all parties happy. Moreover, it is balanced, fair and, above all, cohesive: it connects stakeholders along a path which leads from the past, through the present, to the future.

On the subject of cohesion, all stakeholders (staff, students, governors, the community, etc.) need to be involved in agreeing the vision but this does not have to mean a long and convoluted process of wrangling over every word. Instead, the senior team – or perhaps a working party representing as many different areas of the organisation as possible – should draft a vision for wider consultation. That consultation should be clearly framed: what aspects of the vision are leaders consulting on, what are the dividing lines? Leaders need to make it clear what is open for debate and what is not. Do they want to debate every word, or do they want to debate broad principles? Leaders need to make clear what form they expect the consultation to take and how they will garner feedback. They need to make clear how they will respond to that feedback. People need to feel listened to but, equally, leaders should not promise something they cannot deliver.

As well as the organisation's existing vision, motto or values, the vision should be informed by the current school improvement plan which in turn is likely to be informed by the latest inspection report, the latest exam results and so on.

Kotter says that the process of creating an effective vision often starts with an initial statement from a single individual, reflecting both his or her dreams and real marketplace needs. The first draft is always modelled over time by a guiding coalition of senior leaders or an even larger group of influential people. Teamwork is important. The group process never works well without a minimum of effective teamwork. The head and the heart have roles of equal importance: analytical thinking and a lot of dreaming are – Kotter says – essential throughout the process of creating a vision.

The process can often be messy because vision-creation is usually a process of two steps forward and one back, movement to the left and then to the right. Vision is never created in a single meeting. The activity takes months, sometimes years. The process results in a direction for the future that is desirable, feasible, focused, flexible, and is conveyable in five minutes or less.

Robinson says that, in terms of creating a vision, three conditions need to be in place. People need to feel personally committed to the goal and believe they have the capacity to achieve it. The goal also needs to be specific so people can monitor their progress towards it. Vision creation (or 'goal setting' as Robinson calls it) works by creating a discrepancy between the current situation and an attractive future. This discrepancy motivates people to focus their effort and attention on the activities required to reach the goal and to persist until they achieve it.

People commit to a vision that they believe is important. Robinson says that the pursuit of the goal becomes attractive because it provides an opportunity for reducing the gap between the vision and the current reality. This means that two things are required for goal commitment. The goal needs to provide an opportunity to achieve what is valued, and people need to accept that the current situation falls sufficiently short of that vision to warrant pursuit of the goal. This is why it is important that a vision is a collective goal rather than that of a single leader and that it emerges through discussion rather than being imposed.

The second aspect of gaining goal commitment, according to Robinson, is acceptance of the gap between the goal and the existing state of affairs. "Many leaders...focus only on the desirability of the goal and not on the difference between what they envisage and the present situation," she argues. One solution, Robinson says, is to engage in 'constructive problem talk': "Such talk involves naming, describing, and analysing problems in ways that reveal the possibilities for change. Constructive problem talk builds trust because people respect leadership that can own problems and take responsibility for solving them."

Creating a vision works best when people are committed to goals which they believe they have the capacity to achieve. Commitment and capacity are highly interdependent because people will not commit to goals which they believe they cannot achieve.

"When the responsible system lacks the capacity to achieve a particular goal," Robinson says, "leaders should initially set learning rather than performance goals". Performance goals are about "the achievement of a specific outcome". A learning goal, by contrast, focuses on the "discovery of the strategies, processes, or procedures to perform the task effectively". With a learning goal, attention is directed to learning how to do the task rather than to achieving a specific outcome.

According to Robinson, a vision is specific when it "include[s] criteria by which progress and achievement can be judged". Ensuring the vision has a set of SMART targets or objectives attached to it makes sense because people cannot regulate their performance if they are unclear about how to assess their progress.

However, Robinson argues that there are occasions when the call to set SMART targets is inappropriate: "In order to set a SMART goal, you have to know quite a lot about how to achieve it. When goals involve new challenges, how can you possibly know if it is achievable, if it is realistic, and how long it will take you to achieve it?"

A vision should also be clearly focused because if it has too many goals it will defeat the purpose of giving clear messages about what takes priority.

An additional challenge in achieving goals is developing the routines that enable teachers to integrate goal pursuit into their daily work. Without such routines, a 'business as usual' mentality and approach will drive goal achievement.

Writing a mission statement

Let us now to consider the mission statement...

As I say above, the vision is the destination and the mission is the means of transport. The mission is necessarily longer than the vision statement because it is a detailed declaration of what an organisation will do in order to achieve its vision. A mission statement should try to cover all the important aspects of an organisation's working practices. In the case of schools and colleges, for example, it might cover: How it uses data; what kind of curriculum it has or aspires to have; what the atmosphere should be like; how it caters for vulnerable students; how it engages with the local community; and so on.

As a starting point, you may wish to consider the following statements:

Our school/college is a place where...

- There is a shared vision of what the school is trying to achieve
- Data is understood and acted upon appropriately
- Pupils make good or better progress within each year and key stage, academically, emotionally and socially
- There is a rich curriculum taught by skilled, well-motivated teachers
- There is a purposeful, organised working atmosphere, pupils are valued, and their contributions are appreciated
- Resources, including quality ICT provision, are well-matched to the curriculum
- Pupils are challenged and encouraged to do their best
- Vulnerable children are identified early, and support mechanisms are put in place
- Parents are fully informed and are welcomed contributors to school life
- There is a sense of involvement in the local community and visitors and outside agencies provide contributions to the school
- All staff are valued and are supported in their own personal and professional development
- Standards reflect the status of the pupils: there is no coasting, and realistic achievement targets are consistently met
- The school is held in high esteem by the local community
- There is appropriate and interesting extra-curricular provision.

How to realise the vision and mission

Once the vision and mission have been agreed, they need to be officially ratified by governors and/or trustees. Once ratified, they should not be filed away in a dusty drawer and forgotten about. Rather, they should be placed centre-stage. They should be referred to as frequently as possible, in as many different ways as possible, and should underpin everything the organisation does.

In practice, this might mean:

- Including the vision statement on letter-headed paper, in a prospectus, and in newsletters and leaflets
- Using the vision to frame the organisation's 3-year strategy, aims and objectives
- Including the vision and mission on the front page of the school improvement plan (SIP) and using it to frame that plan: a section for each aspect of the vision, broken down into specific actions which will help to realise the vision
- Including the vision and mission on the front page of the self-evaluation form (SEF)
- Including the vision and mission in faculty or departmental action plans
- Including the vision in performance management documentation and using the vision to provide a broad basis for staff appraisal objectives

But, most importantly of all, and certainly for our present purposes, the vision and mission should guide our quality assurance processes...

After all, if the vision articulates what you want the quality of education to be like, then surely quality assurance is a means of testing whether or not the vision is being achieved? It is a means of identifying good practice and then sharing it more widely to ensure it becomes uniform and consistent, and a means of identifying practice that falls short of the expected standard and thus pinpoints areas for development. In short, the vision/mission and quality assurance are inextricably linked.

In Student-Centred Leadership, Robinson, for her part, says that, "once clear goals are established, the second dimension of effective leadership – resourcing strategically – comes into play". In other words, the vision or goal should be used to determine what to spend an organisation's precious time and money on.

"Scarce resources – money, time, teaching materials, and instructional expertise – [should be] allocated in ways that give priority to key goals," she says. "As such, strategic resourcing and strategic thinking are closely linked: strategic thinking involves asking questions and challenging assumptions about the links between resources and the needs they are intended to meet."

Kotter says that a vision can get lost in the clutter of everyday working life if leaders fail to communicate it effectively. The total amount of communication going to an employee in three months, he argues, is approximately 2,300,000 words or numbers. The typical communication of a change vision over a period of three months equates to just 13,400 words or numbers (that is, the equivalent of one 30-minute speech, one hour-long meeting, one 600-word article in the firm's newspaper, and one 2,000-word memo). This means that the change vision captures only 0.58 per cent of the communication market share.

In order to communicate the vision more effectively, then, leaders need to ensure communications are simple – all jargon and technobabble must be eliminated. Leaders need to make use of metaphor, analogy, and example: a verbal picture, after all, paints a thousand words. Leaders need to use multiple forums such as meetings (big and small), memos and newsletters, formal and informal interaction – all are effective means of spreading the word. Repetition is also key: ideas sink in deeply only after they have been heard many times - seven times in seven different ways is a good rule of thumb.

Leaders need to lead by example because if the behaviour of important people is inconsistent with the vision, it will overwhelm all other forms of communication. Leaders need to explain seeming inconsistencies because, if inconsistencies go unaddressed, they will undermine the credibility of all other communications. And finally, leaders need to allow for a bit of 'give-and-take', a bit of two-way communication because a dialogue is always more effective than a monologue. It's the 'con' in 'conversation', after all: 'con' meaning 'with' in Latin.

So, use the vision to frame every conversation and speech, to focus every meeting, to inform every decision. Use it as a mantra. It will remind people of their ultimate goal and refocus them on what's most important; it will convince them that they are playing a crucial role in helping to make the organisation's vision a reality and reassure them that they are helping to shape the future.

Using the vision and mission as your 'north star'

Daniel Coyle, in his book The Culture Code, argues that there are four types of 'catchphrase' which he calls the North Star, Do's, Don'ts, and Identity.

The North Star provides the Why. It has the highest priority because it carries the aim or objective. In other words, the North Star is the vision. The Do's and Don'ts, meanwhile, describe the How. In other words, they articulate how to achieve the aim or objective. The Identity outlines the qualities or traits that distinguish the organisation from the rest of the world. In other words, they articulate the Who - the personality, morals, beliefs and attitudes of the organisation, and what makes them unique.

Taken together, these four types of 'catchphrase' create what Coyle calls the "culture story". This captures the soul of the group — or, as Coyle puts it, "a narrative algorithm that provides the crucial connections between the Why, the Who, the How". In other words, catchphrases - and vision statements - aren't cliched or corny; they are genius because purpose isn't just about inspiration, it's also about navigation. Having a shared purpose is about building a vivid, accessible roadmap with a set of emotional GPS signals that define the organisation's identity and guide the behaviour of its staff.

Let us now return to quality assurance specifically...

Quality standards

Once we have agreed our vision and mission and set our medium-term priorities, the next stage, I would suggest, is to agree a set of 'quality standards'. Whilst the vision is the goal, an articulation of what the quality of education should look like, and the mission is a set of collective actions that we must take in order to achieve that goal, the quality standards are the everyday attitudes, behaviours and values we need our school or college to embody if we are to achieve our vision and mission.

Here are some examples for the purposes of illustration, though – as with the vision and mission – these should be tailored to each school and college's unique context:

1. The curriculum offer is relevant, up-to-date and meets the needs of learners, communities, and the regional economy
2. The curriculum is ambitious for all learners and addresses issues of social mobility
3. Curriculum leaders and teachers identify and provide equal access to the knowledge, skills and experiences learners need to thrive
4. The curriculum is planned and sequenced to ensure positive progression
5. Teaching and assessment ensure learners know and can do more, and remember what they have learned for the long term
6. Learners are supported to become increasingly independent and resilient
7. Learners are prepared for the next stage of their lives and progress to high quality destinations
8. There is a positive learning environment and there are clear expectations for behaviour, attendance and punctuality
9. Bullying, harassment and discrimination is not accepted, and issues are quickly and consistently dealt with
10. Learners are supported to develop research and study skills that help them academically
11. Learners are afforded opportunities for personal development beyond the academic curriculum
12. Learners are given planned opportunities to develop wider skills including through high quality work experience and enrichment opportunities
13. Learners receive effective information and advice about their next steps, including careers guidance
14. Leaders and managers engage with learners, parents, the community and employers to plan and support the curriculum

Once the vision, mission, priorities and quality standards are in place – the QA system, if you like – we need to put them into practice – the QA structure – to ensure they form the backbone of our QA activities.

This process should, I would argue, involve a cycle of self-assessments and reviews - *self*-assessment because effective quality assurance is 'done by' or 'done with' rather than 'done to' subject leaders and teachers. Effective quality assurance is a supportive, developmental process or reflection and improvement planning, not a high stakes judgmental process.

Self-assessment and review

Quality improvement is a cyclical – as opposed to a linear – process and, as such, does not have a natural start and end point. The job is never finished. Perfection does not exist. Each self-assessment informs future planning which informs the actions taken, and each action is reviewed to inform the next self-assessment and so on. However, for the purposes of easy explanation, I will begin with the subject self-evaluation...

Remember that quality assurance is about improving the quality of education that we provide in our schools and colleges. This is why it starts with a vision which sets out, clearly and concisely, what that quality of education should look like at the end, so to speak. It is about supporting subject teams and teachers to improve their planning and teaching so that pupil outcomes are improved and so that all our pupils are prepared for the next stage of their lives.

The main role for senior leaders in this process, one might argue, is to create the culture in which improvements can happen and then to 'get out of the way' and let subject teams and teachers get on with enacting those improvements. If not this, then senior leaders might help subject leaders to identify their areas for improvement by taking on the role of a 'critical friend', helping to challenge decisions and thought processes, and question the status quo from an relative outsider's perspective.

With this in mind, let us consider how the self-assessment process might work...

First of all, effective quality assurance recognises the differences that exist between subject disciplines. The form and format that QA takes in each subject, therefore, will be necessarily different. However, it should have a common goal: the purpose of the subject self-assessment should be to critically reflect on past performance in order to improve future performance.

Self-evaluation, therefore, requires subject leaders and teachers to state their position at the end of each cycle, say an academic year, as well as the actions they took in the previous year to get there, the positive impact of those actions on pupils (each with supporting evidence), and the areas for improvement that remain and that they therefore need to focus on in the year ahead.

The areas for improvement contained within the self-evaluation record should then be carried forward to the curriculum improvement plan and form the objectives for the year ahead...

The curriculum improvement plan should, I think, be a live document used to record the actions required in-year in order to improve the quality of education each subject discipline provides. Each action taken to improve the quality of provision should be added to the plan alongside emerging evidence of its impact on pupils.

To quality assure each subject's provision and to support their improvements, subject leaders should then partake in curriculum reviews during the academic year. There might be three in a year, roughly one per term.

Each curriculum review should be a professional process used to support and challenge subject leaders and teachers. The process should begin and end with the curriculum improvement plan. The plan should be used to determine the nature of the review and to identify key areas of focus for the review. The outcome of the review process should, in turn, be an updated plan. In other words, and to misquote Shakespeare, the plan is the thing! This ensures paperwork is kept to an absolute minimum and that there is a single source of information which will help ensure consistency, clarity and communication.

An effective curriculum review might, I would argue, consist of three stages:

1. A professional conversation about subject purpose and intentions
2. A range of quality assurance activities (on which more below)
3. An action planning meeting to agree next steps

There should, as I argued above, be myriad forms of quality assurance activity that, when triangulated, paint a holistic picture of performance. I'd suggest at least these four cornerstones:

1. Lesson observations
2. Work scrutiny
3. Review of planning
4. Review of resources

Let's take a closer look at what this process might entail...

1. A professional conversation

The process begins, then, with a meeting between members of the subject team which is being reviewed and the reviewers if they are external to the department, such as senior leaders or peer-reviewers from another subject team.

This is a professional dialogue. The review team will use the meeting to better understand subject leaders' and teachers' intentions for their curriculum and to understand what leaders and teachers deem to be their team's current strengths and areas for improvement. This is about context, about what stage of the curriculum development journey the team is at now, not about binary judgments of good and bad practice.

Leaders and teachers, meanwhile, should use the meeting as an opportunity to have their self-assessment and improvement planning decisions challenged through coaching conversations.

At the end of the conversation, the reviewers might ask the subject leader: 'Now show me that in practice...' and thus signal the start of the quality assurance activities.

The quality assurance activities are an opportunity to test out subject leaders' and teachers' assumptions and beliefs about the quality of provision in their areas. Initially, subject leaders will guide reviewers by selecting the teachers and pupils they wish to have observed. But reviewers may then decide to observe other teachers and pupils in order to triangulate their findings. This is not about 'catching people out', but rather about ensuring consistency and helping subject leaders and teachers to test out their assumptions.

2. A range of quality assurance activities

Lesson observations

Lesson observations conducted as part of quality assurance activity might best be carried out jointly. All reviewers should have been trained in how to observe so that they understand what can and what cannot be observed, and in order to ensure they do not make unreliable and/or invalid judgments but, rather, use the opportunity of visiting lessons to discuss with pupils and teachers how the lesson fits into the bigger picture of learning and how typical the lesson is of daily practice. Training is not necessarily about right and wrong but about ensuring a consistency of practice among all those who observe.

Observations should not be used to extrapolate judgments about learning or progress, neither of which can be easily or reliably 'observed' in lessons. Indeed, in Book Two I talked at length about the differences between 'performance' and 'learning'.

Observations should only be used as one piece of a much bigger jigsaw and to better understand the type of provision being reviewed. Further, teachers should be given the opportunity to clarify any aspect of the lesson with the observer to avoid unhelpful assumptions being made.

I would suggest that, if you adopt a set of quality standards similar to those I posited earlier in this chapter, then lesson observations could be used to aid an evaluation of Quality Standards 5-10, namely:

5. *Teaching and assessment ensure learners know and can do more, and remember what they have learned for the long term*
6. *Learners are supported to become increasingly independent and resilient*
7. *Learners are prepared for the next stage of their lives and progress to high quality destinations*
8. *There is a positive learning environment and there are clear expectations for behaviour, attendance and punctuality*
9. *Bullying, harassment and discrimination is not accepted, and issues are quickly and consistently dealt with*

10. *Learners are supported to develop research and study skills that help them academically*

Work scrutiny

Work scrutiny is usually a desk-based exercise but may also be carried out during observations of lessons where pupil work is seen.

Pupil work is reviewed to better understand the frequency and quality of teacher's assessments and feedback, to gain evidence of how pupils respond to feedback and improve their work, and to gain evidence of the quality of pupils' work (including its presentation and the accuracy of spelling, punctuation and grammar) and the quantity of work being completed.

Sometimes it may be possible to extrapolate progress by looking at learners' work from two points in time but often progress is not so easily observed, and therefore caution should always be exercised. Furthermore, where there is uncertainty, teachers' views should always be sought to explain the contents of pupils' work.

Work scrutiny could be used to aid the evaluation of Quality Standards 1 to 7, namely:

1. *The curriculum offer is relevant, up-to-date and meets the needs of learners, communities, and the regional economy*
2. *The curriculum is ambitious for all learners and addresses issues of social mobility*
3. *Curriculum leaders and teachers identify and provide equal access to the knowledge, skills and experiences learners need to thrive*
4. *The curriculum is planned and sequenced to ensure positive progression*
5. *Teaching and assessment ensure learners know and can do more, and remember what they have learned for the long term*
6. *Learners are supported to become increasingly independent and resilient*
7. *Learners are prepared for the next stage of their lives and progress to high quality destinations*

Review of planning

Reviewers should look at evidence of the subject team's curriculum planning to aid its assessment of the subject leader's and teachers' curriculum intentions.

Planning takes many forms, and I do not think that school and college leaders should prescribe a particular method or format. Where it is available, reviews should look at overarching curriculum models and plans, at progression pathways, awarding body specifications, schemes of work and short-term plans. They should also review assessment schedules. They may look at how and why the curriculum offer has changed over recent years.

The review of planning may be used to aid the evaluation of Quality Standards 1 to 4, and 10 to 14, namely:

1. *The curriculum offer is relevant, up-to-date and meets the needs of learners, communities, and the regional economy*
2. *The curriculum is ambitious for all learners and addresses issues of social mobility*
3. *Curriculum leaders and teachers identify and provide equal access to the knowledge, skills and experiences learners need to thrive*
4. *The curriculum is planned and sequenced to ensure positive progression*

10. *Learners are supported to develop research and study skills that help them academically*
11. *Learners are afforded opportunities for personal development beyond the academic curriculum*
12. *Learners are given planned opportunities to develop wider skills including through high quality work experience and enrichment opportunities*
13. *Learners receive effective information and advice about their next steps, including careers guidance*
14. *Leaders and managers engage with learners, parents, the community and employers to plan and support the curriculum*

Review of resources

Learning resources could also be reviewed for their quality and effectiveness. This may encompass those resources stowed online including on the school or college VLE, as well as the presentation slides and other Smartboard resources used by teachers in lessons.

Reviewers may also assess the quality and effectiveness of the published textbooks used in lessons or for independent study, and of the worksheets and handouts produced and/or used by teachers.

Where relevant, reviewers might assess the written materials provided to pupils with additional and different needs such as writing frames and differentiated worksheets.

This review of resources may be used to aid the assessment of Quality Standards 2 and 3, 5 to 7, and 10, namely:

2. The curriculum is ambitious for all learners and addresses issues of social mobility
3. Curriculum leaders and teachers identify and provide equal access to the knowledge, skills and experiences learners need to thrive

5. Teaching and assessment ensure learners know and can do more, and remember what they have learned for the long term
6. Learners are supported to become increasingly independent and resilient
7. Learners are prepared for the next stage of their lives and progress to high quality destinations

10. Learners are supported to develop research and study skills that help them academically

3. An action planning meeting

At the end of the quality assurance review, the reviewers and the subject leader and teachers should meet to discuss their findings and next steps.

This is a professional conversation in which all the staff who are present share their thoughts without fear or favour, the onus being on an honest dialogue about the strengths and areas for improvement in the subject curriculum.

As a result of this discussion, the subject leader should agree a series of actions which they will add to their curriculum development plan. It may also be the case that existing actions are removed or amended in light of fresh evidence. Where actions are removed, it is best if changes are tracked, and comments added to explain why an action is no longer relevant.

The progress made against these new agreed actions will form the focus of the initial meeting at the next curriculum review. As I say, the plan is the thing!

Chapter 19: Performance management

The second apex of our golden triangle, you will recall, is performance management. You will also recall that I favour the term 'performance *development*'. Here's why...

For a long time and in too many cases, teacher performance management in schools and colleges was synonymous with an annual lesson observation. The lesson judgment – which usually took the form of a single number from 1 to 4, modelled on the Ofsted rating system – determined whether or not a teacher passed the appraisal cycle successfully and thus could escape the sanctions of 'capability' and – where relevant – be rewarded with pay progression.

Thankfully, this is much less common today than it once was, say, five or ten years ago. But it is not unheard of and even if *graded* lesson observations have ended, for too many teachers, appraisal cycles are still won or lost in a lesson observation. This is problematic because, as I explained at the start of the previous chapter, lessons observations alone – no matter how professionally and pragmatically they are carried out – do not enable us to accurately judge a teacher's effectiveness in the classroom, let alone their entire professional contribution.

To do that, or at least to do it better, we would need to triangulate what we see and hear in classrooms with other sources of information, not least our teachers' professional judgment.

In other words, as I said earlier, we should measure the quality of teaching – if we need to measure it at all – in a holistic rather than an isolated way. And even then, we must accept that we will not come close to doing justice to it because teaching is highly complex and judgments about its relative quality are fraught with difficulty.

The main thrust of my argument with regards performance management is simple: we should move away from performance *management* and towards performance *development*. In other words, we should avoid instigating a pass/fail system of appraisal that assumes teachers are either good or bad. Instead, we should strive for a system that recognises the complexity of the job, accepts that people have good and bad days, that many more factors affect pupils' progress and outcomes than an individual teacher, and that the goal is to help everyone – no matter their career stage – improve over time (whilst acknowledging that everyone is human, and no one is perfect).

Let me emphasise those key points again because I think they are important and if you take nothing else away from this chapter, I'd like it to be this...

Performance management should:

- Recognise the fact that teaching and learning are highly complex and cannot be reduced to a checklist or rubric
- Accept that a teacher's performance isn't uniform – they have good and bad days, and an ineffective lesson does not mean they have failed
- Acknowledge that pupil outcomes are affected by many factors beyond a teacher's control
- Aim to help every teacher in a school to improve, no matter their career stage or training needs
- Promote collaboration rather than competition, and incentivise team-working and joint practice development

So, put simply, it is my belief that performance management – if it is to 'measure' anything – should measure a teacher's willingness to engage in professional development activity and improve over time.

As a natural progression from this, it is reasonable to assert that an appraisal system could consist quite simply of one professional development target per year and be reviewed at the end of the cycle on the extent to which a teacher has engaged in CPD activity, tried new approaches and evaluated their impact.

I could end the chapter there. But I accept that most schools and colleges want more than this and so I will explore other possible methods.

But I do urge you to bear in mind when reading my thoughts on the balanced scorecard approach or the professional portfolio approach to performance management that, although these can work and are certainly much better than a single high-stakes lesson observation, they are not without their problems. And, perhaps most importantly, are no better than the much simpler approach I have just outlined.

If you want your performance management systems to 'measure' *teacher* quality or *teaching* quality, then what does this look like and how can we measure it?

How to measure teaching

As I explained in the previous chapter, the Measures of Effective Teaching (MET) project by the Bill and Melinda Gates Foundation was a three-year study which sought to determine how best to identify and promote great teaching. The project concluded that it was possible to identify - and therefore measure - great teaching by combining three types of measures, namely:

1. Classroom observations,
2. Pupil surveys, and
3. Pupil achievement gains (or outcomes).

The project report said that "Teaching is complex, and great practice takes time, passion, high-quality materials, and tailored feedback designed to help each teacher continuously grow and improve."

The project's report shows that a more balanced approach – one which incorporates multiple measures such as the pupil survey data and classroom observations – has two important advantages: teacher ratings are less likely to fluctuate from year to year, and the combination is more likely to identify teachers with better outcomes on pupil assessments.

The project posited four strategies we could employ if we are to improve our systems of performance management:

1. We should base teacher evaluations on multiple measures of performance, including data on pupil academic progress.

2. We should improve classroom observations by making them more frequent and robust.

3. We should use or modify an existing observation rubric instead of trying to reinvent the wheel.

4. We should give evaluators the training and ongoing support they need to be successful.

So, if we accept that teaching is a highly complex job and that we should base teacher evaluations on multiple measures of performance, what aspects of teaching should we measure? What elements of teaching matter most to us and lead to the most significant academic gains for pupils and, perhaps more pertinently, what elements of teaching can actually be observed and measured?

What to measure

In attempting to answer this question, there are several useful starting points, I think. Hopkins and Stern (1996), for example, conducted a synthesis of OECD findings from ten countries. They concluded that excellent teachers in all these countries had the following traits in common:

- They made a passionate commitment to doing the best for their students.
- They had a love of children which was enacted in a warm, caring relationship.
- They had strong pedagogical content knowledge.
- They used a variety of models of teaching and learning.
- They had a collaborative working style and regularly worked with other teachers to plan, observe and discuss one another's work.
- They constantly questioned, reflected on, and modified their own practice in light of feedback.

The Teachers' Standards – created by the UK government's Department for Education in 2011 – are intended to inform and support the performance management of teachers working in state schools in England. The standards are gathered under eight umbrella headings. According to the standards, great teachers:

1. Set high expectations which inspire, motivate and challenge pupils,
2. Promote good progress and outcomes by pupils,
3. Demonstrate good subject and curriculum knowledge,
4. Plan and teach well-structured lessons,
5. Adapt teaching to respond to the strengths and needs of all pupils,
6. Make accurate and productive use of assessment,
7. Manage behaviour effectively to ensure a good and safe learning environment, and
8. Fulfil wider professional responsibilities.

There are many such frameworks that seek to set out as succinctly as possible the roles and responsibilities, and the character traits and qualities, shared by the best teachers around the world. One of my favoured sets of standards is The Danielson Framework (2013) which pithily yet comprehensively sets out what great teachers do the world over.

Here is a summary of the Danielson Framework which you may find useful when devising your own set of standards for the purposes of performance management...

The Danielson Framework

The standards are grouped under the following four headings:

1. Planning and preparation,
2. Classroom,
3. Instruction, and
4. Professional responsibilities.

Under '**planning and preparation**', Danielson says that (and I have taken the liberty to abridge and paraphrase this and all that follows) teachers should:

Demonstrate a good pedagogical knowledge

They do this by ensuring that their curriculum plans reflect important concepts in the discipline and accommodate prerequisite relationships among concepts and skills. They ensure they give clear and accurate classroom explanations, give accurate answers to students' questions and feedback to students that furthers learning. And they make interdisciplinary connections in plans and practice.

Maintain a good knowledge of students

They do this by gathering both formal and informal information about students which they use in planning instruction. They learn students' interests and needs and again use this to inform their planning. They participate in community cultural events.

Write learning outcomes that are of a challenging cognitive level

They do this by stating student learning not student activity, by ensuring outcomes are central to the discipline and related to those in other disciplines, and by ensuring outcomes can be assessed and differentiated for students of varied ability.

Maintain a knowledge of resources

They do this using material from a range of sources including a variety of texts, as well as internet resources and resources from the local community. They participate in professional education courses or professional groups.

Provide coherent instruction

They do this by ensuring their lessons support instructional outcomes and reflect important concepts, perhaps by creating instructional maps that indicate relationships to prior learning. They provide activities that represent high-level thinking and offer opportunities for student choice. They make use of varied resources and teach structured lessons.

Assess students

They do this ensuring their lesson plans correspond with assessments and instructional outcomes. They use assessment types that are suitable to the style of outcome and offer a variety of performance opportunities for students. They modify assessments for individual students as needed. They write clear expectations with descriptors for each level of performance. And they design formative assessments which inform minute-to-minute decision making by the teacher during instruction.

Under the '**classroom**' heading, Danielson says that teachers should:

Show respect and rapport for others

They do this by ensuring they engage in respectful talk, active listening, and turn-taking. They acknowledge students' backgrounds and their lives outside the classroom. Their body language is indicative of warmth and caring shown by teacher and students, and they are polite and encouraging at all times.

Create a culture of learning

They do this by believing in the value of what is being learned, by setting high expectations for all that are supported through both verbal and non-verbal behaviours, for both learning and participation. They have high expectations of students' work, too, and recognise effort and persistence on the part of students.

Develop effective classroom procedures

They do this by ensuring the smooth functioning of all routines, with little or no loss of instructional time. They ensure students play an important role in carrying out the routines and that they know what to do and where to move.

Manage student behaviour

They do this by setting out clear standards of conduct which are regularly referred to during a lesson. There is a notable absence of acrimony between teacher and students concerning behaviour. The teacher is constantly aware of student conduct and takes preventive action when needed. They reinforce positive behaviour.

Make good use of the physical space

They do this by creating a pleasant, inviting atmosphere, a safe environment that is accessible for all students. They make effective use of physical resources, including technology.

Under '**instruction**', Danielson says that teachers should:

Communicate effectively

They do this by having a clarity of lesson purpose, articulating clear directions and procedures specific to the lesson activities. They give clear explanations of concepts and strategies and use correct and imaginative use of language.

Make good use of questioning and classroom discussion

They do this by asking questions of high cognitive challenge. They use questions with multiple correct answers or multiple approaches, even when there is a single correct response, and make effective use of student responses and ideas. During discussions, the teacher steps out of the central, mediating role, and focuses on the reasoning exhibited by students, both in give-and-take with the teacher and with their classmates. There are high levels of student participation in discussion.

Engage students in learning

They do this by promoting enthusiasm, interest, thinking, and problem solving. Learning tasks require high-level student thinking and invite students to explain their thinking. Students are highly motivated to work on all tasks and persistent even when the tasks are challenging. Students are actively working rather than watching while their teacher works. There is a suitable pacing of the lesson: it is neither dragged out nor rushed, and there is time for closure and student reflection.

Use assessment wisely

They do this by paying close attention to evidence of student understanding, by posing specifically created questions to elicit evidence of student understanding, and by circulating to monitor student learning and to offer feedback. Students assess their own work against established criteria, too.

Be flexible and responsive

They do this by incorporating students' interests and daily events into a lesson, and by adjusting their instruction in response to evidence of student understanding (or indeed the lack of it).

And under '**professional responsibilities**', Danielson argues that teachers should:

Reflect on their teaching

They do this by adjusting their practice so that it draws on a repertoire of strategies. They maintain accurate records. They establish routines and systems that track student completion of assignments.

Communicate with families

They do this by sending appropriate information home regarding the curriculum and student progress. Communication is two-way and there are frequent opportunities for families to engage in the learning process.

Participate in the professional community

They do this by regularly working with colleagues to share and plan for student success. They take part in professional courses or communities that emphasise improving practice and engage in school initiatives.

Grow and develop their practice

They do this by regularly attending courses and workshops and engaging in regular academic reading. They take part in learning networks with colleagues, freely sharing insights.

Show professionalism

They do this by forging a reputation as being trustworthy. They frequently remind colleagues that students are the highest priority and challenge existing practice in order to put students first.

Performance management systems

Once you have agreed a set of expectations or standards against which teaching, learning and assessment – and other aspects of a teacher's professional practice – can be measured for the purposes of performance management, it is important to build a workable system of recording, monitoring and tracking performance against those measures which leads to professional conversations and to the offer of support where performance is deemed to fall short.

The professional portfolio

One solution is the professional portfolio approach. This is not to be confused with a tick-box approach which mandates subject teams or teachers to self-assess against a fixed set of criteria, often feeling the need to engineer evidence where none exists. Rather, it is about teams and staff taking genuine responsibility for their own development and taking their professional practice seriously.

It is not essential that teams or teachers gather evidence against every criterion. Instead, they take a pragmatic approach to identifying their development needs and to monitoring and evaluating the impact of their efforts to improve their practice.

The portfolio should be a living document, added to throughout the academic year so that it becomes a true record of developing practice as well as a means of reflecting on that practice, rather than being hurriedly compiled the day before an appraisal meeting.

The balanced scorecard

Another possible solution is the 'balanced scorecard' approach – which works when criteria are quantifiable rather than qualitative – which is a means of aggregating a range of data. That data – soft and hard, narrative and numerical – can be drawn from in-year pupil progress, end-of-year pupil outcomes including value added scores, pupil voice surveys, a team's engagement in professional development, a scrutiny of marked pupil work, evidence of curriculum planning, and so on. The wider the net is cast, the more accurate, fair, and holistic the picture of the quality of the provision will be.

Of course, such systems are premised on the understanding that no measure of teaching, learning and assessment is perfect because education is highly complex. Such systems are also premised on the understanding that data is more than a spreadsheet; it is a conversation. In other words, the data recorded in a scorecard is just that – data. And data is the start of a discussion not its conclusion. Through discussion, data can be converted into meaningful information that will support improvements in teaching, learning and assessment and, moreover, improvements in outcomes for pupils.

Whilst accepting its limitations, one advantage of a scorecard – and indeed a portfolio – is that it can focus attentions where they're needed most, and it can help drive positive behaviours.

Formative assessment

A balanced scorecard – or a portfolio – is only part of the process, however. The best systems of performance management will lead to formative feedback which helps teachers to improve their practice.

In other words, the best performance management systems do not merely draw lines in the sand but rather provide a roadmap to excellence and are intrinsically linked to professional development.

Hence why I stated at the start of this chapter that the best systems are not about performance *management* at all; rather, they are about performance *development*.

When giving performance feedback, it's important to remember – common sense, I know, but it's often forgotten in the heat and urgency of the moment – to be polite, professional, and friendly throughout. Even if performance is less than we desire, whatever that might mean, there is nothing to be gained by being confrontational or rude. As such, it's worth contemplating the language we use: our choice of words cannot be in direct conflict with any judgment or outcome.

It's wise to remember that the observed lesson or the scrutinised paperwork was a mere snapshot and not wholly representative of overall performance. Our feedback should make this point explicit - just as we would differentiate between a pupil and their actions when chastising them for misbehaving, we should also differentiate between the team as professionals, and the snapshot of their performance we've seen.

As well as accepting the limitations of the snapshot, we should remember the Hawthorn Effect, too: by observing something we are changing its very nature.

Once performance feedback has been concluded, we should move towards action. Whatever the outcome, there is always need of a follow-up.

If performance is excellent – again, whatever that might mean – then the action might be to enlist teachers to share their good practice, to help colleagues improve the quality of their teaching. Perhaps teachers could lead a CPD session or video their lessons to share with colleagues in a staff meeting.

If the performance has been less than desired then the action might be to engage the team or individual teachers in some professional development activities, perhaps observing a colleague and trying out some new approaches in their own classroom.

Either way, the outcome of performance management is to inform future professional development activity. Talking of which...

Chapter 20: Professional development

In Chapter 19, I argued in favour of a new approach to appraisal, moving from a system of performance *management* to one of performance *development*.

Rather than relying on high-stakes, graded lesson observations, I said, we should adopt a 'balanced scorecard' approach whereby we aggregate a broad range of data in order to paint a more accurate, fair and holistic picture of a teacher's performance. Or perhaps use a portfolio approach whereby teachers collate evidence of their professional contributions against a set of expectations. Or, my favoured approach, we should only set one appraisal target per cycle: to engage in targeted professional development activity and evaluate its impact.

I also argued that performance management data should lead to performance feedback aimed at helping teachers to improve in targeted ways.

Performance management systems, in other words, should not merely draw a line in the sand but provide a roadmap to excellence.

In short, the outcome of performance management should be to inform future professional development activity.

In this chapter, therefore, I'd like to explore the next stage of the process – and the third and final apex of my golden triangle: teacher professional development...

Let us start, then, with this important – yet often forgotten – truth about education: teachers – and what happens in their classrooms – are the only real drivers of positive change in our schools. The only way to improve the quality of teaching, therefore, is to improve the quality of our teachers. And the only way to improve the quality of our teachers is to treat them fairly and with respect, and to train them well and continue to develop them throughout their careers.

Improving the quality of teachers requires systems of collaboration so that professional development becomes an everyday, collaborative exercise not an end of year 'sheep-dip' activity 'done to' teachers by school leaders.

Improving the quality of teachers requires professional development to be personalised, tailored to meet individual needs, so that it is made meaningful and encompasses all aspects of self-improvement activity – such as engaging with academic research, watching colleagues teach, working with a coach, and engaging in lesson study – not just attending a formal training course.

Improving the quality of teachers also requires professional development to recognise hard work in all its forms – even the quiet, 'just doing my job' kind – and to encourage rather than stifle teamwork, promoting collaboration over competition.

In short, improving the quality of education in our schools and colleges is about building a mature, adult culture in which teachers and school leaders work together in the best interests of their pupils to improve their practice without fear or favour.

So how can schools and colleges ensure that they provide high quality professional development for their staff and do so without drilling a big hole in their diminishing budgets?

As I explained in Chapter 18, the Standard for Teacher Professional Development (2016) - together with the ETF Professional Standards and the DfE Teachers' Standards - might just provide the answer.

The five strands of the Standard, you will recall, are:

1. Professional development should have a focus on improving and evaluating student outcomes.
2. Professional development should be underpinned by robust evidence and expertise.

3. Professional development should include collaboration and expert challenge.
4. Professional development programmes should be sustained over time.
5. Professional development must be prioritised by senior leadership.

I shared my thoughts on what all this means in practice earlier so won't do so again here. But what more can we say about effective professional development?

The purpose of CPD

Robert Sternberg, the American psychologist, argues that "The major factor in whether people achieve expertise is not some fixed prior ability, but purposeful engagement." The Professor of Psychology at Stanford University, Carol Dweck, meanwhile, believes that "Your basic qualities are things you can cultivate through your efforts. Although people may differ in every which way...everyone can change and grow through application and experience." And the author Dan Heath asserts that "To practice isn't to declare, I'm bad. To practice is to declare, I can be even better." To which sentiment we might add Doug Lemov's statement that "With practice you'll get stronger results if you spend your time practising the most important things."

Professional development provides teachers with opportunities to practice and, through practice, to improve.

Teaching is not a job; it is a profession. As such, teachers and school leaders should take seriously the continuous development of their knowledge and skills. After all, we wouldn't want to be operated on by an unqualified, unskilled surgeon with out-of-date knowledge. We wouldn't want to fly in a plane piloted by an amateur. So why would we want our students to be educated by unqualified, unskilled teachers and our schools to be run by unqualified, unskilled leaders?

International comparisons teach us that the most successful education systems in the world – such as the oft-cited Finland which I was lucky enough to visit a couple of years ago and, as such, through my research can confirm the following to be true – recruit the best teachers, train them well, and continue to value and develop them throughout their careers.

Judith Little, an American educational researcher who works at the University of California, Berkeley, says that the most successful schools tend to have four things in common and these shared traits might, I think, be key to the kind of quality, staff-driven professional development I am advocating...

1. Teachers talk about learning.

Professional development activities are dedicated to talking about lessons, about students, and about teaching and learning in general. CPD opportunities are rarely used to discuss administrative matters, this is done by other means such as email, memos, a chat in the corridor, and so on.

2. Teachers observe each other.

Professional development provides opportunities for teachers to engage in a planned programme of peer learning reviews and feedback. Peer learning reviews are then followed by constructive, focused professional conversations about how teachers can improve and about how teachers can share good practice and celebrate each other's skills and talents. Peer learning reviews and unseen observations, along with learning walks, allow teachers to take genuine snapshots of what happens every day, snapshots which can provide helpful suggestions for improvement as well as recognise and then reward genuine success.

3. Teachers plan together.

Judith Little talks of teachers writing lesson plans together, teaching the same lessons, then discussing them. I do not believe that it is necessary to have individual lesson plans because detailed session-by-session plans can encourage rigidity and 'teaching to the plan', not the kind of teaching which responds pragmatically to students' needs.

Little's 'teachers plan together' could be interpreted as teachers talking to each other about their medium- and long-term planning, and about their marking and students' work. Professional development could involve teachers routinely scrutinising each other's work and moderating each other's assessments, perhaps engaging in a process of peer review of each other's mark-books and students' work.

4. Teachers teach each other.

Professional development events and meetings are transformed into professional learning communities (such as those I described in Chapter Fourteen) which provide opportunities for teachers to share practice and comment on what they've tried and what worked and what didn't. These sessions are staff-led, collaborative enterprises not opportunities for leaders and managers to stand and deliver.

The focus of CPD

If we agree that professional development is important, then what should be the focus of teachers' development activities? What teaching approaches or strategies are proven to lead to the largest academic gains for students?

The best professional development is sustained. In other words, it focuses on one thing at a time and does so over a long period. Why? Because being an expert teacher – like being an expert at anything – takes a lot of hard work and effort. However, when a teacher practises their trade they must do so for a long period of time and must do so deliberately because, as Doug Lemov says in his book Practice Perfect, practice does not make perfect, it makes permanent. In other words, if teachers practice the wrong things or the wrong techniques then they will simply embed these bad habits into their everyday practice; they will not get better.

Deliberate practice is a focused and collaborative exercise. Deliberate practice is what top athletes do. Top athletes are coached in one area of their performance at a time – say, their backhand, their golf swing, their positioning on the starting blocks – and are given immediate feedback by their coach, before reflecting on that advice and making small corrective adjustments.

This is a process not dissimilar to what teachers do as trainees and newly qualified teachers. They constantly receive feedback and reflect on their own performance before making tweaks. Their mentor acts as a critical friend.

Teachers should, I think, continue in this vein throughout their teaching careers not just during their training. They should not be allowed to become isolated or to start developing bad habits. Of course, this is not easy because engaging in deliberate practice, to continually reflect on your performance, is to expose yourself to your own failures, to pick apart your mistakes. Deliberate practice is also time-consuming and takes real effort and resilience.

Doug Lemov suggests that effective professional development should be about the following three things:

1. Practising the 20%

Lemov argues that teachers should apply 'the law of the vital few' because, with practice, they'll get better results if they dedicate most of their professional development time to practising the 20% of things which create 80% of the value (or, in a different interpretation, the 20% of things which have the same value as the other 80% combined). In other words, teachers need to prioritise their professional development content.

2. Designing the drills

Through focusing on fewer things at any one time, it is possible to work on those things with a greater level of intensity. Designing the drills is about thinking through the ways in which teachers can best practise the 20%; it is about designing methods which will have the biggest impact on everyday performance. In other words, teachers need to find the best form for their professional development to take.

3. Shortening the feedback loop

Once teachers have chosen their 20% and decided on the methods by which they're going to improve them, they need to find ways of getting regular feedback on their improving performance because one of the most effective ways of improving their teaching practice is to improve the quality and immediacy of the feedback they get.

Teachers therefore need to ensure that professional development provides opportunities to get feedback on their teaching which can help them 'tweak' what they do and can be put into immediate use.

In other words, they need to routinely evaluate their performance and evaluate the effectiveness of the professional development in which they engage.

The format of CPD

So far, we have explored the purpose and focus of CPD activity. But what is the best form for it to take?

The honest answer, I think, is that it should take myriad forms.

Firstly, I think CPD should provide opportunities for external expertise to be injected into a school and so take the form of INSET events led by a guest speaker. This is important because schools must not become isolated from the outside world. If they do, they are in danger of becoming 'sausage factories' which keep churning out the same results precisely because they keep putting in the same ingredients.

External speakers, trainers and advisors can help schools to challenge the status quo, to question hitherto unquestionable practices, and to sense-check their work against other schools. They can also provide a new way of thinking about ideas and approaches.

Secondly, I think CPD should also be external in the sense of teachers accessing conferences, training courses and networking events outside the school gates. Such events provide an opportunity for teachers to stop, think and reflect on their current practices and to talk to colleagues from other settings and thus share ideas.

Thirdly, I think CPD should take myriad forms and not be limited to formal training courses. As I said earlier, CPD can include engaging with academic research, networking online, and trying out new strategies in the classroom then evaluating their impact. In the case of vocational teachers in FE settings, CPD can – and indeed should – take the form of workplace visits to ensure their industry knowledge is kept up-to-date and relevant.

And finally, I think CPD should be teacher-led and thus afford teachers the opportunity to share best practice with colleagues from their own departments and schools and seek help and advice from colleagues who teach in the same setting. Peer-observations and peer-teaching are particularly helpful here. A note of caution, though: It is important that there is a structure and a clear focus for any teacher-led CPD in order to avoid it becoming simply a 'talking shop'.

On the latter point, one structured form that teacher-led CPD can take is the professional learning community...

Professional learning communities

Professional learning communities are a way of engaging colleagues in the process of sharing best practice and developing their professional practice...

Professional learning communities provide teachers with the time, space and – perhaps most importantly of all – the safety net they need in order to feel able and supported to take risks and to try out new teaching methods without fear or favour.

In Joyce and Showers' report, 'Student achievement through staff development' (2002), the authors argue that teaching has at least three times the effect on student achievement as any other factor and assert that teaching is best improved through experimentation. In other words, teachers need to be accorded the opportunity to try out new teaching strategies and then to candidly discuss with colleagues what worked and what did not. They advocate using the professional learning community as a means of doing just this and suggest the following method:

Identify training needs:

Here, teachers ask themselves 'What do we feel are our most pressing needs? And 'What do our results tell us? Then a list of 10-20 ideas for improvement is drawn up, combined, compromised and prioritised into one common goal. This common goal is focused on a process designed to produce better outcomes which will directly affect students' experiences.

Training is devised:

At this stage, training is planned in the following sequence...

- Knowledge – new theories and rationale are explained
- Demonstration – new theories are modelled
- Practice – teachers try out the theories for themselves
- Peer coaching – teachers work together to solve the problems and answer the questions which arise during the 'practice' stage.

Training is delivered:

Now, the above training takes place over a period of time and is continually evaluated.

Joyce and Showers found that teachers must practice new methods 20-25 times if they are to learn how to use them as effectively as they do their usual methods.

There is a lot of research which underlines the importance of deliberate practice in achieving mastery and all insist that practice must be carried out over a long period of time. Most notably there is the '10,000-hour rule' propounded by Malcolm Gladwell in Outliers and Matthew Syed in Bounce. The argument here is that in order to become an expert you must accrue at least 10,000 hours of practice. Anders Ericsson, from whose seminal study of violinists in Berlin the 10000-hour rule purportedly arises, has said he never insisted on this figure as a hard and fast rule – the number of hours of practice required to achieve mastery, he says, depends upon the individual's starting point, the skill being practiced and the nature of the practice. However, Ericsson does still insist that it is only the amount of practice that distinguishes the novice from the expert.

As well as dedicating a significant amount of time to practising a new teaching strategy, Joyce and Showers also warn that the first few attempts at trying out a new classroom technique might fail but that the teacher must remain positive and keep trying. This process of experimentation works best – according to Joyce and Showers – when teachers:

- Practice the use of the new methods repeatedly over a period of time
- Monitor the effect of the new methods on students
- Ask students their opinions on the new methods, garnering further suggestions
- Bring issues to peer coaching sessions for discussion

- Help and support others with their experimentation

It is important that leaders support experimentation by modelling what Joyce and Showers call an 'improvement and renewal' style of leadership. That is to say, they display an emphatic belief that it is always possible to get better, no matter how good you already are. And they display the belief that the factors which most affect student outcomes are in students' and teachers' control. They do not blame achievement on socio-economic factors nor suggest that ability is innate. They do not accept low standards.

Leaders can also promote improvement by:

- Promoting collaboration
- Ensuring improvement meetings are frequent and well-attended
- Expecting a high standard of peer coaching
- Expecting experimentation to be supported by evidence
- Being positive and promoting the importance of teachers

Geoff Petty, an education writer, has also shared a useful model for improving teaching. It goes like this:

1. Explore the context: understand the key issues in ensuring success for all
2. Explore present practice: understand how we teach at present
3. Explore the pedagogy: understand what other teaching strategies could improve teaching
4. Plan experimentation and implementation: decide ways to teach better
5. Improve and coach-in strategies: develop strategies whilst receiving support from a peer coach
6. Monitor: monitor experimentation to ensure they make a difference to students
7. Share and celebrate success: report on experiments and share strategies
8. Embed practice: new strategies are agreed and put into planning for the whole team to implement

What professional learning communities do best, I think, is encourage risk-taking. Because they are about developing teaching expertise rather than judging teachers' abilities, they encourage colleagues to try out new ways of teaching, some of which will work and some of which will not. Risk-taking and innovation are key to the long-term development of teaching because they help us as professionals to keep on getting better over time.

As lead learners, teachers should model the process of learning for their pupils. We need to show our pupils that we are also learning all the time and that we are unafraid of trying new things even if that means we sometimes make mistakes. Actually, not "even if that means we make mistakes" but "exactly *because* it means we make mistakes" ... After all, to make mistakes is to learn; to learn is to increase our IQs. As Samuel Beckett wrote back in 1884, "Ever tried? Ever failed? Try again. Fail again. Fail better." Teachers need to model the 'growth mindset' approach pioneered by Carol Dweck.

Professional learning communities also encourage teachers to do exactly what we want all of our pupils to do in order to achieve success: namely, to work outside their comfort zones, to try something difficult. And setting tough tasks is also to be encouraged because challenge leads to deeper learning and greater achievement.

Challenge is, after all, a central feature of effective learning. If you think back to a time when you've felt challenged either personally or professionally, you'll probably recall feeling discomfort. But, once you'd overcome the challenge and achieved your goal, the sense of success with which you were rewarded felt far greater than it would have done if you'd achieved something easy without even breaking into a sweat.

Dylan Wiliam suggests a six-part structure for running professional learning community workshops. He advocates following the same structure each time so that all colleagues come to know what is expected. This structure is as follows:

1. Introduction.
Approximately five minutes to share learning intentions for the workshop.

2. Starter.
Approximately five minutes as a warm-up or to share some recent positive and negative experiences.

3. Feedback.
Between twenty-five and fifty minutes for colleagues to talk about what they've done since the last workshop, perhaps by talking through their professional development plan. It is important that all colleagues prepare for this session and are clear and detailed in the experiences they talk about including outlining what went well and what did not, and what they have learned from the experience.

4. New learning.
Between twenty and forty minutes to discuss new learning, learning which can then be put into practice between this workshop and the next one. This might involve watching a video, discussing a book, and so on.

5. Professional development planning.
Approximately fifteen minutes to update professional development plans and organise with colleagues any future peer observations and work scrutiny activities.

6. Review of learning.
Approximately five minutes to recap on the core learning from this workshop.

Each workshop, Wiliam says, should last between seventy-five minutes and two hours.

Garmston and Wellman share 7 Ps of effective collaboration which may be useful in setting a supportive tone at these professional learning community workshops:

1. Pausing

This is about allowing all participants time to think, reflect on what's been said and develop their understanding.

2. Paraphrasing

This is about the workshop leader reiterating key points, repeating back what others say in order that all participants can hear and understand what is being said.

3. Probing

This is about the workshop leader asking questions and requesting participants develop their ideas further.

4. Putting ideas on the table

This is about welcoming everybody's input and greeting ideas with respect; it is also about the workshop leader accepting that there are different points of view which need to be considered and thought through without prejudice.

5. Paying attention to self and others

This is about thinking through how to say something in a way that does not offend others nor incite argument.

6. Presuming positive intentions

This is about presuming others mean well and trying to prevent argument.

7. Pursuing balance between advocacy and inquiry

This is about striking the right balance between inquiring into others' ideas before advocating your own.

Dylan Wiliam says that the most effective professional learning communities run for two years, meet monthly to discuss new ideas and to share experiences, and identify dedicated time between meetings for colleagues to carry out peer observations and to plan collaboratively.

Wiliam also advocates starting with the *content* then moving on to the *process*. Content is about choosing the appropriate evidence, formulating the initial ideas; process is about according people with choice and flexibility, encouraging them to take small steps forward with support but also with accountability. In other words, content is about the what? and process is about the how?

Another way of looking at it is this...

As a collective, we should decide on the strategy – what aspect of pedagogy we need to focus on first; and then individual teachers should decide on the techniques – how they intend to embed this strategy, what practical changes they plan to make. For example, a school may decide that its first collective focus should be on improving the quality of the formative feedback given to pupils by teachers and by pupils themselves. Then individual teachers are given the autonomy to trial new methods of giving and acting on feedback in their classes. In other words, individual teachers take ownership of their own professional development. After all, teaching is in part about personality. Every teacher has a different personality and therefore a different way of teaching. Such differences should be embraced not eradicated. We want human beings at the helm of our children's learning not automatons, after all.

Part Seven: The new normal

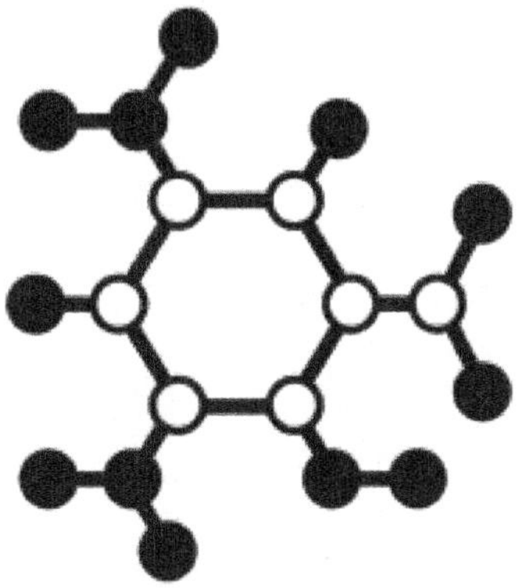

Chapter 21: Ethical leadership

Since I started writing this book, the world has tilted on its axis in ways we could never have anticipated... unless, that is, we'd taken the film *Contagion* to be documentary rather than drama.

The publication was the second book in this series was delayed due to the onset of the Covid-19 pandemic in early 2020 and this book was written largely in lockdown. (And yet, despite being house-bound, I was still late submitting the final draft to my publisher!)

Although, as I was putting the finishing touches to this book in March 2021, schools and colleges re-opened to all pupils and it looked like the vaccine would slowly allow us to return to our normal ways of life by the summer, it would still be remiss of me, I think, not to mention the pandemic and not to look again at our education system through this lens.

Even if the virus is controlled and becomes akin to seasonable flu, our pupils and students will be living with the consequences of the pandemic for some time.

Between March 2020 and March 2021, there were three national lockdowns in England, with similar restrictions in place in Scotland, Wales and Northern Ireland.

As such, many pupils were unable to attend school in person for many months. And thus, those young people who start their secondary school journeys in September 2021 will not have a full year of schooling since they were in Year 4.

There are various aspects to consider, therefore:

1. What can we do to help pupils re-engage with education and achieve their full potential?
2. What can we learn from the lockdowns about better ways of working?
3. How might we embrace technology in the future to take advantage of the gains made with online learning?

In this final part of the book, I would like to do several things; some directly related to Covid-19 and others not.

Firstly, I would like to explore a leadership approach that I think can help us rebuilt our school and college communities after Covid-19 and provide a moral compass to guide all future decision-making. That approach is ethical leadership. I believe that, from this point forwards, ethical leadership should be our guiding star as school and college leaders.

Secondly, I would like to explore the importance of parental engagement – again, both now as we seek to rebuild our schools and colleges following a crisis but also long into the future. I believe that schools and colleges are far more successful when they work in partnership with parents/carers and their communities. I believe that we are 'stronger together'. And I believe that parental engagement is about ensuring parents and others are not only *informed* about the work of our schools and colleges but are also *involved* in the work of our schools and colleges.

Of course, as pupil return to school and we try to respond to 'lost learning' and the widening of many disadvantage gaps, it is more crucial than ever that we engage with pupils' homes.

Thirdly, I would like to explore the lessons we have learned from the recent pandemic, both in terms of better working conditions for all our staff and in terms of improved effectiveness.

Fourthly, I would like to explore the notion of 'lost learning' and consider ways of helping pupils to 'catch up'. There is a reason I place those two terms in inverted commas as you will discover later. Suffice to say, I don't think doom-mongering and employing a deficit model will be helpful.

Fifthly, I would like to explore the lessons we have learned from our experiences of online learning so that we are better prepared for such an eventuality in the future whereby pupils cannot attend school in person (gone, I suspect, are 'snow days!) but also so we can utilise technology all the time, including for homework, independent study and revision.

Finally, I'd like to offer some advice for future crisis management so that we might be better prepared to roll with the punches when they strike.

So, let us start with ethical leadership...

Ethical leadership in education

Ethical leadership in education is driven by a respect for values and an unfaltering belief in the dignity and rights of others.

Ethical leaders build school cultures governed by fair, clearly articulated expectations, rather than cultures driven by personalities or politics.

In an ethically led school, there is a clear vision and mission, and a set of shared values and principles, that are understood and owned by everyone who works there.

Every action that is taken is sense-checked against this vision and mission – if completion of said action would not aid the pursuit of the vision and mission, it isn't deemed important; as well as against these values and principles – if completion of said action would not uphold the values and principles, it isn't considered valid.

Every element of the school, from performance management appraisals to staff professional development, from expectations of pupil behaviour to the resourcing of the curriculum, reflects this vision and mission, and these values and principles.

Ethical leaders cannot pick and choose which situations call for moral judgment or leave their principles at the door whenever it's convenient; an ethical code provides the very foundations on which these schools are built and function day-to-day.

In practice, ethical leadership is, I think, anchored in five principles:

1. Honesty
2. Justice
3. Respect
4. Community
5. Integrity

Honesty

If school leaders are dishonest, a culture of mistrust soon creeps. This, in turn, leads to a loss of faith, not just in the leaders themselves, but in the whole school and what it stands for and seeks to achieve.

Ethical leaders are always honest and upfront, even when they must have difficult conversations or take unpopular decisions. They articulate the rationale and reasoning behind their decisions and set out the supporting evidence. What's more, they afford colleagues a right of reply, they don't close down dissent.

Justice

If leaders are unjust, an insidious sense of unfairness pervades. Ethical leaders treat everyone equally and ensure that fairness governs their decision-making. They don't give some colleagues special treatment except when a particular situation demands it for the purposes of justice.

Respect

If leaders do not respect their colleagues, they rarely win others' respect in return. Like authority, respect is earned through one's actions not guaranteed along with a job title.

Ethical leaders believe that everyone has value, both as individuals and as members of the wider school community; as such, they listen carefully to others' opinions and ideas, value everyone's contributions, and work hard to ensure colleagues feel worthwhile.

Ethical leaders don't run hierarchical institutions where the word of a senior leader is unquestionable and final. Though schools are not democracies, neither should they be dictatorships – collaboration and cooperation are key to their long-term success.

Community

If leaders do not foster a sense of community and engender collective, professional autonomy, colleagues rarely feel like they belong, and thus they do not develop a sense of ownership of the school's vision and mission. In short, they do not feel compelled to help achieve the vision.

Community breeds a sense of purpose, a belief that each member of the team is a part of something bigger than themselves and has a crucial role to play in that community's success.

Ethical school leaders build such communities by caring about the health and happiness of their colleagues and by empowering others through genuine delegation; they also invest in their people's professional development and instil a sense of collective autonomy or collegiality.

Ultimately, ethical leaders regard it as their legacy to build a school that will continue to succeed in their absence – they put in place sustainable systems and structure, policies and procedures that do not rely on the cult of personality.

Integrity

If leaders do not act with honour and integrity, they quickly lose the trust and respect of all those around them and will struggle to recruit. Trust is non-negotiable.

Ethical leaders possess a strong moral purpose and an overriding sense of honesty. They lead by example at all times and act with conviction.

Ethical leadership in a post-Covid world

The five principles of ethical leadership – honesty, justice, respect, community, and integrity – have, in my view, always been important (and I first wrote about the need for such principles a decade ago when macho school leadership, defined by bullying tactics and high staff attrition, was the preferred model) but I would argue that they should now carry particular weight as we seek to rebuild our school and college communities following the Covid-19 pandemic.

A British Psychological Society report called 'Back to school: Using psychological perspectives to support re-engagement and recovery' (2020), which I will explore in more detail in Chapter 23, says that "research following other community crises have highlighted the importance of clear, open and decisive leadership in building resilient communities".

The basic principles of good leadership, the report says, are: Listen, learn and *then* act.

As I will argue in Chapter 23, listening and learning are particularly important whilst we are in the process of rebuilding our schools following the coronavirus crisis. Despite the many obvious negative consequences of Covid-19, not least the loss of loved ones, it is possible to find some positives too if only we listen to and learn from all our colleagues and stakeholders.

Indeed, Post Traumatic Growth Theory research highlights the potential for positive growth and development as a consequence of trauma and challenging experiences.

Staff and pupils are likely to be feeling vulnerable and may be worried about what school will hold for them in the coming months.

Many members of our school communities will have experienced difficulties being locked down and home-schooled and, worse, may have lost loved ones to the virus. Some staff and students may have had distressing experiences leading to safeguarding issues or mental health crises. Many will be concerned about the possibility of contracting the virus now they're back in school or struggle to adapt to our new ways of working.

Now more than ever, then school leaders need to adopt the principles of ethical leadership and act with strong moral purpose.

What can we do?

We can further help staff and pupils by adopting ethical leadership behaviours such as:

- Leading by example
- Communicating moral values
- Making ethical decisions

Leading by example

Putting ethical leadership into daily practice is, I think, about 'walking the walk'. Ethical leaders have high expectations of their pupils but, crucially, hold themselves to the same standards.

It's important, therefore, that leaders talk openly about their concerns and put people at ease about their worries.

Communicating moral values

Ethical leaders tend to be good communicators. They are comfortable speaking in public, leading meetings and writing communications that clearly articulate what they are trying to convey.

Ethical leaders are effective at building these relationships via communication, too. It's important, therefore, that they communicate clearly, concisely and often, and keep everyone informed.

We have seen from the government's own mixed and confused messaging during the pandemic how trust can be easily lost. Schools must try to avoid falling into the same trap. School leaders therefore need to be on top of policy and set out clearly and concisely what is expected of everyone and why these expectations are consistent with the school's values and principles.

Making ethical decisions

Ethical leaders assess each decision before implementing it in order to make sure that the decision accords with their school's vision and mission, and values and principles. They only initiate such decisions if the ethical criteria are met.

They should, therefore, ensure that they consult with as broad a range of stakeholders as possible before making decisions that affect people's work and lives, and then act in the best interests of our pupils, staff and communities.

Sometimes this means being bold and brave and doing what it right for their school context and for individual pupils, irrespective of what other schools are doing.

When they communicate their decisions, they should explicitly link them to their school values so that parents/carers know they are acting in good faith and in accordance with their long-held principles.

Finally, we should, I think, be kind leaders...

Kindness

Ethical school leaders routinely recognise and reward success. For ethical leaders, celebrating others' achievements is an everyday part of what they do rather than an afterthought or rarity.

Ethical leaders also give quality time to people, have an open-door policy – which does not mean being available twenty-four hours a day, but rather being able to meet with staff as soon as possible and listening and responding to what they have to say.

Ethical leaders are protective of their staff, showing empathy, respecting people's privacy, remembering birthdays, and granting personal leave – without question – when staff have important or urgent personal matters to attend to such as family funerals. They also set as their default position a genuine belief that everybody wishes to do well and will try their best, rather than assuming the worst of people.

Kindness and gratitude are, I think, needed now more than ever.

Using technology to support staff

Many schools have continued to harness the technology they discovered during lockdown for, amongst other things, virtual meetings and online on-demand CPD in order to ensure that part-time staff and those with outside commitments such as childcare are not at a disadvantage and can fully participate in school life.

Flexible working like this is, I think, one way to improve staff wellbeing – which, in turn, is a means of tackling teacher retention.

After all, according to a CooperGibson Research report (DfE 2018), flexible working is generally viewed positively by teachers as a way to secure a better work-life balance.

A majority of primary teachers are female (75% according to the DfE's latest figures) and many have young children (54% according to Teacher Tapp, 40% of which have children under the age of 8). As such, flexible working can be particularly impactful in primary schools.

Whilst the pandemic has undoubtedly brought to light some positive solutions to the issue of staff wellbeing, it has also exacerbated those issues...

More than half of primary school teachers (59 per cent) and 49 per cent of secondary school teachers told a YouGov TeacherTrack survey, commissioned by the charity Education Support, that they were experiencing higher than usual levels of stress and anxiety because of the lockdown. And more than half of the calls to the Education Support confidential helpline are currently related to coronavirus, the charity says.

And it's not only affected staff, of course. Research by the Prince's Trust has found that more than a quarter of young people felt unable to cope with life amid the pandemic and almost a third had had panic attacks. More than a third said they were struggling to think clearly. In October 2020, an investigation by The Guardian newspaper revealed that prescriptions for sleeping pills for under-18s had increased by 30% between March and June compared with two years ago.

Meanwhile, one of the largest private eating disorder services, the Priority Group, has reported a 71% rise in admissions in September compared to the same period a year ago. And Place2Be, a charity that offers counselling, has said that reports of safeguarding issues, and in particular self-harm, are up 77% among secondary pupils, whilst suicidal ideation increased by 81%.

Ann Longfield, the Children's Commissioner for England, told The Guardian the situation was "really concerning" and that schools "need an NHS-trained counsellor". Providing more support for pupils' health and wellbeing was "something that needs to be prioritised", she added.

So, what – beyond using technology to facilitate flexible working – can schools do to promote good health and wellbeing for their staff and pupils?

Staff wellbeing

Firstly, as I say above, school leaders can develop ethical leadership practices.

In practice, and in addition to what I suggest above, ethical leaders might promote staff wellbeing by taking some of the following actions...

Firstly, in order to help reduce teachers' workload, ethical leaders can...

- Ensure teachers are given more than the statutory 10% of planning, preparation and assessment (PPA) time, or non-contact time, as well as offer all staff with additional responsibilities protected leadership time
- Ensure meetings are kept short and productive, are only called when essential and stick to an agreed agenda
- Offer all staff career development opportunities, as well as access to quality CPD
- Ensure school policies and procedures are workable and fair, and not overly bureaucratic... especially when it comes to assessment

Secondly, in order to protect staff health and wellbeing, ethical leaders can...

- Ensure there is a safe space for staff to get together and talk without fear or favour
- Provide free refreshments for staff
- Provide healthcare for staff, including flu vaccines
- Plan regular staff social events and do so at different times and in different locations so as to cater for all staff

- Be flexible when it comes to affording staff access to family events such as children's Christmas concerts
- Make sure staff get time back that they spend on extra-curricular activities such as going on educational visits
- Operate clear communications protocols such as for the use of email to help achieve a work life balance

Thirdly, ethical leaders can help provide purpose and focus for all staff by...

- Having clear job descriptions and person specifications which are followed
- Having clear policies and expectations
- Consult as much as possible and on as many issues as possible, ensuring every voice is heard and respected
- Making sure hard work is recognised and success is celebrated

Pupil wellbeing

To promote pupil wellbeing in the aftermath of Covid-19, Trauma Informed Schools UK suggested we do the following (which I have taken the liberty to paraphrase):

- Be calm – we should be steady and matter of fact in order to reassure pupils
- Be positive – we should remind pupils of all the ways they have learnt to keep themselves safe such as washing their hands and staying in their own space
- Be supportive – we should reassure pupils who may have separation anxiety that we have missed them too and that their parents will miss them but that they'll be there for them later in the day
- Be curious – we should listen and try not to dismiss pupils' fears but validate how they're feeling
- Be thankful – we should help pupils to think of things they're looking forward to such as being with friends and learning exciting new things
- Be prepared – we should help pupils to understand the changes that have happened in the classroom environment and rehearse routines such as the start and end of the day in order to maintain social distancing where possible

A report by the World Health Organisation entitled 'Building Back Better: Sustainable Mental Health Care After Emergencies' (2013), says that during emergencies, mental health requires special consideration.

This is, they say, due to three common issues:

1. Increased rates of mental health problems,
2. Weakened mental health infrastructure, and
3. Difficulties coordinating agencies providing mental health and psychosocial support.

It is certainly true that many of our pupils will have experienced trauma during in recent times including as a result of bereavement, and that – as the above data attests – mental health issues are likely to be more prevalent. It is also true that many pupils with existing mental health problems will have had less support during the pandemic and that accessing specialist support will have been – and will continue to be – more difficult.

So, what can we do to support our pupils' mental health and wellbeing?

A British Psychological Society report called 'Back to school: Using psychological perspectives to support re-engagement and recovery' (2020), says that, in order to support pupils' social, emotional and mental health needs, we should first acknowledge that they are going to experience a range of emotions. This may include a mixture of excitement, happiness and relief but it may also include anxiety, fear and anger.

In most cases a whole community response aimed at promoting positive reintegration and building resilience will, the BPS say, help to resolve their difficulties; for others, the use of school-based social emotional and mental health resources and expertise will help.

The BPS report also advocates building vulnerable pupils' resilience. The report says that resilience is not something that someone either does or does not have, it comes from how all the important parts of a person's life interact – their friends, family, school and local community.

As such, we need to make sure that children have a strong sense of belonging, strong relationships, a sense of agency, high expectations, and that they can meaningfully contribute to their community.

The BPS say that, during this crisis, there is a risk that the narrative around changing policies and school transition becomes dominated by the language of risk and trauma. Coping is important to protect ourselves from stress and it is important to connect with the ways in which we are coping with this challenge. Psychological perspectives and approaches to resiliency also give space for talking about strengths and hope.

A framework to promote resilience includes:

1. Creating positive goals
2. Planning how to track positive change
3. Working to reduce risk while enhancing strengths

Chapter 22: Parental engagement

As I said at the start of Chapter 21, as well as being more ethical in our leadership practices, and protecting staff and pupil wellbeing, we can try to improve parental engagement in our post-Covid schools and colleges in order to ensure that parents/carers and the wider community are partners in education and are not only informed about, but actively involved in the work we do.

So, what can schools and colleges do to ensure they fully engage with parents and carers? In this chapter, I will explain why parental engagement matters and outline a two-way process of communication. I will examine how best to communicate with parents, including in written and verbal forms. And I will explore the role that technology can play in this process. I will also take a look at ways of dealing with complaints from parents and at resolving conflict when it arises.

Why parental engagement matters

When my daughters transitioned from primary to secondary school, I think I was more nervous than they were.

Whilst they were at primary school, I felt fully informed in their academic and pastoral progress. In fact, if I'm honest, I sometimes felt a little *too* informed. I was bombarded by daily emails and texts, weekly newsletters, PTA flyers, invitations to quiz nights and barn dances, and... well, you get the idea.

My daughters' primary school regularly invited me over the threshold for assemblies, charitable events, discos, open evenings, sports activities, you name it. It got to the point I think I saw my daughters' teachers more than I saw some of my closest friends.

But when they transferred to secondary school, I felt abandoned. Like the prisoner who develops Stockholm Syndrome, I had become accustomed to and reliant upon the daily deluge of information about my daughters' education. Yes, when they moved to secondary school, I attended my daughters' induction evenings and received bi-annual progress reports, and of course I attended parents' consultation evenings once or twice a year. But most of the contact I had with my daughters' secondary school was in the form of demands for money.

Of course, schools have less need to make contact with parents as children grow older and more independent, and so secondary schools should not try to emulate the parental engagement policies of their primary partners.

But many secondary schools may be able do more to engage their pupils' parents and carers and to ensure that they are *involved* in, not just *informed* about, school life.

It is in a school's best interests to ensure staff make regular contact with parents because when pupils' families become partners in the education process, they are more likely to support the school when times get tough, as well as stand shoulder-to-shoulder with teachers in celebrating the good times. Put simply, if schools and parents work as a team for the benefit of young people, life is easier for everyone and pupils' life chances are enhanced.

Evidence suggests that, when schools work effectively with parents and carers, pupils benefit from higher academic achievement, good attendance and punctuality, and better behaviours and attitudes to learning.

For more, see Butler et el (2008), Haynes et al (1989), and Henderson (1987) who found that effective parental engagement is associated with higher academic achievement.

Butler and Haynes also claim that effective parental engagement leads to increased rates of pupil attendance.

Becher (1984) and Henderson et al (1986), meanwhile, claim effective parental engagement can have a positive effect on pupils' attitudes to learning and on their behaviour in class.

Research has also shown that improving parental engagement can lead to:

- An increased level of interest amongst pupils in their work (see, for example, Rich [1988] and Tobolka [2006])
- Increased parent satisfaction with their child's teachers (Rich)
- Higher rates of teacher satisfaction (MetLife Survey [2012])

Let's take a closer look at what the research literature has to say on the subject...

What the research says

Researchers have found evidence of the positive relationship between parental communication and pupil outcomes (see, for example, Fan & Williams, 2010; Rumberger, 2011; Sirvani, 2007). Research also shows that pupils' engagement in school is continuously shaped by their relationships with adults and the quality of their learning environment (see, for example, Connell, 1990; Finn & Rock, 1997).

It's well documented and commented upon that teachers play a crucial role in shaping pupil engagement (see Battistich, Solomon, Watson, & Schaps, 1997; Furrer & Skinner, 2003; Ryan & Patrick, 2001). But perhaps less well known is the fact that parents also play a central role in shaping their children's behaviour and engagement in school. For example, research by Barnard (2004) and Seitsinger et al. (2008) has shown that involving parents in their children's schooling can improve students' academic achievement.

Kraft, M. A., & Dougherty, S. M. (2013), meanwhile, in a paper entitled 'The effect of teacher–family communication on student engagement: Evidence from a randomized field experiment', estimated the causal effect of daily teacher-parent and teacher-pupil communication on pupil engagement during one week of a mandatory summer academy for entering 6th and 9th grade students at MATCH Charter Public School. They found large and immediate effects of communication on homework completion rates, classroom behaviour and participation in class. The willingness and ability to complete homework, to be on-task and to be active participants in lessons are, Kraft et al argued, key mediators of academic achievement in school.

So parental engagement can improve pupils' motivation and engagement in school life. And motivation, in turn, is a powerful predictor of academic outcomes...

For example, there's a significant body of research (see, for example, Connell, Spencer, & Aber, 1994; Connell & Wellborn, 1991; Deci, Vallerand, Pelletier, & Ryan, 1992; Finn & Rock, 2007; Klem & Connell, 2004; Marks, 2000; Skinner, Wellborn, & Connell, 1990) documenting the strong positive relationship between pupil engagement and learning outcomes. There's an equally large body of research suggesting that pupils' intrinsic and extrinsic motivation, along with their sense of efficacy, are malleable and are likely to influence their levels of engagement in school (see, for example, Bandura, 1997; Connell, 1990; Connell & Wellborn, 1991; Deci & Ryan, 1985, 2000; Gillet, Vallerand, & Lafreniere, 2012).

In short, improving parental engagement can, in turn, improve pupil outcomes.

Starting principles of parental engagement

So far, we have discovered the importance of parental engagement. Before we delve into some specifics, let's consider a few starting principles you may wish to bear in mind...

Firstly, **parental communication needs to start early** and continue throughout a pupil's journey through school. The parents of pupils moving from nursery to primary school, or from primary to secondary, will not want to receive information halfway through the summer holiday at which point it will be deemed too late. Schools need to engage with parents early and clearly set out their expectations and requirements.

Secondly, **parental communication needs to be a two-way process**: as well as the school staying in touch with parents, parents also need a means of keeping in contact with the school. One way to do this is to create a frequently asked questions (FAQ) page, as well as a Q&A facility and a parents' forum on the school's website. This will need to be monitored carefully, of course, or perhaps pass through a 'gatekeeper' in order to be vetted before comments are made 'live'. In order for it to be viewed as worthwhile, the school will also need to communicate its response to parental comments and suggestions, perhaps through a 'You Said, We Did' page.

Thirdly, **parental communications need to be appropriately timed, relevant and useful** and one way to do this is to utilise the experience and expertise of pupils and their parents. For example, the parents of current Reception or Year 7 pupils will be able to share their thoughts on what information they needed when they went through the transition process with their child not so long ago, as well as when they needed it most, whilst current Reception or Year 7 pupils will be able to offer their advice about how to prepare for primary or secondary school by, to give but two examples, providing a reading list for the summer and sharing their advice on how to get ready for the first day of school.

Fourthly, **parental communication should take many forms and embrace new and emerging technologies**. The use of technologies such as email, texting, websites, electronic portfolios and online assessment and reporting tools have – according to Merkley, Schmidt, Dirksen and Fuhler (2006) – made communication between parents and teachers more timely, efficient, productive and satisfying.

Of course, doing all of this effectively takes time and yet it is important to balance the needs of parents with those of hard-working teachers. You do not want the unintended consequence of effective parental engagement to be an unworkable teacher workload. So, how can you ensure you remain mindful of workload concerns whilst meeting the needs of parents?

The DfE advises that schools do the following:

- Consider why you are communicating. Think about all the communications you make in the day and review if they are making a difference – if not, stop.
- Establish and publish a communications policy or protocol planned around pinch points in the year.
- Start small with little activities that chip away at the time in a working day. Find out which areas of the school generate the

most paper, slips or forms and consider if they are necessary, or if alternative systems can be used.

- Consider running a communications workshop.
- Review staff meetings. Reduce meeting times. Have clear start and end times with timed agenda items. Consider the number of meetings in place each week and provide flexibility. Have a nominated person look over departmental/phase/staff meeting agendas and reject them if they are not focused on pedagogy. Consider using tools like Google Forms to book meetings online.
- Use a variety of communication channels with parents and carers. Add frequently asked questions or 'decision tree' options to the school website to direct users, e.g., a short email may be as appropriate as a phone call, or a phone/video call could replace a face-to-face meeting.
- Apps and software can be used to send letters and reminders home, as well as collecting forms, making payments and booking appointments.
- Consider use of email. Set out times after which staff should not check, send or reply to work emails (whilst being mindful of urgent needs, for example, in relation to safeguarding).
- Use distribution lists and functions such as out of office messages and delayed delivery. All emails should have a descriptive heading with a status assigned to it to signify its urgency.
- Consider a daily/weekly bulletin using cloud services, and alternative messaging tools to reduce emails or categorise messages.
- Review the number and effectiveness of parental events. Consider the impact on pupil progress of each event as well as attendance from parents and balance the range of events on offer. Monitor staffing at events – decide on the supervision required and create a rota to reduce the number of events that staff are required to attend.
- Agree with staff what is a reasonable number of out-of-hours events (taking into account directed time) and prioritise your programme around the capacity you have.
- Review your approach to written reports. Assess the time and impact of current practice. Explore alternatives to written reports. Compare your current approach with the requirements for reporting to parents and the considerations in the Making Data Work report. Consider how reports could be made more succinct (e.g. limiting the word count) and meaningful (e.g.

focusing on key strengths and areas for development), as well as how the right technology can help to automate reporting where possible.

A pragmatic parental engagement policy

There's a growing trend for parents to be given teachers' direct email addresses and for teachers to make a set number of phone calls to parents each week.

Whilst it is undoubtedly helpful for parents to have easy access to their child's teacher, and regular contact between the school and home is a good thing for pupils as we have already seen, it's important, as I say above, to consider the possible unintended consequences of this approach, particularly on a teacher's workload and wellbeing.

I read a tweet just before the pandemic that brought this into sharp focus for me: a teacher tweeted that she'd opened her work email on a Sunday evening just before returning to school after the half-term break to find awaiting her a very long email from a disgruntled parent which, she assumed, had taken most of the holiday to write. The teacher said this had made her feel stressed and sleepless as a result.

Of course, we want parents to work in partnership with us; for them to be involved in – not just informed about – our schools. So, in addition to the DfE advice I shared in the previous article, how might we improve parental engagement without it adversely affecting teachers' workload and wellbeing...?

First of all, school leaders need to remember that they are the gatekeepers: for example, in the case of face-to-face meetings, they should protect their teaching staff and should not let an angry parent see a teacher until there is a noticeable reduction in their aggression (and even then, it may not be the best course of action).

Here, it is worth adopting a clear policy regarding meetings with teachers which has the following caveat at its heart: a teacher's first duty is to teach his or her classes and not to meet with parents; appointments, therefore, have to be arranged in advance and parents without prior appointments will not be seen.

Honesty in the best policy

An effective – and clearly understood - parental engagement policy can solve a lot of these issues. Such a policy should set out what you expect parents to do. Here's an example...

We encourage parents to:

- Be supportive
- Be informed
- Maintain a direct involvement in their child's progress
- Understand what the school is trying to achieve for their child
- Take a positive position - contribute to initiatives like home visits and information-gathering events such as parents' consultation evenings
- Visit school and be informed about issues and initiatives
- Support events that promote the school efforts
- Be aware of and support any home/school agreements

A parental engagement policy should also outline how your school intends to communicate with parents and how it will consult with parents on key decisions. It may be useful to start with a statement of intent such as this:

Our school, in order to be effective, must acknowledge, appreciate and respond to the views of parents. It needs to take informed decisions following consultation.

Your school will communicate with parents in a variety of ways including:

- Parents' consultation evenings
- Open evenings
- Information meetings
- Parents' workshops and discussion forums
- Parents' associations or committees
- Formal questionnaires and market research products
- Regular newsletters
- The school website
- Online reporting and the parents' portal
- Text messaging
- Email

Your school will need a clear strategy for communicating effectively and expediently in each of these circumstances.

As well as writing letters (I'd suggest your school agrees a policy dictating your 'house style' and that letters should be checked and formatted by the admin team), it is likely you will use email and text messaging to communicate with parents. Before relying on email and texts to impart important information, it is vital you understand access arrangements: do all parents have internet and mobile phone coverage and do all parents have the financial means to utilise it? Will you disadvantage some parents if you rely solely on email and texts? You may need to adopt a 'belt and braces' approach to communication by sending a text and/or email to indicate that a letter is on its way.

And what of the school website? Your school should also agree a policy explaining how it will use its website to aid communication. It is likely it will be used for publishing news articles, celebrating school successes and reproducing the school calendar. It may also – and to be an effective school which extends the boundaries of learning, I think it should – use the website for setting work and for providing help and advice to pupils. The website may provide an overview of each course and syllabus being taught in school and may have links to homework tasks and extension tasks should pupils and parents wish to do extra work in order to secure the learning or to revise.

As well as a policy for how your school communicates with parents, it will need a policy for how staff use these means of communication to ensure accuracy, timeliness and appropriateness.

A two-way process – informing *and* involving parents

As we've already seen, effective communication with parents can improve pupils' academic achievement, attendance, punctuality, and their behaviour and attitudes towards school.

In order to be effective, parental communication needs to be two-way, allowing parents to communicate with the school as well as helping the school to communicate with parents. And parental engagement must transcend information-sharing and ensure that communication leads to parents being both informed *and* involved in school life.

I'd like to explore some mechanisms you could use to ensure communication is two-way and enables parents to become involved in the running of your school...

Two-way communication might include:

- Parent conferences or forums
- Parent-teacher associations or school community councils
- Sending home portfolios of pupil work every week or month for parents to review and comment
- Phone calls from teachers and school leaders
- E-mails or updates via the school website
- Text messages

Face-to-face communication, including in the guise of forums, conferences, home visits, open evenings and information evenings are often the most effective form of communication and help to avoid misunderstandings and the escalation of conflict.

However, parental engagement has become increasingly complex as society has changed and as communication methods have evolved and expanded.

This means it's no longer feasible to rely on a single method of communication that will reach all homes and all parents and carers with a single message. Rather, it's essential that a variety of strategies and means of communication, adapted to the needs of particular families and their schedules, are utilised.

Some such strategies might include:

- Parent newsletters
- Annual open days / evenings
- Curriculum information nights
- Home visits (where applicable)
- Meetings in a neutral location such as community facilities
- Phone calls
- Text messages
- Emails

- Annual school calendars
- Inserts in local newspapers
- Governor letters
- Meet the governor events
- PTA letters and leaflets
- Homework helplines / emails
- School website
- Workshops for parents
- Communications that are focused on wider family members with responsibilities such as grandparents, siblings etc

In order to be effective, these communications need to be:

Clear – Information should be given in plain English and avoid room for confusion or misunderstanding.

Timely – Information should be given at appropriate times when action is needed and not too far in the future.

Consistent – Information should be logical and in line with the school's policies, and it should reflect the school's values and attitudes. Information should, ideally, emanate from a single source or be passed through the school office, to avoid contradictory messages being given.

Acted upon – Information requests should be followed up and all promises kept. This might mean being more realistic about what can be achieved in set timescales rather than promising parents the earth in order to appease them.

Parental communication can also be improved by making a habit of positive praise. For example, weekly 'good news' telephone calls to parents by teachers and leaders can help build rapport and establish a strong partnership. When a phone call from school conveys good news, rather than always being about poor behaviour, attendance or progress, the relationship between the home and the school will improve.

However, sometimes, particularly for new teachers, it can be difficult to make that first phone call to a parent or carer. Preparing the call will make it easier and rehearsing the opening lines can alleviate some of the anxiety. For example, before making a call, the teacher could write down the reasons for the call. Here are some other suggested guidelines to help teachers prepare a phone call:

- Introduce yourself – what's your name, what's your role in school and what's your relationship to the pupil
- Tell the parents what their child is studying in class – what's the current topic, how does this fit into the wider curriculum?
- Comment on their child's progress to date – in what ways have they improved over time, what do you predict of their achievements this term/year?
- Comment on their child's behaviour and attitude to learning – are they attentive, keen, hard-working, polite, helpful towards others, etc?
- Inform them of their child's achievements – have they won any awards, received any house points, etc.?
- Inform them of their child's main strengths or share an anecdote about their performance in class
- Ensure the parent knows they can contact you to discuss their child any time in the future and remind them of the ways in which they can stay in touch with school

Using technology

To summarise my advice so far, I would say that there are, to my mind, four cornerstones of effect parental communication:

1. Communication needs to start early and continue throughout a child's schooling.
2. Communication needs to be a two-way process: as well as the school staying in touch with parents, parents also need a means of keeping in contact with the school.
3. Communication needs to be appropriately timed, relevant and useful to parents.
4. Communication needs to take myriad forms.

And one of the best ways to achieve all four of these aims is to embrace new and emerging technologies...

The use of technologies such as email, texting, websites, electronic portfolios and online assessment and reporting tools have – accordingly to Merkley, Schmidt, Dirksen and Fuhler (2006) –

made communication between parents and teachers more timely, efficient, productive and satisfying.

Here are a few suggestions for how technology could be used to help you communicate with parents and, indeed, vice versa:

- Parents could send teachers an email to let them know when the home learning environment may be (temporarily or otherwise) holding a pupil back.
- Likewise, teachers could send parents an email to let them know when issues arise at school which may have a detrimental effect on the pupil, such as noticeable changes in behaviour or deficits in academic performance.
- Teachers could text parents at the end of the day on which a pupil has done something particularly well or shown real progress or promise. Instant and personal feedback like this is really valuable and helps make a connection between the teacher and a child's parents.
- Teachers could send half-termly or monthly newsletters via email to parents to inform them about which topics they are covering in class in the coming weeks, what homework will be set and when, and how parents can help.
- The school could use text, email and the school website to keep parents updated on forthcoming field trips, parent association meetings and other school activities.
- Teachers could use email to send out regular tips to parents on how they might be able to support their child's learning that week/month. For example, they could send a list of questions to ask their child about what pupils have been learning in class. They could also send hyperlinks to interactive quizzes or games.
- The school could use the school website to gather more frequent and informal parent voice feedback about specific topics. For example, they might post a short survey after each open evening and parents' evening.
- The school could provide an online calendar via its website to allow parents to volunteer to help in class, say as reading mentors or helpers at special events.
- An online calendar could also be used as a booking facility to enable parents to make their own meetings with school staff rather than having to phone the school, which many people find daunting.

- The online calendar could prove useful for booking slots at parents' evenings and other open evenings and events, enabling parents to be in control of the times at which they attend school rather than relying on a child and their teachers to agree suitable slots.

Dealing with conflict and complaints

Now let us turn our attentions to when parental engagement goes wrong!

No matter how effective our parental engagement policy and procedures are, there will be times when parents wish to complain or when we have to deal with conflict. So, how can we best resolve disputes? It starts by understanding why conflict might arise...

The human brain is locked in a perpetual fight. In the red corner, we have the limbic system – the primitive 'fight or flight' part of our brain that responds intuitively and emotionally to situations we regard as potentially threatening (whether they be physically threatening – let's say someone wants to punch us in the face, or emotionally threatening – let's say someone wants to pull our trousers down in public). And in the blue corner, there's the frontal lobe which is more logical and rational than the limbic system.

The limbic system is often referred to as 'the chimp' because it is a part of the brain we developed early on our evolutionary journey and first utilised when we had to battle for our daily survival by attacking or outrunning our predators or competitors.

The frontal lobe is often referred to as 'the human' part of the brain because it developed much later as we acquired the art of logic, of thinking through situations rationally, predicting a range of possible outcomes and making informed decisions.

The fight being waged in our heads, then, is between the chimp and the human, between our primitive instincts and our more rational thought processes.

The problem is, it's not a fair fight. The frontal lobe has its hands tied behind its back...

The limbic system - because it is instinctive - is far quicker to act than the frontal lobe and so, by the time the 'human' starts thinking logically about how best to respond to a situation, weighing up the pros and cons of various possible actions, the 'chimp' has already entered into 'fight or flight' mode and is either throwing punches or running for the hills screaming.

Before we evolved, in the fight for our daily survival, the fact the limbic system is fast was a very good thing. After all, as a scary caveman ran towards us brandishing a spear, we didn't want to stand stock-still considering why that person wanted to harm us, what we had said or done to upset them so, and how best we might articulate to them that it's not such a good idea to impale us after all. Rather, we wanted to get out of their way and hide pretty sharpish.

But in the modern world, the limbic system is not quite so helpful.

The brain's battle and conflict management

In terms of dealing with parental conflict, then, it's important we remember this internal battle between our limbic system and our frontal lobe.

When a parent threatens us in some way – by, for example, vocally disagreeing with us or refusing to do as we've asked – our limbic system kicks in first and we respond emotionally. We take it personally, as a slight on our good name and as an insult to our hard work and good judgment. We regard the dissent as threatening to our professional standing and feel angry and hurt.

As well as being alert to our own limbic system, it's important that we also remember that the nature of the attack – and sometimes even the substance of it – is likely to be down to our attackers' own inner chimp. For example, they may be attacking us because they feel threatened by something we've said or done and have therefore responded emotionally rather than rationally because they are in fight or flight mode. Perhaps they are scared of failure. Perhaps they don't understand something but are too embarrassed to say so.

So, what can we do about it? How can we take control our own chimp and how can we manage parents' chimps?

Firstly, although we cannot prevent our limbic system from kicking in first – it's natural and unavoidable – we can actively acknowledge its existence and make it a habit, when conflict arises, to pause before responding to it. There's a reason we are counselled to 'count to ten' whenever we're irritated or angered, after all.

Secondly, we can divorce the personal from the professional. We should never confuse an attack on our decisions as an attack on us as a person. We should remember that any ostensible attack of us is – at worst – an attack on the office we hold, on our job title and role, and not on us as a human being. More likely, it's not an attack at all but, as I say above, a symptom of someone feeling threatened in some way.

Thirdly, we can apologise when our limbic system does get the better of us – as it inevitably will from time to time because we've human and fallible – and acknowledge the way we responded was inappropriate and unhelpful. By doing this, we are showing others that we are human and make mistakes, and yet we are willing to acknowledge, accept, apologise for and learn from those mistakes rather than dig our heels in. By modelling all these things, we are also setting a good example for others to follow. We are, albeit retrospectively, being professional and rational.

The road to breakdown

Often, conflict with an angry parent doesn't erupt suddenly and without warning; rather, it is the result of a slow-burning problem that slowly and incrementally bubbles up towards the surface before exploding.

Conflict might start with a discussion, which leads to a debate then to an argument, before things finally break down.

This 'road to breakdown' is characterised by a desire for one person to change the other, or by one person blaming the other... however...

1. Trying to change someone rarely results in change. Change is more likely to come from understanding. Wanting to change someone implies there is something wrong with that person and, naturally, this only leads to them becoming defensive and argumentative.

Seeking to understand, however, suggests the other person's point of view is valid and reasonable. This is the approach that creates collaboration and mutual problem-solving.

2. Trying to blame someone is reactive and looks to the past, attempting to discern who was right and who was wrong. A better approach is to focus on the future and on how the situation can be resolved. This is the difference between arguing who left the stable door open after the horse has bolted and going out to try find the horse. One approach is reactive, futile and damaging; the other is proactive and solution oriented.

You should remember at all times that your aim is to identify any underlying problems, establish rapport and then find, where possible, a resolution. You can do this by personalising your language: use names and refer to your relationship. You can also reassure the other person: offer them praise where possible.

Sometimes it might be tactical to ignore certain behaviours or incendiary language.

Active listening is a useful skill - give the parent your undivided attention, use eye contact and nod your head to signal you're paying attention. Paraphrase and summarise their points of view by repeating key statements back in your own words and then seek clarification, check your understanding.

Comment on your feelings and their feelings. Use open questions such as, 'Tell me about ...' in order to invite further exploration of the problem.

If a problem persists and an argument escalates, you may need to de-escalate and limit the problem. You can do this by withdrawing your compliance with phrases such as, 'Please stop doing that'.

You could also try to re-direct and/or re-engage the other person's thinking by keeping the person talking or, conversely, by allowing silence to create the space needed for the other person to regain control.

If the meeting is face-to-face, you could sit down which might remove the power disparity but, if so doing, take care not to put yourself at a disadvantage or reduce your ability to escape.

You could encourage a pattern of positive responses: the more 'yes' answers you can obtain, even to less important requests, the more likely it is that the other person will comply with your requests for them to stop difficult behaviours.

You could stay calm which will diffuse the aggressor's anger. Or you could use self-disclosure, reminding the other person that you are human too, not just a job title.

Here are some tips to help disarm someone's anger:

- Listen to what they have to say, don't interrupt and don't jump to conclusions. Stay silent if necessary.
- Make empathetic statements where possible. Try to establish rapport.
- Try to maintain rapport by using open and friendly body language and a calm, considered tone of voice.
- Feedback and clarify what you hear, perhaps by listing the key points as you understand them. Take notes if necessary. Check your understanding and be prepared to be corrected. Don't get defensive, apologise and admit mistakes.
- Remain focused on finding a solution throughout.

You could also use lots of bridging language such as:

- Us, We, Our
- Can, May, Might, Could
- Let's talk
- Appreciate, Understand
- Alternatives, Options, Perspective
- What do you need?
- What do you think?
- How can we?
- Help me understand
- What would you say to...?
- How do you want things to be?
- I want to resolve this with you

...and avoid using barrier language such as:

- Me, I, Everybody
- Should, Need to, Have to, Got to
- Waste of time
- Your problem is
- Opinion
- You always, Never
- Yes BUT
- Why are you?
- Out of the question
- That's my final word, non-negotiable
- You don't understand, listen
- I've heard all this before
- You wouldn't understand

Chapter 23: Learning lessons from lockdown

So far in this final part of the book, we have explored the part ethical leadership might play in our post-Covid schools and colleges, and we have examined the central tenets of effective parental engagement.

Now let us turn to some more specific lessons we have learned as a consequence of the coronavirus pandemic...

Covid-19 was undoubtedly a global crisis. Not since the Second World War have nations been compelled to take such drastic action to protect their peoples.

So, what might we learn from recent experiences about how to improve our schools and colleges over the longer-term...?

Building back better

'Build Back Better' is an approach to post-disaster recovery aimed at increasing the resilience of nations and communities to future disasters and shocks. As a guiding principle, it was adopted by the UN Member States as one of four priorities for disaster risk reduction in the Sendai Framework.

The concept of building back better has its roots in the improvement of land use, spatial planning, and construction standards through the recovery process. But the concept has since broadened to represent a wider opportunity, not just to restore what was damaged or lost to the impact of disasters, but to build greater resilience in recovery by systematically addressing the root causes of vulnerability.

As our schools start the long and difficult process of adjusting to life after Covid-19 and we begin to adjust to a 'new normal', we too might wish to embrace the spirit of 'build back better' by rethinking the way we operate in order to learn lessons from the lockdown.

I am not suggesting that the pandemic will – or indeed should – revolutionise the way our schools and colleges work for this would be to suggest that, before the outbreak, they were in some way broken and of course they were not. Nor I am suggesting that we abandon our traditional ways of teaching in favour of wholesale digital learning simply because we've gained more experience of remote teaching. But I do think we'd be wise to give pause and reflect on what we've learnt and make a commitment to do some things better in the future.

Three stages of recovery

In 2013, writing on ReliefWeb, an information service provided by the United Nations Office for the Coordination of Humanitarian Affairs (OCHA), Melissa Crutchfield suggested that there were three recognisable stages in the process towards recovery: survival, resilience and reconstruction.

Phase 1: Survival

This phase, says Crutchfield, involves immediate responses to the emergency, efforts to minimise the damage and to rescue people. At this stage, people have little capacity to think beyond issues of survival and there is little point in thinking about long-term reconstruction.

"People take one day at a time, retreating into a defensive core, armed against adversity," she says.

And hunkering down is, she adds, an effective strategy. After all, in order to retain inner equilibrium under extreme stress, it is vital to focus on what is within your control – what you can do and what you can change, whilst seeking to ignore everything else.

I would contend that our schools and colleges were at the 'survival' stage in the early days of the coronavirus outbreak as they prepared for partial closure and for the provision of home learning.

Schools necessarily focused on the short-term and, in the case of teaching and learning, this meant identifying the children of key workers and the most vulnerable and working through plans to remain open in order to provide childcare for these youngsters. It also meant providing some short-term study materials to aid the home-schooling of all other children.

But, in so doing, it meant accepting that education in the traditional sense had to be put on hold and that pupils' safety and health and wellbeing were the primary foci. In most cases, schools became childcare facilities, and the teaching of the curriculum was suspended.

Phase 2: Resilience

The second phase of the process of recovery is about the development of 'disaster resilience'. This is the ability of individuals, communities, and organisations to adapt to and recover from disaster without compromising long-term prospects for development. Increased resilience enables people to transition into a recovery phase, in which systems are in place to guarantee survival and people can turn to rebuilding their lives in accord with a 'new normal'.

At this point, some balance has been restored, so that it is possible to begin to plan for the future.

During Covid-19, this stage began with an acknowledgement that schools would remain closed for a significant period of time and that 'busy tasks' were therefore insufficient, and that teaching would have to resume in a more substantial manner and be more closely linked to the national curriculum and qualification specifications.

Schools and colleges therefore redoubled their efforts to provide meaningful work for children to do at home and many schools moved towards providing more 'live' teaching via videoconference software, as well as more online instructional videos and interactive materials. This involved the building of online platforms and in some cases the facility for children to interact with each other in order to maintain friendships and support their mental health and wellbeing.

This stage continued into 2021 as schools considered wider re-opening including how to maintain social distancing and limit transmission of the virus.

Phase 3: Reconstruction

The third stage in Crutchfield's plan is about the long term. Of course, it is difficult to think about the long-term whilst still in the middle of a crisis, not least because all our time and energies were taken to crisis management (just keeping on top of the daily deluge of documents from the DfE was a full-time job).

But post-lockdown and with a programme of vaccinations promising a return to some sense of normality, we are at this stage and this schools and colleges face a choice between trying to rebuild the systems we had before (and return to 'normal') or building new ones (and establishing the 'new normal').

If we do not consider the long term now, we will, I think, be in danger of simply defaulting to 'business as usual' and opportunities could be missed to 'build back better'.

Innovations in working practices

Post Traumatic Growth Theory research highlights the potential for positive growth and development as a consequence of trauma and challenging experiences.

The notion of Post Traumatic Growth Theory is echoed by Build Back Better – an approach to post-disaster recovery aimed at increasing the resilience of nations and communities to future disasters and shocks that was adopted by the UN Member States as one of four priorities for disaster risk reduction in the Sendai Framework.

As I say above, the concept of 'building back better' has its roots in the improvement of land use, spatial planning, and construction standards through the recovery process but it has since been broadened to represent a wider opportunity, not just to restore what was damaged or lost to the impact of disasters, but to build greater resilience in recovery by systematically addressing the root causes of vulnerability.

So, what can schools learn from the coronavirus crisis about the ways in which they operate? What can be 'built back better' in terms of their working practices? And more specifically, how can schools harness technology to improve teachers' work life balances?

These are some of the questions I posed via social media in the eye of the Covid storm. Here is a snapshot of some of the responses I received to the question of what new working practices were effective and should be retained when schools return to normal:

"Remote meetings [with colleagues]."

"Remote meetings with external partners [which] save on travel and time."

"The flexibility to actually work from home should you need to."

"Online, on-demand CPD [which] has been a revelation."

"Remote training [which is] a great way for our team of part-time staff, who work in different places, to keep in touch."

So, let's take a closer look at what we've learned about meetings, flexible working and online CPD...

Virtual meetings

One multi-academy trust Deputy CEO from the midlands told me that the experience of Covid-19 has helped her MAT to appreciate the possibilities available to it to connect with staff from across their trust in more effective and convenient ways.

She told me that weekly Zoom meetings between the central trust team and the Principals and Heads of Academies, virtual governing body meetings, and fortnightly sessions with staff from all year groups really helped support and teaching staff to connect and professionally develop.

Using technology in new ways during the lockdown had also, she explained, increased engagement with families and communities, for example, via Twitter and Facebook daily challenges, films from school staff with positive messages, welfare telephone calls home, working with local welfare charities, and so on.

In short, the use of technology, she said, has been a revelation.

Ironically, by having virtual meetings, many schools and trusts and have been able to meet with more staff which has really enhanced the feeling of being part of the and has allowed leaders to be more efficient with time and costs on meeting face to face for some.

A subject leader at a school in Yorkshire told me that meetings had improved during lockdown because her school came to realise that many meetings could be done online and at various times, which is particularly helpful for those colleagues with families and other after-school commitments.

Online meetings also allow parents to have the pleasure of collecting their own children from school and then enjoy some quality family time as well as being fresher for the meeting.

As well as improving the efficiency of staff meetings, and making meetings with colleagues from different schools in a trust more workable, our recent experiences of lockdown have highlighted the possibility of using technology to enable more flexible working for staff...

Flexible working

Facebook has said it plans to shift towards a more remote workforce as a long-term trend.

Mark Zuckerberg reportedly told staff it was "aggressively opening up remote hiring" in July and that he expects half of Facebook's workforce to do their jobs outside the company's offices over the next five to ten years.

It follows moves by other tech firms in Silicon Valley, including Twitter, which said employees can work from home "forever" if they wish.

Flexible working policies can certainly help retain good staff who wish to work more flexibly for a range of reasons including for childcare.

Meanwhile, New Zealand's Prime Minister Jacinda Ardern has suggested the country may move to a four-day working week, partly to boost tourism in the country.

Ms Ardern has suggested a four-day working week to help boost the economy and address work-life balancing: "I hear lots of people suggesting we should have a four-day work week. Ultimately that really sits between employers and employees. But as I've said there's just so much that we've learnt about Covid and that flexibility of people working from home, the productivity that can be driven out of that."

Our recent experiences of lockdown have the potential to lead to changes to our school day and to working patterns for our staff, too.

For example, many schools can harness the technology they're invested in during lockdown, such as virtual meetings and online on-demand CPD, to ensure that part-time staff are not at a disadvantage and can participate fully in school life. What's more, this, in turn, may lead to more schools recruiting part-time staff or allowing existing staff to work more flexibility.

Flexible working like this is, I think, one key to resolving the teacher retention crisis engulfing the education system.

After all, as I say above, flexible working and part-time contracts are generally viewed positively by teachers and likely to improve recruitment and retention. And 42% of teachers have said they'd like to reduce their hours, with 78% saying they'd prefer a 4-day week.

There is little doubt that technology can help bring these changes about. It can also help provide more flexible access to CPD...

Professional development

One casualty of the lockdown has been teacher CPD in the sense that face-to-face training, such as school INSET days, conferences and open courses held in hotels, have been cancelled or postponed in order to ensure social distancing rules can be observed.

However, in the place of these more traditional forms of CPD, new ways of professional learning have emerged.

Many of these 'new' forms of CPD are not actually new, of course, but were rarely used in the past as most schools and teachers stuck with what they knew best – a face to face training course.

Face-to-face courses are often highly valuable and a way of networking as well as learning from an expert trainer. But they are also time-consuming and expensive, not least in terms of lesson cover, travel and accommodation.

Now, thanks in part to the lockdown, many more teachers are engaging in online on-demand CPD, virtual conferences, and professional development in other forms such as reading academic research and engaging in online networks.

On-demand training can provide greater flexibility than a face-to-face course and can be accessed and worked through at a time and pace suitable to the delegate, making it much more personalised. Online CPD does not impact on teaching commitments, either, making it less disruptive and less costly for schools.

Staff wellbeing

As well as improving access to, and the quality of, teacher professional development, our experience of lockdown could also help us improve our approach to staff wellbeing and welfare.

And staff wellbeing will be more important than ever in the coming months and years because the coronavirus crisis has put teacher's mental health and wellbeing under intense pressure.

Recently, more than half of primary school teachers (59 per cent) and 49 per cent of secondary school teacher told a YouGov TeacherTrack survey, commissioned by the charity Education Support, that they were experiencing higher than usual levels of stress and anxiety because of the lockdown. And more than half of the calls to the Education Support confidential helpline are currently related to coronavirus, the charity says.

Education Support say that this is because teachers have been struggling to juggle online learning with school rotas and many have also been trying to home-school their own children.

Technology may be able to help here, too. As well as providing more flexibility in the way teachers work and facilitating a healthier work life balance as a result, staff can use tech to help them keep in touch with each other and to offer support to colleagues. Tech can also be used to provide helpful information. Many schools have, for example, used tech to create social gatherings for staff so that they have been able to connect on a personal level with colleagues and alleviate some of the stresses of lockdown.

Talking of technology...

Harnessing technology in schools and colleges

Although there is no substitute for face-to-face teaching, the pandemic has highlighted the advantages of educational technology (ed tech) and helped us to realise the potential to extend learning beyond the classroom.

We certainly need to accept that technology will continue to play a part in pupils' learning for the foreseeable future and, rather than reluctantly trying to make it work as best we can, I think we should now embrace it and make a success of it.

So what does good ed tech look like...?

Firstly, I think we should be mindful of the fact that technology is not a panacea. In fact, technology can often detract from learning and the best teaching tends to take place when an educated, experienced expert – a human being – stands at the front of a class of other human beings and engages in effective teacher explanations and modelling.

But there are undoubtedly advantages to blended and flipped approaches and the experience of lockdown has brought these to the fore. It has, of course, also brought some of the issues to the fore, too. So, let us explore some of the advantages and disadvantages of ed tech before we consider our next steps upon re-opening...

The good, the bad and the ugly (truth) about ed tech

As I say, schools and colleges can no longer ignore educational technology – it's been ubiquitous during the lockdown – but that's not to say that all technology is equal or that the use of technology is always preferable to more traditional 'analogue' forms of teaching.

The challenge for schools in the coming months and years will be knowing when to invest in tech, and when to say no to the new.

The good

Firstly, using technology in the classroom can allow for more active learning. For example, the teacher can increase pupil engagement through online polling or asking quiz questions with instantaneous results. Digital textbooks that embed links to relevant materials or pupil-maintained course wikis can also make information more dynamic and engaging.

Secondly, technology in the classroom can help promote fuller participation. Online polling and other tools help to engage all pupils, including shy pupils who wouldn't normally raise their hand in class. Online engagement systems also allow the teacher to check in with pupils at regular intervals in order to receive feedback on their learning.

Thirdly, at the beginning of the lesson, technology can be used to help the teacher gauge pupils' prior knowledge and understanding of a subject. For example, a quick, anonymous onscreen quiz which can inform and direct what the teacher needs to focus on next. Setting the same quiz at the end of the lesson allows pupils to gain a sense of the progress they've made and allows the teacher to assess the effectiveness of her lesson.

Fourthly, classroom 'gamification' – the use of competitive scenarios, and the distribution of points and rewards – can make the classroom more fun and engaging and more relevant to young people's lives outside of school. Games also encourage pupils to accept challenge without fear of failure because they instinctively know that gaming means learning from your mistakes.

Fifthly, technology can afford pupils instant access to new, up-to-date information. There is much value in having high quality, expertly edited textbooks and other printed materials. However, information online is usually more up-to-date and young people used to Google are more likely to engage with it.

Finally, our pupils live in a digital world, are so-called 'digital natives', and developing their use of technology is an important life skill.

In short, we can't ignore tech in the classroom when it is ubiquitous outside of it. Creating presentations, learning to differentiate reliable from unreliable sources on the Internet and maintaining proper online etiquette are all vital skills that pupils can learn in the safe and supported environment of the school classroom.

The bad

For all these advantages, however, we'd be wise to remember that educational technology can also be damaging...

Firstly, technology in the classroom can be a distraction. Research suggests that pupils learn less when they use computers or tablets during lessons than when they rely on more traditional resources such as class debates, textbooks, and pen and paper.

Writing in the New York Times, for example, Susan Dynarski, Professor of Education, Public Policy and Economics at the University of Michigan, said: "The research is unequivocal: Laptops distract from learning, both for users and for those around them."

Secondly, technology can disconnect pupils from social interactions. Many people are sceptical of technology and what it does to pupils' (and everyone else's) ability to verbally communicate.

Thirdly, technology can foster cheating in class and on assignments. While pupils have always found ways to cheat, the digital age makes it even easier - from copying-and-pasting someone else's work to hiring an essay-writer from an online essay factory.

Fourthly, as we seen starkly in recent months, pupils don't have equal access to technological resources outside of school due to socio-economic differences. Expecting all pupils to use technology for remote learning, flipped learning or homework, therefore, can perpetuate the disadvantage gap between rich and poor.

As well as issues around equal access, technology poses safeguarding concerns that cannot be ignored, particularly around cyber-bullying and child protection issues. Furthermore, it is harder to differentiate when using technology – some pupils may have special educational needs that hinder their use of certain technologies and therefore are disadvantaged by its use in class or for homework tasks.

Finally, the quality of online research and sources are variable and hard to verify. The information on Wikipedia, for example, is famously dubious because anyone can contribute to it! The internet is both a blessing and a curse for academic research and school study. Pupils may need guidance on identifying proper sources and unreliable sources.

The ugly truth

There are many pros and cons associated with educational technology so how can schools decide whether to invest further in it as they return to a 'new normal' following the coronavirus pandemic, and, if so, know what's best for pupils and teachers?

The key to technology in the classroom, I would argue, is the teacher-pupil relationship, because that's where education happens – in the space between a teacher and her pupils.

Technology can be a highly effective tool, but that's all it is – a tool. In today's hyper-connected world, sensible use of technology can enhance education but if used poorly or without appropriate instruction and supervision, it can always be harmful and detract from learning.

Technology is not meant to replace the teacher. The evidence around distance learning and flipped learning, for example, is far from encouraging – when technology is used in the absence of a teacher, it is rarely effective.

Ultimately, the success of educational technology depends upon how technology is applied to keep pupils engaged and active. It can be frustrating and time-consuming, it can distract and detract from learning if regarded as a gimmick or game, but in the end technology in education can also open doors to new experiences, new discoveries, and new ways of learning and collaborating.

The future of ed tech

So, what does all this mean for schools and colleges in the coming months and years...?

For the long-term, in terms of teaching and learning technology, we might wish to consider which aspects of remote teaching and learning worked well and should be embraced.

Could we, for example, make better use of digital resources for homework and independent study?

Could we "front-load" some teaching by providing instructional videos for pupils to watch outside of lessons and therefore dedicate more class time to interactions with pupils in the form of discussions, questioning, redrafting work in response to feedback, etc? The recording of such videos seems to have been one of the success stories of education during the lockdown.

Could we provide more retrieval practice activities online or in learning packs to aid long-term learning but without losing too much curriculum time?

If we decide to embrace some form of remote teaching and learning, not just in the medium-term, but in the longer-term too, then we might do well to reflect on what has worked best in recent months...

Remote learning: what works?

In 2020, the Educational Endowment Foundation (EEF) examined existing research from sixty systematic reviews and meta-analyses for approaches that schools could use to support the remote learning of pupils.

When implementing strategies to support pupils' remote learning, or supporting parents to do this, the EEF found that key things to consider include the following:

- Teaching quality is more important than how lessons are delivered
- Ensuring access to technology is key, especially for disadvantaged pupils

- Peer interactions can provide motivation and improve learning outcomes
- Supporting pupils to work independently can improve learning outcomes
- Different approaches to remote learning suit different types of content and pupils

Let's take a closer look at a couple of those points...

Teaching quality is more important than how lessons are delivered

The EEF said that pupils can learn through remote teaching. Ensuring the elements of effective teaching are present – for example clear explanations, scaffolding and feedback – is more important than how or when they are provided.

The EEF found that there was no clear difference between teaching in real time (so-called "synchronous teaching") and alternatives ("asynchronous teaching").

For example, teachers might explain a new idea live or in a pre-recorded video. But what matters most is whether the explanation builds clearly on pupils' prior learning or how pupils' understanding is subsequently assessed.

Supporting pupils to work independently can improve learning outcomes

Pupils learning at home will often need to work independently. Multiple studies reviewed by the EEF identified the value of strategies that help pupils work independently with success. For example, prompting pupils to reflect on their work or to consider the strategies they will use if they get stuck have been highlighted as valuable.

Wider evidence pooled by the EEF related to metacognition and self-regulation and suggested that disadvantaged pupils are likely to particularly benefit from explicit support to help them work independently, for example, by providing checklists or daily plans.

And finally...

In planning the use of ed tech for the longer-term, if we are to consider continuing with some form of remote learning, the following questions may be helpful:

- What level of access do our pupils have to devices and connectivity?
- How much can we ask of our parents and families?
- How much can we ask of our staff and how will we balance the provision of online learning with classroom-based lesson planning and teaching?
- Do we want remote learning to consolidate pupils' existing knowledge, or teach new content?
- Is some form of remote learning desirable and sustainable for everyone over the longer-term?

I will return to the subject of online learning in the next chapter and offer my own suggestions for making a success of remote teaching approaches.

But now I'd like to focus on how we might support pupils who have been most disadvantaged by the pandemic and explore ways to helping them readjust to school-life and address any knowledge gaps that have emerged...

Supporting disadvantaged pupils post-Covid

Vulnerable, disadvantaged and SEND pupils are likely to have suffered the most during lockdown and attainment gaps are likely to have widened.

So, what can we do to support these pupils and help them to catch up with their peers as our schools and colleges begin the long and difficult process of returning to normal?

Our support should, I think, take two forms:

1. Pastoral
2. Academic

Supporting disadvantaged pupils pastorally

In terms of pastoral support, we need to talk to pupils about the lockdown. We cannot simply resume 'business as usual' and assume pupils are ready and able to continue their schooling as if nothing has happened save for an extended holiday.

The lockdown – and the coronavirus pandemic more generally – will have affected pupils to different degrees and in different ways. But we can be certain that they will all be affected in some way and we must therefore acknowledge this and address it.

In so doing, we need to be aware of our pupils' different experiences. Some will have had supportive home environments and may even have enjoyed aspects of the lockdown such as spending more time with loved ones, exercising more, getting out into the sunshine, lie-ins and late nights, and so on. Others may have had deeply distressing experiences including bereavements and, undoubtedly for some, living in stressful, abusive homes.

We should, I think, when discussing the pandemic with groups of pupils, focus on good news and on sharing and celebrating the kindness and self-sacrifice children and others have displayed.

For example, we can talk about how the world has responded, acknowledge the hardship and loss of life, but celebrate the best of humanity too, learn from the way people supported each other, for example by thanking key workers, displaying rainbows and cuddly toys, looking out for vulnerable neighbours, donating to hospitals and care homes etc.

Of course, we also need to address the worst aspects of the experience too. We can talk generally about how to deal with bereavement with groups of pupils but many of the more difficult conversations are, I would suggest, best had with individual pupils.

Addressing pupils' worries including about bereavement

The charity Winston's Wish has produced a number of useful resources to help support schools with difficult conservations with pupils about the coronavirus in general and bereavement in particular.

Firstly, they advise that we teachers acknowledge pupils' worries, concerns and anxieties. A child may understandably be concerned or worried by what they have seen, read or heard in the news regarding the coronavirus, and this anxiety can be heightened for children and young people who have had someone important die. As such, as pupils return to school, it is important to acknowledge their worries.

Winston's Wish say that it's good to talk to children honestly but calmly about what is happening, and not ignore or shield them from what is going on in the world. We should remember that we don't need to have all of the facts and answers.

A gentle conversation can reassure a pupil that they can talk to you so that they don't feel like they're on their own. Children and young people who have been bereaved or are facing the death of someone important, especially during coronavirus, will appreciate people acknowledging their particular concerns.

Secondly, Winston's Wish suggest we reassure pupils. It is natural, they say, that children and young people who have experienced the death of someone important may worry that something will happen to someone else in their family. They will spot false reassurance, but it is reasonable to put what is happening into context in a reassuring way.

It may be helpful to remind pupils that some people only experience mild coronavirus symptoms and reassure them that more people are recovering from the virus than dying from it.

Thirdly, Winston's Wish suggest we talk to pupils about coronavirus. We shouldn't be afraid to have conversations with pupils about Covid-19 – indeed, not talking about something can sometimes make children worry more. After all, other children will be talking about it and they may hear about it on the news or social media.

We may need to gauge their level of understanding or interest first in order to decide what level of detail we need to go into when explaining what is going on.

Supporting mental health

A report by the World Health Organisation entitled 'Building Back Better: Sustainable Mental Health Care After Emergencies' (2013), says that during emergencies, mental health requires special consideration.

This is, they say, due to three common issues:

1. Increased rates of mental health problems,
2. Weakened mental health infrastructure, and
3. Difficulties coordinating agencies providing mental health and psychosocial support.

It is certainly true that many of our pupils will have experienced trauma during the pandemic including, as I say above, as a result of bereavement, and that mental health issues are therefore likely to be more prevalent. It is also true that many pupils with existing mental health problems will have had less support during the lockdown and that accessing specialist support will have been – and will continue to be – more difficult.

A British Psychological Society report called 'Back to school: Using psychological perspectives to support re-engagement and recovery' (2020), says that, in order to support pupils' social, emotional and mental health needs as they return to school, we should first acknowledge that they are going to experience a range of emotions. This may include a mixture of excitement, happiness and relief but it may also include anxiety, fear and anger.

Supporting disadvantaged pupils academically

As well as supporting our vulnerable, disadvantaged and SEND pupils *pastorally*, we will need to address *academic* gaps, too.

Addressing the social and digital divide

The coronavirus pandemic highlighted a deep social divide in the UK. Death rates in the poorest communities were double that of the richest.

Many families live in overcrowded accommodation without outdoor access. Other children and young people live in contexts with difficult and challenging family dynamics, including domestic abuse.

As such, school can be a haven for them.

Considerable numbers of families faced significant financial hardship due to the pandemic, too, and some struggled to feed their children. Many parents lost their jobs or did not qualify for government grants whilst unable to work and earn.

Data from the Institute of Fiscal Studies highlighted how the period of home schooling in 2020 accelerated the attainment gap. The study reported that the most advantaged pupils accessed 75 minutes more educational input each day than their poorest peers. This amounts to more than one and a half weeks more education during the first lockdown than their poorest peers.

With most learning moving online during lockdown, the need to access the internet was also vital. The 'digital divide', therefore, clearly exacerbated the attainment gap.

Community cohesion

We saw writ large throughout the pandemic the crucial role that schools play in their local communities. For example, many schools organised food parcels and supermarket vouchers for those on free school meals, and rallied around local hospitals and refuges, providing essential care packages and so on. Schools were also the main conduit of information for many families, providing a trustworthy voice of reason often lacking from central government.

When planning together and developing support plans to ensure that staff, parents and children feel safe and are supported to readjust, the BPS recommend the following may be useful:

- Establishing an implementation team to organise and monitor new systems and structures.
- Identifying families that might need extra support and inviting families who might have experienced trauma and loss to come forward in confidence.

- Identifying key workers to support people who have experienced financial, social, personal, emotional or safeguarding issues
- Inviting parents to tell school about any worries or concerns they have about their children.

In order to support our disadvantaged pupils post-pandemic, reconnecting with local support services – such as educational psychologists, education welfare officers, children's social services, peripatetic teachers and child and adolescent mental health teams, and mental health practitioners – is also vital.

The trauma gap

In May 2020, the children's charity Barnardo's warned that children had been exposed to "an unprecedented level of trauma, loss and adversity", with those who were already vulnerable likely to have been badly affected.

A report from the charity called 'Time for a clean slate' said the coronavirus crisis and our measures to tackle it "exacerbated existing inequalities", especially for children in unsafe home environments.

The report argued that a return to 'business as usual' could be very damaging for many young people and called instead for a "readjustment period".

It said this might include a more flexible curriculum, time for children to "re-socialise with friends", and a change to the school day to focus more on pastoral care, play, outdoor activities and creative outlets.

Some approaches planned by schools, according to the report, included:

- Planning a gradual, phased return, with a flexible curriculum.
- Risk-assessing children on their return and enabling the most vulnerable children to return first.
- More focus on mental health and wellbeing in lessons.
- Dedicated time for children and young people to talk about their Covid experiences.

- More time for children and young people to play, be creative, and reconnect with their peers.
- More pastoral provision, including one-to-one support for pupils.
- Physical spaces for staff and pupils, e.g., quiet rooms and remembrance gardens.

In the next chapter we will explore the notion of 'lost learning' further. But first we will consider the lessons we have learned about making a success of online learning...

Chapter 24: Online teaching

In the previous chapter I talked about technology and explored the good, the bad and the ugly truth of ed tech.

In this chapter I would like to home in on what we now know works – and doesn't work – when it comes to online teaching and learning...

When the Covid-19 pandemic first struck in early 2020, schools had to adapt quickly to a situation whereby a majority of pupils were forced to stay at home and access remote learning. The monikers given to this form of teaching – that which takes place in the child's home – were varied and, to my mind, not always particularly helpful.

The most common, and the term often used by the UK government, was 'remote learning'. But this, I think, has a number of negative connotations that imply a sense of disengagement – pupils adopting an intellectual and emotional distance (and not just physical distance) from their teachers and their education – and therefore, in my experience, is not 'remotely' accurate.

The term 'home-schooling' is also, to my mind, inaccurate because it suggests teaching has been wholly delegated to parents/carers and families. It also implies that parents are expected to emulate the school-day which, for most, even those parents who are themselves teachers, is an impossible ask.

'Online learning', though perhaps less fraught with negative connotations than 'remote learning', is no more helpful because it suggests that learning from home takes place entirely online – which, in turn, has two misleading implications: firstly, that teaching should be conducted entirely 'live' via video-conference software; and, secondly, that learning should be carried out entirely onscreen, through a laptop, tablet or mobile device.

Although 'distance learning' is still in its infancy and the academic research on the matter is both nascent and inconclusive, we do now know with some certainty, I think, that the learning that takes place away from the school site works best when it is much more nuanced than any of these terms suggest.

I'd therefore like to offer my 3Ms of home learning: mechanisms, mode, and methods. I do so in the hope that, should we need to rely on home learning again in the future, and I think it's inevitable that we will, even for short bursts of time such as during floods or heavy snowfall, we will be better prepared and more successful.

Let us begin, then, by exploring the mechanisms we use to deliver distance learning and ask: should it be online or offline?

1. Mechanisms

Online or offline?

Spoiler alert: my answer is 'both'. I think that some learning should be carried out online, and some offline. Why? Well, it is my belief that we should provide some offline learning because...

Firstly, we need to manage pupils' screen time. Excessive amounts of screen time can have a detrimental effect on pupils' health and wellbeing. For example, staring at a backlit device for lengthy periods of time can be harmful to pupils' eyesight, leaving their eyes dry and potentially leading to retinal damage and blurred vision. Too much screen time can also inhibit sleep and interfere with sleep patterns, leading to a number of physical and mental health issues.

Secondly, we need to be mindful of the digital divide. Many pupils do not have access to a device or broadband internet and thus are at a disadvantage when learning online. Even families we might not ordinarily consider to be disadvantaged may struggle to provide devices to all the children and adults in the house and/or may find Wi-Fi speeds prohibitive. Furthermore, taking part in online lessons, particularly live lessons, requires a quiet workspace in which pupils can concentrate – and many households may not be able to provide this.

So, some offline learning is important but, whereas a diet of online learning alone is not ideal, it is still beneficial as part of a blended approach. In particular, we should provide some online learning because...

Firstly, relying solely on offline resources such as textbooks or worksheets makes it more difficult to monitor pupils and assess them and provide feedback. Even if paper-based work is submitted somehow, this takes more time and prevents timely feedback from being given. Progress is more visible when there is some live – therefore 'online' – interaction.

Secondly, it is harder to motivate pupils when they are working entirely offline and it is more difficult to promote a positive work ethic offline because the pace of their progress and the amount of time that they commit to their studies is not, or at least not as immediately, visible to their teachers. If work is entirely offline, teachers may assume that the work they set is being completed on time but have no easy way of checking this. And pupils have no easy way of getting feedback and of asking for help.

So, some online learning is also important.

And thus, in terms of the mechanisms of home learning, I would advise we plan learning activities that make use of *both* online and offline mechanisms. For example, we might offer a carefully planned blend of live lessons delivered through video-conferencing software, pre-recorded lessons whereby pupils can access clear and concise teacher explanations and modelling at a time which best suits them and as often as they need, pausing and rewinding the videos so they're able to process the information effectively, and textbooks or worksheets, together with physical activities such as exercise.

Let us now explore the particulars of both online and offline learning in more detail. We'll start with online learning...

Firstly, let's look at the different <u>modes</u> that online learning can take...

2. Modes

Online learning: synchronous versus asynchronous

Broadly speaking, there are two modes of online learning: synchronous and asynchronous.

Synchronous learning is 'live' in that the teacher and their pupils are present at the same time and in the same online 'place'. The most common form of synchronous learning is a 'live lesson' delivered using video-conferencing software such as Zoom, Microsoft Teams, Google Meet, and so on.

The advantages of synchronous learning are, I would argue, as follows:

Firstly, it promotes engagement because the teacher can encourage – and indeed compel – pupils to contribute to the lesson just as they would in the classroom.

Secondly, it provides a means of supporting pupils in their learning by answering questions, explaining difficult ideas, offering encouragement and praise, and listening to pupils' concerns.

Thirdly, it proffers a means of assessing pupils and giving them timely feedback. Although work completed asynchronously and offline can also be assessed, this is not usually as timely and tends to be more formal – written comments on pupils' work, say – rather than 'live' low stakes assessments which are conducted as an integral part of teaching, such as in the form of retrieval practice activities, class questioning, and the sharing of worked examples. Feedback can be more impactful when given live, too, because it can be acted upon immediately and whilst the teacher is present.

Finally, synchronous teaching allows pupils to interact with each other, as well as with the teacher, and thus provides the opportunity for peer-assessment and feedback, for passing questions around the class whereby pupils can comment on and add to each other's responses. And synchronous teaching enables social interactions which are crucial to pupils' motivation, engagement, and general health and wellbeing.

All of which is not to suggest that synchronous learning is the gold standard, of course. Rather, synchronous teaching should form just one part of home learning and indeed only a part of online learning...

As well as synchronous learning, online learning should encompass asynchronous activities, too...

Asynchronous learning – whilst still taking place online – does not require 'real time' interactions and does not occur at the same time and place.

The advantages of asynchronous learning, then, are as follows...

Firstly, pre-recorded clips whereby the teacher films short instructional videos and uploads these to the cloud sharing platform for streaming at a later time, allows the teacher to deliver high quality – clear and concise and chunked – explanations of key concepts. These can be streamed at a time and, crucially, a pace that suits each pupil, and as many times as they need to.

Thus, pupils' access to a device and to broadband internet can be better regulated and managed within the family. A quiet space can more easily be found when the timing is flexible. And pupils can manage their own learning more effectively when in control of the video content rather than constrained by the timing and pace of a live lesson.

Secondly, pre-recorded videos which show worked examples can also harness the power of teacher modelling whereby the teacher deconstructs examples of excellence for pupils, showing them how to emulate excellence themselves, rather than presenting 'here's one I made earlier' which is often unhelpful for pupils who are left with little clue as to how to get from where they are to where the finished product is. The best models involve the teacher 'thinking aloud', making their decision-making and other thought processes visible to pupils, and pre-recorded videos allow teachers to do this and allow pupils to listen to those thought processes as often as they need to.

Thirdly, pre-recorded videos can be used for the purposes of re-teaching and re-capping on key ideas, such as threshold concepts, that enable pupils who are progressing at different speeds to fill in any gaps in their knowledge and address any misconceptions or misunderstandings, and thus move forwards in their learning.

Of course, asynchronous learning does not have to originate – or at least not entirely – from the class teacher; rather, to help manage teachers' workloads and provide variety, we might make use of existing high quality online materials such as those provided by BBC Bitesize and commercial software companies such as TTRockstars and Purple Mash.

One further point about online learning before we consider offline materials...

As well as synchronous and asynchronous learning, online learning platforms such as Microsoft Teams and Google Classroom can be used for the issue and collection of work, as well as a means for pupils to ask questions and for teachers to provide ongoing help and feedback. This can be done during live lessons but also asynchronously through chat rooms and forums.

Asynchronous learning does not have to be entirely online, of course. Indeed, as I have already argued, it is advisable to balance pupils' screen time with work set and completed offline.

So what might offline learning look like...?

Offline learning: reading

Firstly, one of the most impactful activities in which pupils can engage is reading. As Jackie Kennedy once said, "There are many little ways to enlarge your child's world. Love of books is the best of all".

We can help parents and carers to develop their children's reading skills whilst studying at home by providing them with some easy-to-follow tips. And we can make sure pupils have easy access to lots of books, including via local library ebook services.

The best way to help children develop their reading skills is to start by modelling fluent reading – in other words, to show them how we read. Accordingly, we should encourage parents to read aloud to their children to demonstrate how they make good use of pace (including pauses) and intonation (emphasising certain words for effect).

Modelling fluent reading also means showing children that in order to read a book in a way that makes sense, we read ahead, we anticipate or guess what's coming next, and we make educated guesses based on the context. (That's how you knew, in the last sentence, to pronounce 'read' as 'reed' and not 'red'.)

Modelling involves two things: showing children how we do it; and narrating our thoughts and decisions by 'thinking aloud'. So, we should also encourage parents to read a page of a book aloud for their children, then get their children to read the same page aloud to them.

Contrary to what many of us used to think, children's reading capabilities are best improved by repeatedly reading the same short texts rather than by reading one long book after another. That's not to say that children shouldn't be challenged to read a whole novel and to do so for pleasure, but if the goal is to explicitly develop reading comprehension, then short texts are best.

Accordingly, we should encourage parents to use – and indeed we could provide – short extracts or passages and save novels for children's private reading pleasure. Once parents have modelled reading fluently and listened to their children reading aloud to them, we should encourage them to move on to comprehension skills. For example, we could encourage parents to ask their children to read a short text then test their understanding of that text.

Here, the goal is to help children develop the following comprehension skills:

- **Predict**: whilst they're reading aloud, ask children to guess what might happen next – this will also make sure they pay more attention to the text

- **Question**: ask children to think of questions they'd like to ask about the text, ask why they'd ask those questions and at those points in the text; ask children to tell us anything they're unsure about in the text and ask them how they might gather further information to help them become more certain

- **Summarise**: ask children to briefly describe what's just happened in the text or, alternatively, ask them to create a timeline showing how the plot is developing, or to write pen portraits of key characters

- **Infer**: inference is about drawing conclusions from what is suggested in a text. For example, if someone said, 'Please can you close the window?', we might infer that it was cold in the room. They didn't explicitly say it was cold, but we made an educated guess. Here, ask children to infer the meaning of sentences from their context, and the meaning of words from spelling patterns. Or ask them to infer what characters really mean by what they say.

- **Connect**: the more children know about the world, the easier it is for them to learn more. So, to help them, ask children to tell us what they already know about the topic of the text we are about to read, or are reading, and ask them to make links. Schema theory teaches us that there are 3 useful links to make here: between the text and other texts children have read before, between the text and children's own life experiences, and between the text and what children know of the wider world.

Next, we might want children to read a longer passage or perhaps a chapter of a book by themselves and, depending on their age, in silence. To ensure they continue to pay close attention to the text and understand what's being said, parents can stop them at certain points and ask them questions.

Here, parents can help children to develop their reading comprehension skills by using the PEER framework which, again, you could copy and paste and provide as a guide to parents:

P*rompt your child to say something about the book*
E*valuate their response*
E*xpand their response by rephrasing or adding information to it*
R*epeat the prompt to help them learn from the expansion*

The prompts that make up the P of PEER can be remembered using the acronym CROWD:

***C**ompletion—leave a blank at the end of a sentence for children to complete*
***R**ecall—ask children about something they have already read*
***O**pen-ended—often with a focus on pictures in books*
***Wh**—prompts that begin with 'who', 'what', 'where', 'why', and 'when'*
***D**istancing—connects the book to children's own life experiences and provides an opportunity for high quality discussion.*

Offline learning: textbooks

Secondly, good quality textbooks can be highly effective because they provide ready-made lessons with accompanying reading materials, worked examples, retrieval practice activities and tests. The reading materials tend to be well-selected and the presentation of the materials well-thought-out.

Textbooks are written by experts in their field and in a language that is appropriate to the age of the pupil. Textbooks are also logically planned and thus learning is sequential.

Textbooks are also easy to manage in the home – certainly easier than online resources. Many textbooks have answers at the back which makes the task of monitoring progress and giving feedback easier – and less stressful – for parents and carers.

Textbooks are far easier to manage than online resources which require devices and internet connections and can be completed anytime anywhere. Textbooks also provide time away from the screen and, as well as being good for the eyes, they help limit the number of distractions a pupil is faced with such as social media and gaming.

In addition to textbooks, teacher-produced worksheets and other handouts can be used to provide paper-based activities and assessments. The advantage of teacher-produced resources is that they can be tailored to the class and to the topic being taught. They can complement online learning and provide effective retrieval practice activities.

Offline learning: IRL

Recently, I played a game of Trivial Pursuits with my youngest daughter and was asked to explain what several internet-based acronyms stood for. Not being 'down with the kids', I failed miserably. Though I knew what LOL meant – certainly better than former Prime Minister David Cameron did – I struggled with TTYL among others. But, in my defence, I did know what IRL meant: 'in real life'. IRL refers to what happens in the physical world as opposed to on a computer. As such, I think we need to provide learning opportunities that allow pupils to interact with the real world...

Thirdly, then, offline learning can – and, I would argue, *should* – extend education beyond the screen and beyond pen-and-paper. Physical activities including exercise can be used as an antidote to desk-based tasks and offer a means of keeping pupils healthy. They can also ensure pupils engage with the world around them.

When the UK entered its first lockdown as a consequence of the Covid-19 pandemic in March 2020, I wrote an article for an education magazine in which I suggested our first priority should be to try help keep children physically and mentally healthy. And that advice still holds...

In terms of keeping physically healthy, I said, we should encourage daily exercise. There are plenty of online workout videos to choose from.

In terms of keeping mentally healthy, I said, we could provide mindfulness activities and we should remember that our pupils are likely to miss their classmates and so, if possible, we should find ways of helping them to safely maintain contact with their friendship groups.

One other way in which we can help to support our pupils' physical and mental wellbeing is to encourage them – and, in the case of younger children, their parents – to establish a routine including what time children get up, get dressed and have breakfast. Pupils need to be reminded that they are not on holiday and need to 'attend' learning sessions, work hard and meet deadlines.

We might encourage pupils to work to a timetable – but, if so, we need to be cautious and pragmatic about this. Not all pupils will be able to stick to a rigid plan and many will lack the support or home environment conducive to such a formal approach.

Instead of a rigid timetable, however, I would advise we provide pupils with a list of tasks to be completed by the end of the day or week, rather than time-stamped 'lessons' such as '9am English, 10am Maths, etc.', because those timings may become a millstone around our – and their – necks.

A 'to-do' list approach will also afford children – and their parents – some control over what they do and when, and that element of choice should help to motivate them. If they get bored of their maths worksheet, they can stop and play some educational games or follow an exercise video and come back to the maths later in the day.

Whatever approach is taken, I argued in March 2020 and still believe today, we need to allow plenty of free time for games and practical, creative activities. If we can encourage parents to combine the work that we set with educating children about household tasks and home economics, as well as current affairs, then all the better. For example, pupils might be encouraged to bake, to garden, to use their daily exercise to conduct research in the local community or conduct a treasure hunt, to partake in shopping for food, planning and costing meals, and so on. Learning opportunities in the home are practically endless and almost all useful in preparing young people for their later lives.

So far, we have explored the mechanisms – online and offline – and the modes – synchronous and asynchronous – of home learning. Now let us turn to my third and final 'M': methods.

3. Methods

We will begin with the methods of effective online synchronous learning...

Online synchronous learning methods

It is helpful, I think, to start every 'live' lesson with an orientation screen, perhaps in the guise of a presentation slide we can display to pupils by sharing our screens via video conferencing software. Such a slide might contain the learning intentions for the session, instructions for engaging and interacting with others during the session, and a list of tasks. It might also contain reminders regarding mics and cameras, and the use of 'chat' functions and so on. Starting each 'live' lesson with the same screen is a good way of reinforcing rules and routines, and will eventually automate some of these instructions, thus establishing good learning habits.

Along similar lines, we may get into the habit of setting a starter task as soon as pupils join the 'live' lesson, perhaps in the form of a retrieval practice activity such as a multiple-choice quiz, in order to activate prior learning, assess pupils' knowledge, and get the lesson off to a quick, purposeful start.

To ensure starter tasks are effective and engage all pupils, it is advisable to establish habits regarding how pupils will be assessed. For example, if you begin with a short multiple-choice quiz, you may ask pupils to type their answers into 'chat' but only press 'enter' when instructed to do so in order to ensure that every pupil takes part and does not simply copy their peers' responses. Or you may 'cold call' on some pupils to answer questions, thereby ensuring every pupil knows they must be prepared to answer when asked.

In classroom learning, we use pupil names often. Live online lessons should be no different. It helps to develop engagement and motivation to use pupils' names online as much as possible, both verbally but also in the 'chat' function.

Targeting questions in 'chat' at named pupils ensures they all remain in readiness and helps to assess individual progress, rather than repeatedly hearing feedback from the most loquacious pupils in the group.

When asking questions, either verbally or via a slide or the 'chat' function, it is helpful to allow sufficient 'take up' time, just as we would build 'wait time' into our classroom questioning. Take-up time not only allows pupils time to think through their responses and then consider how to articulate those responses, but it also helps ensure more pupils can answer the question and thus leads to more varied answers being given.

In some ways, the unfamiliar nature of online learning hinders pupils' cognition and so there's an argument for allowing more 'take up' time online than we would ordinarily do in the classroom.

It is important that 'live' lessons make use of the fact that the teacher and pupils are present at the same time and thus, as well as asking questions and assessing progress, there should be frequent checks of understanding, too. These can be done verbally, perhaps using the 'cold call' and 'show call' methods outlined in the book, Teach Like a Champion, but also in the 'chat' function. Checks of understanding should be both individual and whole class. Talking of which...

There should, I think, be a balance of individual and whole-class feedback during 'live' lessons. Whole-class feedback might take the form of worked examples using one pupils' work, identifying common misconceptions or mistakes made by the class. Individual feedback can be given verbally in response to specific responses, and also via 'chat'.

I've developed a mnemonic to help improve the assessment of pupils' work during online lessons.

The mnemonic is PACED, and it stands for:

Plan: Know where you want learners to go then assess where they are now

Activate: Start each online session with learners writing down/telling you what they already know about the topic

Cogitate: Ask questions that require learners to think and will provide insights into their understanding

Engage: Answers need to be garnered from all or most learners to inform future instruction

Develop: Aim to improve the learner not the work, fix the future not the past; use live mark-up

The strategies I outline above, you will have noticed, are not dissimilar to those I would recommend we use during face-to-face classroom teaching. And that is an important point: online learning is not significantly different to classroom learning and so what we know works in traditional classroom settings should also work online. What's more, we do not want to throw the baby out with the bathwater and start designing wholly different curricula or brand-new assessment systems because that is not only time-consuming but likely to fail.

At its simplest, as per my mnemonic above, during online lessons we want to move pupils forwards and that requires knowing where pupils are now and where we want them to be. That, in turn, requires two things: a means of assessing pupils' current knowledge and skills, and a curriculum plan that clearly identifies the knowledge and skills we need pupils to acquire by the end of each lesson or sequence of lessons.

One of the best ways to assess starting points – and also activate prior learning – is to begin each session with a retrieval practice activity. As I say in my mnemonic, this could be as easy as sharing the learning intentions of the session then asking pupils to write down what they already know about a topic.

To help ensure pupils then focus on the curriculum content we have planned for them to learn that session, we need to make sure they pay active attention to that content – and thus avoid any distractions – and think hard about that content.

As well as sharing learning intentions, we can aide this process by asking questions that require pupils to think about the curriculum content we need them to learn and ensure we survey as many responses as possible so that we know whether or not pupils are making progress and whether or not we need to reteach or recap or can move forwards.

Online asynchronous learning methods

If we decide to use pre-recorded instructional videos, and other asynchronous methods of learning online, then it might help to structure this in order to ensure that pupils 'attend' sessions and process what they have watched.

When engaging in classroom-based learning, I advocate following a 4-step teaching sequence for introducing pupils to new information. I covered this in Book Two so, briefly, those four steps are as follows:

1. Telling
2. Showing
3. Doing
4. Practising

Telling – or teacher explanation – works best when the teacher presents new material to pupils in small "chunks" and provides scaffolds and targeted support.

Showing – or teacher modelling – works best when the teacher models a new procedure by, among other strategies, thinking aloud, guiding pupils' initial practice and providing pupils with cues.

Doing – or co-construction – works best when the teacher provides pupils with "fix-up" strategies – corrections and "live" feedback.

Practising – or independent work – works best when the teacher provides planned opportunities in class for extensive independent practice.

Of course, the learning process does not end here. Rather, pupils need to garner feedback on their independent practice and then act on that feedback in order to improve by increments.

Let's take a more detailed look at each step before considering how we might adapt this sequence for online asynchronous learning...

Telling

The most effective, expedient way for pupils to acquire new information is for the teacher – that educated, experienced expert at the front of class – to tell them what they need to know.

This is not to suggest that sometimes, for some purposes, other approaches are not also effective, but teacher explanations remain the most efficient method of teaching – not to mention the least likely to lead to misconceptions among pupils and a misunderstanding by the teacher of what pupils can and cannot do. So, what are good explanations made of?

First, good explanations involve metaphors and analogies because this enables the teacher to contextualise new information so that abstract ideas or hitherto alien concepts are made concrete, tangible, and real, and so that they are related to pupils' own lives and experiences.

Second, good explanations make effective use of dual coding. In other words, teachers' verbal instructions, as well as any text-based explanations displayed on the board or in handouts are paired with and complemented by visuals such as diagrams, charts, graphics and moving images.

And finally, good explanations are reciprocated, with pupils explaining concepts back to the teacher as well as to each other. This works on the basis that only once you teach something have you truly learned it. Learning by teaching works because, by teaching, pupils gain feedback and make better sense of a topic. Learning by teaching also works because it is a form of learning by doing, of practising, and thus provides a source of both intrinsic and extrinsic motivation.

Showing

Once teachers have explained something, they should make effective and plentiful use of models – exemplars of both good and bad work, as well as exemplars from a range of different contexts – which show pupils what a final product should look like and what makes such products work.

Good models demonstrate what works as well as what doesn't. It is important to show pupils what excellence looks like by sharing models of the very best work, giving them something to aspire to, and an understanding of how to produce high-quality work of their own.

But it is equally important to show pupils models of ineffective work, work that isn't quite the best (or perhaps is so very far from being the best) so that pupils can learn what not to do and how to avoid making the same mistakes themselves.

All the models that are shared should be dissected in front of pupils, with the teacher demonstrating the dissection process.

For example, if a model of a persuasive speech is shown on the board, the teacher should analyse it using text marking, pointing out and then annotating how it works, what makes it effective, breaking it apart to identify and discuss each of its component parts. Then the teacher should reconstruct the speech, explaining how the component parts hang together to create an effective argument, how the whole becomes something much greater than the sum of its parts.

Once pupils know how to dissect models, they should be afforded the opportunity to do so without the teacher's guidance, perhaps by teaching other pupils. In order to prepare pupils for this, it is important that the teacher offers encouragement, gives specific instructions, uses thought or sentence stems to provide pupils with the right language, and – as I say above – directly demonstrates the process first.

Doing

Once the teacher has modelled something at the front of class, it is important to do so again but, this time, with pupils' help. Co-construction (or joint construction) works well because the teacher engages pupils' thought processes and helps them by questioning their decisions and by prompting further decision-making.

The teacher's role is not to construct another model herself but to ask targeted questions of pupils to encourage them to complete the model together, as well as to provide corrections and feedback along the way, and drip-feed key vocabulary into the mix.

For instance, and to return to the example above, if a teacher has explained to a class how to write a persuasive speech and then modelled doing so on the whiteboard while thinking aloud, she might then ask the class to produce a persuasive speech of their own.

The teacher may begin by asking the class to determine an audience and purpose for the speech, then prompt pupils to debate and decide upon the tone of the writing.

The teacher might ask a pupil to come up and write the first sentence and then ask other pupils to comment on it. She might drip-feed technical vocabulary into the conversation where appropriate (reminding pupils, for example, that placing two contrasting ideas side-by-side is called "juxtaposition") and she might encourage pupils to repeat it and use the correct term in future. She might ask pupils to model their thought processes, thinking aloud as they write, explaining the reasons for their choices.

The teacher, therefore, will mostly be engaged in asking open questions, such as: "Why did you choose that word? "Is there another word which might fit better or have more impact? Why is this word better than this one? Should we use a short sentence here? Why/why not? What is the effect of this, do you think?"

Practising

Once the class has constructed a model together, they need to do so independently.

Independent practice not only provides a crucial third opportunity for pupils to practise – after teacher modelling and co-construction – it also enables pupils to demonstrate their own understanding and for the teacher to assess the extent to which they have "got it".

Until a pupil completes a task by themselves, we – and perhaps they – cannot be certain that they can do it or that information has been encoded in long-term memory.

If pupils succeed, the teacher can move on. If not, the teacher can use the feedback information to guide further teaching of the subject, perhaps re-teaching key elements of it or engaging those pupils who have succeeded in teaching those who have not.

The feedback loop

The four-part teaching sequence is not the end of the learning process, because once pupils have practised new learning, we need to provide planned opportunities for them to be assessed (by themselves, by each other, or by us) and receive feedback on what they have mastered and what they still need to practise. Then, crucially, we need to provide planned opportunities in class for them to act upon that feedback.

Most of the above advice can of course be applied to online learning, too, including 'live' lessons. But it might be helpful to adapt it for online asynchronous modes of learning.

For asynchronous learning, I would suggest this five-step process instead:

1. Explain it
2. Note it
3. Model it
4. Support it
5. Revise it

Here are those top 5 tips in more detail...

1. Explain it

Although it may be possible, particularly for small cohorts of older students, to make a success of video-conferencing software in which the teacher delivers a 'live' interactive lesson and in which pupils participate, it's hard to get this right and, for many pupils, it will only distract them from their learning.

When pupils interact online, it's also important to consider the safeguarding implications.

But, whilst live videoconferencing can be a minefield, pre-recorded video can be used effectively to deliver teacher explanations.

Here, the videos are made available for pupils to watch at a time suitable to them, but within set timescales. It is possible on some platforms to monitor who 'attends' each video (and watches in full) to ensure full participation.

The videos usually work best when they are short, focused on a small amount of information at a time, given in clear steps, i.e. chunked, and when the explanations are clear and concise.

I've learned from experience that teaching via video is very different to standing in front of a class.

For example, I've learned that explanations should be delivered in short chunks, with longer pauses for punctuation than you would ordinarily think to give when face-to-face with pupils. The language needs to be simpler, too, and body language should be kept simple.

It also works best when you complement a video of yourself talking with slides and other materials. In order to achieve this, most platforms allow you to share your screen.

It might be helpful to provide a knowledge organiser using Google Classroom or Microsoft Teams before pupils watch the video on which pupils can make notes (on which more in a moment) and perhaps complete a pre-quiz to activate prior learning and assess starting points.

As with teacher explanations delivered in the classroom, as outlined above, direct instruction via video works best when it includes **metaphors and analogies** because this enables the teacher to contextualise new information so that abstract ideas or hitherto alien concepts are made concrete, tangible, and so that they are connected to pupils' own lives and experiences.

Video-based explanations also tend to work best when the teacher makes effective use of **dual coding**. In other words, verbal instructions are paired with and complemented by visuals such as diagrams, charts, graphics and moving images.

Here, screen-capture software is useful because it allows teachers to record their explanations over the top of presentation slides, a virtual whiteboard or other text-based resources, and to do so in 'real time' and in a natural manner. Many video-conferencing software packages also allow teachers to 'share their screen' so that they can complement their verbal instruction with visual resources.

2. Note it

Once pupils have watched a pre-recorded video, they should be required to write about what they've learned.

As I say above, we might support this process by providing a knowledge organiser in advance, or perhaps just a simple, partially pre-populated Cornell note-taking pro-forma.

Writing about your learning is a form of self-explanation which is proven to be an effective study aid.

Whether pupils use a partially pre-populated worksheet or just write freehand in a cloud document, say, is up to you and will be informed by the pupils' ages and abilities.

The key is to ensure pupils write in order to learn and that this writing is shared with you and possibly the whole class.

Mind-maps and other visual aids might also be used, in addition to notes, to help pupils process and structure their thoughts.

A health-warning, though: If you expect pupils to use something like Cornell, it's important they are taught how to do so first.

If research and study skills were not explicitly taught in the classroom before online learning takes place, it can be done via a short video tutorial now and it might be worth curating a digital library of short 'how-to' videos on generic skills like this. You'll find some online but may favour recording your own.

The final product is not necessarily important, though; rather, it's the act of writing about one's learning that matters here...

Steve Graham, Sharlene A. Kiuhara, and Meade MacKay from Arizona State University and the University of Utah recently performed a meta-analysis called *The Effects of Writing on Learning in Science, Social Studies, and Mathematics* in which they examined if students' writing about content material in science, social studies, and mathematics facilitated learning.

They concluded that writing about content reliably enhanced learning (effect size = 0.30). It was equally effective at improving learning in science, social studies, and mathematics as well as the learning of primary and secondary school pupils.

3. Model it

To complement and extent our pre-recorded video explanations, we might also share models of excellence with pupils, perhaps in the form of worked examples.

These can be shared via video, say by us producing a model on a virtual whiteboard, or as additional written resources shared via Google Docs or Microsoft Teams.

Good models demonstrate what works as well as what doesn't. We might, therefore, show pupils what excellence looks like by sharing models of the very best work, giving them something to aspire to, and an understanding of how to produce high-quality work of their own.

But we might also show pupils models of ineffective work, work that isn't quite the best (or perhaps is so very far from being the best) so that pupils can learn what not to do and how to avoid making the same mistakes themselves. Perhaps they could be tasked with identifying mistakes or aspects of the work that could be improved.

What is important is that these models are dissected for pupils, with us demonstrating the dissection process either 'live' via video or as a worked example where we show our thought processes or 'workings out' on paper.

4. Revise it

Once we've delivered teacher explanations via pre-recorded video, encouraged pupils to write about their learning, and shared worked examples to model the process we want them to follow, we need pupils to practise the learning...

We can help pupils to practise prior learning by helping them to engage in self-quizzing, elaboration, generation and calibration...

Self-quizzing

Self-quizzing is about retrieving knowledge and skills from memory and is far more effective than simply re-reading study notes.

When pupils read a text or their notes, we need to encourage them to pause periodically to ask themselves questions – without looking in the text – such as:

- What are the key ideas?
- What terms or ideas are new to me? How would I define them?
- How do the ideas in this text relate to what I already know?

We should encourage pupils to set aside a little time each week to quiz themselves on the work they've done, as well as what they learned in school before closure.

Once they've self-quizzed, pupils need to check their answers and make sure they have an accurate understanding of what they know and what they don't know.

Pupils need to know that making mistakes will not set them back, so long as they check their answers later and correct any errors.

We should help pupils pace out their retrieval practice. This means studying information more than once and leaving increasingly large gaps between practice sessions. Initially, new material should be revisited within a day or so then not again for several days or a week.

When pupils are feeling more certain of material, they should quiz themselves on it once a month.

They could also interleave the study of two or more aspects of a related topic so that alternating between them requires them to continually refresh their memories of each aspect.

Elaboration

Elaboration is the process of finding additional layers of meaning in new material. It involves relating new material to what pupils already know, explaining it to somebody else, or explaining how it relates to the wider world.

We could encourage pupils to explain their learning to their parents or to us and each other via Google Classroom, Microsoft Teams, etc.

One way to elaborate is to use flashcards with a question on one side and the answer on the other. Websites like Quizlet allow pupils to create and share the flashcards and to test themselves repeatedly.

Generation

Generation is when pupils attempt to answer a question or solve a problem before being shown the answer or the solution.

The act of filling in a missing word (the cloze test) results in better learning and a stronger memory of the text than simply reading the text. Before pupils read new material (e.g., that provided by us on Google Classroom, MS Teams, or online), they should be encouraged to explain the key ideas they expect to find and how they expect these ideas will relate to their prior knowledge.

Reflection

Reflection involves taking a moment to review what has been learned. Pupils need to ask questions such as:

1. What went well? What could have gone better?
2. What other knowledge or experience does it remind me of?
3. What might I need to learn in order to achieve better mastery?
4. What strategies could I use next time to getter better results?

Calibration

Calibration is achieved when pupils adjust their judgment to reflect reality – in other words, they become certain that their sense of what they know and can do is accurate.

Often when pupils revise information, they look at a question and convince themselves that they know the answer, then move on to the next question without making an effort to actually answer the previous one.

If pupils do not write down an answer, they may create the illusion of knowing when in fact they'd find it difficult to give a response.

We need to encourage pupils to remove the illusion of knowing and actually answer all the questions even if they think they know the answer and that it is too easy.

Here are some other study skills we might want to encourage our pupils to use at home:

- Anticipate test questions during study.
- Read study guides, finds terms you can't recall or don't know and learn them.
- Copy key terms and their definitions into a notebook.

- Take practice tests.
- Reorganise class material into a study guide.
- Copy out key concepts and regularly test yourself on them.

5. Support it

Some pupils will need more help than others. As such, although whole class videoconferences are unlikely to be effective for most cohorts, it might be worthwhile scheduling days and times when you'll be online and available for pupils (and possibly their parents) to log on and talk to you.

You should stick to set times and not make yourself available 24/7 and you should set clear parameters –good digital hygiene, if you like – about what is acceptable behaviour that must be obeyed. You need to think carefully about safeguarding and about protecting yourself if making direct contact with pupils whilst working from home.

You could complement this 'surgery' style of support, with regular scheduled phone calls to the most disadvantaged pupils and their parents, as well as those with additional and different needs.

Finally, keep it simple...

We need to avoid placing barriers in the way of our pupils' – and their parents' – home learning.

One way to do this is to choose one platform and try to create a 'one-stop-shop' so that pupils are not required to navigate through the labyrinthine corridors of several different systems. In other words, try to stick with Google *or* Microsoft rather than a combination of systems.

If you do need to use different standalone platforms such as TTrockstars and Mathletics, then curate these on one page of your website so that different services are always just one click away. And consider quick and easy ways of parents accessing their usernames and passwords, and of requesting IT support from school.

Further advice

We have now explored my 3Ms for home learning: mechanisms, modes and methods.

I'd like to share some further tips for making a success of home learning...

A. Variety

Once we have settled upon the best mechanism, mode and methods for teaching pupils remotely, we want to ensure that the work we set them to do at home is varied, both in terms of fulfilling a 'broad and balanced' curriculum, and in the form and format it takes. For example, although there are many excellent online platforms and services, as I have already argued, we want to manage children's' screen time. We also need to be cognisant of the fact that some pupils will not have a device or internet access. It would be wise, therefore, not only to provide digital resources for those in need, but also to ensure some work is paper-based and/or requires children to be active, moving around the house.

B. Autonomy

We should also be mindful that many children will not have support at home and so we should not rely on parents being able to help. As well as providing a means for pupils to seek help from us, their teachers, we should try to ensure most work can be completed independently and the best form of independent work is retrieval practice – in other words, the active revision of prior learning.

C. Workload

We don't want to reinvent the wheel – not least because to do so in time-consuming during a period of anxiety for teachers. Therefore, we should make full use of all the free resources available to us. As well as utilising commercial online learning platforms and BBC Bitesize, we should also make use of existing learning plans and resources in school, not regard the situation as a blank canvas. Do we have work already on our VLEs we can use? Can we tweak existing schemes of work and lesson plans for home learning?

Teacher CPD

Of course, if we are to deliver effective online learning, we must ensure that teachers are helped to develop the requisite knowledge and skills. Any professional development aimed at helping teachers to improve their online teaching should, I think, be the following:

- **Subject-specific** – just as teaching in the classroom is determined by the subject discipline being taught, because every subject takes a different shape, online learning must look different in each subject. No one size fits all. As such, we must make sure that teacher CPD on online pedagogies has a subject-specific element and is not entirely 'off the peg'.
- **Teacher-led** – there needs to be balance of academic research, external expertise and peer-to-peer training and support. Teachers must be afforded the opportunity to share good practice with colleagues and to learn from each other's practical experiences of teaching in their contexts.
- **Flexible and accessible** – online learning, certainly during a pandemic, is exhausting and intrudes into teachers' home lives. Teacher CPD, therefore, needs to be flexible both in terms of when and how it is accessed, and at what pace it is completed. It also needs to be easily accessible from the home and with little prior knowledge or skill in specific software packages. Teacher CPD must help not hinder teachers and thus must not be too time-consuming or add to their busy workloads.
- **Practical and impactful** – all teacher CPD works best when it is anchored in the daily lives of teachers and thus leads to tangible take-away actions which can be put into practice immediately and be evaluated. Teacher CPD on online learning should be no different: it needs to be related to the everyday task of teaching online, be practical not too theoretical, and lead to demonstrable impact.

The 5 principles of home learning

I have long shared five principles of home learning, usually shared in the context of improving the effectiveness of homework. But those five principles apply here, too. Those principles are as follows:

1. Home learning should be clearly related to what pupils have been doing in school
2. Home learning should be varied and manageable
3. Home learning should be challenging but not too difficult
4. Home learning should allow for individual initiative and creativity
5. There should a mechanism for pupils to receive guidance and support, and for recognition or reward for work done.

Assessing lost learning after home-schooling

Now pupils have returned to classroom-based learning, we might wish to turn our attention to the issue of their so-called 'lost learning'... although I am uncomfortable with the term 'lost learning', and all the rhetoric around it, for several reasons... let me explain...

The problems with 'lost learning'

Firstly, any talk of 'loss' is, I think, to adopt a deficit model.

I am not suggesting that the Covid-19 pandemic, for example, has been a positive experience; of course, it has not. Many of us lost loved ones and many had difficult lockdown experiences – isolation, mental health crises, domestic violence, and so on.

But to adopt a deficit model is, in my opinion, to double-down on the problems that led to us relying on home learning methods in the first place.

If we talk to pupils about their lost learning, about their lack of progress, and about gaps in their knowledge – as well as about the devastating consequences of the pandemic – we only serve to heighten their anxieties and thus delay their return to 'normality' and stunt their future progress.

Secondly, how do we know if pupils have 'lost' any learning at all? How are we quantifying this loss? Is such data accurate and is it helpful?

A joint study by the Nuffield Foundation and the National Foundation for Educational Research (NFER) published on 1 September 2020 and based on a weighted sample of almost 3,000 school leaders and teachers across over 2,200 mainstream primary and secondary schools in England, had a somewhat damning conclusion:

"Nearly all teachers estimate that their pupils are behind in their curriculum learning, with the average estimate being three months behind. Over half of teachers estimate that the learning gap between disadvantaged pupils and their peers has widened."

The report also found that teachers in the most deprived schools were over three times more likely to report that their pupils were four months or more behind in their curriculum learning than teachers in the least deprived schools.

I don't doubt the integrity of the researchers nor that of the school leaders and teachers who took part in the survey but how accurate can this data be? It all seems a little spurious to me. How are teachers quantifying lost learning – what is a month of learning? – and are they all using the same metric?

Pupils may have 'lost' a few months of classroom teaching and therefore they might not have been taught parts of the planned curriculum, and home-schooling experiences will undoubtedly have been varied, but does this equate to 'lost learning'? Do we really know how effective home-schooling and online learning was? Do we really know what pupils have retained and what they have 'forgotten' over the course of lockdown? And do we know what effect the parts of the planned curriculum we did not cover before the summer will have on pupils' long-term learning and progress?

Thirdly, do we actually mean 'lost learning' at all? Or are we talking about something else entirely?

Above I placed the word 'forgotten' in inverted commas because learning (and forgetting) is, we know, a complex beast.

Paul von Hippel, an associate professor in the LBJ School of Public Affairs at the University of Texas at Austin, studied summer learning loss in 2019. He found that it might not be as pronounced as we first thought and may, in fact, not exist at all.

So, von Hippel says, we can't presume a learning loss just because pupils aren't in school.

Writing in EdWeek in August 2020, Dylan Wiliam, meanwhile, expressed his doubts over reports of lost learning:

"Psychologists who research memory, like Bjork, point out that how easy it is to retrieve something from memory is different from how well something has been learned – what they call retrieval strength and storage strength, respectively.

"When we test students at the beginning of a school year, we are testing retrieval strength, which, if the students have not been reviewing the material they learned in the previous year, will have declined over the summer.

"But how well something is learned – storage strength – does not decline, and restudying the material increases both retrieval strength and storage strength.

"In other words, what students can do on their first day back in school – whether face to face or online – is a poor gauge of what they have actually learned."

More importantly, Wiliam concluded, restudying material increases storage strength more when retrieval strength is low, "so an hour spent restudying material after the summer break will have more impact on long-term learning than the same time spent studying it before the summer break".

I can attest to this. I studied French at GCSE. I did well but didn't continue my studies at A Level. It is now 30 years, therefore, since I last studied the language. However, during the first lockdown, I decided to brush up on my French using a language learning app.

I started with lessons in the 'basics' because this was recommended for beginners. However, after taking a few exercises, I was quickly prompted to skip this stage and move onto more advanced questions because, rather than being a beginner with no prior knowledge, I found that my knowledge had not been 'lost' – it was still stored in my long-term memory – but had instead become hard to retrieve, less readily available.

The content I was being tested on was familiar and much of it came back quickly with a little prompting. It was less learning loss, more learning decay.

I suspect it is the same for our pupils. They will not have lost learning during lockdown, or at least not very much – what we taught them prior to lockdown will still be in there somewhere. Rather, it will have decayed slightly and require some retrieval practice to dust it down and make it more readily accessible. But with some retrieval practice, they could find themselves back on the same trajectory pretty quickly.

Lockdown could have served to help incubate their learning, to help forge new connections and develop more schemata, or at least provided some time for reflection.

So, 'learning loss' implies something that was previously learned has now been lost. However, what is more likely is that pupils have suffered an opportunity cost – pupils have missed out on the opportunity to learn new things.

What should we do about it?

To help our pupils get back on track, we should, I think, eschew formal assessments. Instead, we should make sure our pupils feel welcomed and safe; we should attend to safeguarding and mental health concerns. And then we should put quality teaching first: through good teaching, formative assessments can identify any academic concerns. If nothing else, I am doubtful that lots of formal assessments will be helpful and may add to the stresses of the lockdown.

Yes, there may need to be some form of 'recovery curriculum' but only in the sense of helping pupils to re-establish routines and fine motor skills, and to help them adjust to school life once more. But not in the sense of recovering lost learning. Rather, we should get back to teaching the curriculum and attempt to cover as much depth and breadth as we ordinarily hope to achieve.

Dylan Wiliam also says that the use of standardised tests is unlikely to be of much help:

"Standardised tests can tell us how far along a continuum of achievement a student is but knowing that a student is at the 30th percentile of achievement for his year tells us nothing about what kinds of instruction we should provide.

"Worse, because many such standardized tests adjust the items a student is asked to answer according to how well the student answered previous items (sometimes called "adaptive tests"), we don't even know which items the student answered correctly. All we can do is place the student somewhere along a line of increasing achievement."

Wiliam suggests that, firstly, unless you want to be able to put next year's test results in context by having data that show how little pupils remembered from the previous year, then standardized tests aren't going to be of much help.

Secondly, he says, school leaders and teachers must decide whether material that has not been covered from last year needs to be covered: "While some authors have argued forcefully the desirability of starting students on this year's curriculum, that aspiration must be tempered in the case of more hierarchical subjects like math. After all, if students cannot generate sequences of equivalent fractions, then they are unlikely to be able to master addition of fractions with any understanding."

Thirdly, he says, instead of relying on commercially produced tests, teachers would be better advised to use quick surveys of student achievement: "These sort of assessments could take various forms, from using single, well-designed multiple-choice questions to gauge a class' recall of the prerequisites for the next lesson, to getting students to use finger-voting (one finger for A, two for B, and so on), to using the chat facility when teaching online. This will provide teachers with useful information about where to pitch their instruction (and also provides students with retrieval practice!)."

In short, we should avoid talk of learning loss and help our pupils to adjust to school life, including by re-establishing good habits and study skills. Then we should get on with teaching the curriculum, using ongoing formative assessments – which double as retrieval practice tasks – to ascertain what our pupils know and what they do not yet know.

As David Ausubel said in 1968: "If I had to reduce all of educational psychology to just one principle, I would say this: The most important single factor influencing learning is what the learner already knows. Ascertain this and teach him accordingly."

Chapter 25: Crisis management

In this final chapter of this section of the book entitled the 'new normal', I'd like to explore the role of crisis management in our schools and colleges...

As we have seen writ large on the previous pages, the Covid-19 pandemic has provided school and college leaders with a crash-course in crisis management.

Although I'm sure we all hope we don't have to use these new-found skills any time soon, I think it is worth unpacking what we've learned because crises, though certainly not commonplace, do inevitably plague us from time to time.

During my tenure as a senior school and college leader and as a headteacher, I had several crises to deal with including the murder of one pupil by another, the sudden death of a much-loved colleague, fires and floods, bomb threats, and of course 'snow-day' closures.

None of these crises compares with the scale of the Covid pandemic, of course, and I have nothing but admiration and respect for every colleague who's worked hard to keep their schools calm and orderly and to protect their pupils over the last year or so.

So, what can school and college leaders do to help prepare for the unexpected and to manage a crisis as it unfolds?

First, let's define our terms... what is a crisis?

Raphael (1986) identified the following characteristics of 'crises':

- Rapid time sequences
- An overwhelming of the usual coping responses of individuals and communities
- Severe disruption, at least temporarily, to the functioning of individuals or communities
- Perceptions of threat and helplessness and a turning to others for help.

Originating in the work of Caplan (1964), many organisations use a *prevention, preparation, response, recovery* model (PPPR) of crisis management which describes three levels of intervention:

1. Primary intervention, which consists of activities devoted to preventing a crisis from occurring (this would equate to *prevention* in the PPPR model)

2. Secondary intervention or the steps taken in the immediate aftermath of a crisis to minimise the effects and keep the crisis from escalating (this would equate to *response*)

3. Tertiary intervention, which involves providing long-term follow-up assistance to those who have experienced a severe crisis (this would equate to *recovery*)

I'll adapt steps 1 and 2 from this model and articulate some best practice advice on how to manage a crisis *before* and *during* the emergency occurs...

Before the crisis

There are two key actions I would recommend taking by way of preparation for an emergency:

1. Write a crisis management plan
2. Put together a crisis management team

A crisis management plan tends to work best when:

- It is developed in a consultative, participative manner to ensure it is realistic and achievable, and that everyone understands it and is committed to enacting it.

- The individuals and agencies who will be involved in implementing the plan are involved in its initial development.
- It is accompanied by risk assessments which aid the planning process.
- It considers liability issues, response plans, people's roles during and after the emergency, and the support resources available.
- It addresses and define the tasks and responsibilities of all positions and all organisations likely to become involved.
- It identifies positions of responsibility (i.e., job titles) rather than people's names.
- It is based on appropriate expectations of how people are likely to act/react.
- It is regularly reviewed and updated, including with key contact information.
- It begins with a flowchart showing what action is taken by whom and when.

Before implementing the plan, it should be discussed with the key staff who are nominated within it in order to ensure they are fully aware of their roles and responsibilities.

A staff meeting should be scheduled to share this with all staff. Training should be considered for appropriate staff in relation to some of the main types of incidents they are likely to face.

A hard copy of the plan should be kept in a central location. A member of staff should be responsible for ensuring emergency contact information is kept up to date.

Current lists of contact phone numbers should be available in hard and electronic versions – both staff and student details. The headteacher and nominated staff should keep a copy of the current plan and all contact details at home, albeit obeying GDPR legislation, because emergencies can happen when the school is not occupied.

In order to minimise the effect of any emergency, a school should thoroughly prepare to ensure that all emergencies are dealt with smoothly and efficiently, with the minimum of stress to pupils, staff and others.

The establishment of a crisis management team should be one of the first steps taken. This team needs to include staff from a variety of job roles within school, and not just senior leaders and teachers. A member of admin staff, site staff and learning support should be included so that all areas of school life are considered and are helped to prepare for an emergency. Having a representative team will also ensure more effective and efficient communication when disaster hits.

It may be helpful for the senior leadership team to run through a hypothetical crisis situation during a team meeting, modelling their 'real time' response, in order to identify the short, medium and long-term actions that need to be taken and which external agencies need to be involved.

Although finding time to perform such a modelling exercise during the busy school term will be difficult, it will pay dividends. Not only will be prove valuable CPD for leaders; it will also save time in a real crisis when it matters most.

<u>During</u> the crisis

Here are some suggestions for how you might mitigate some of the worst effects of a crisis and help others cope with an emergency as it unfolds...

Be empathetic

Appreciate that, during a crisis, staff, pupils and parents/carers will be under immense stress and as such may not always act as professionally or courteously as you'd like or expect them to do, and they may occasionally take their frustrations out on you. It is not personal; you must not take it to heart. You are a figurehead, a community leader, and it is what you represent, not who you are, that sometimes makes you a target for their vitriol.

You need to understand staff's pressure-points and provide help dealing with stress and managing mental health. You need to be acutely aware of changes in any colleague's general demeanour and behaviour, and you need to make sure all staff know where to go for help and repeatedly signpost staff to appropriate services.

Be patient and forgiving

You also need to be understanding if some parents/carers don't want to follow the party line. Some parents will disagree with you whatever decision you take during a crisis, and some will feel the need to vent their anger publicly. Others will simply ignore your advice or direction and undermine you.

Again, you need to try to appreciate that this is a very testing time for everyone, and people need your patience and understanding more than ever. People need your leadership during a crisis and good leaders are magnanimous and benevolent. And, ultimately, when it is over, your detractors will need to be forgiven for any poor choices they make in the eye of the storm.

Be visible

It's tempting at times of heightened stress to descend to your bunker. And you'll certainly need time to think through and make important decisions, as well as to craft regular communications to all your stakeholders. But, as I say above, people really need your leadership during a crisis and that means you need to lead from the front. So be visible, be available, and be kind. If it's possible, get out and walk the floor. Be outside school at the start and end of the day to field questions and concerns from parents. If you can't be, make sure a member of the senior team is always visible and available.

Keep communicating

People will need to know what's happening and they will need to feel informed and involved. Regular, measured communications are therefore vital during this crisis.

You should try to sound human in your written communications so don't just copy and paste the official line; rather, put it into friendly language that reflects your local context and sounds like you.

Whilst avoiding the verbatim parroting of the official line, do still share useful links to official sources.

Beware of the tone and potential mis-readings of your written communications. Often, it's best to word lengthy communications as FAQs because these can help reduce the possibility of there being misunderstandings and will also help keep your messages focused and relevant.

You should be open to questions and suggestions – indeed, use each communication to positively invite feedback. But, having said this, it will also be important to address misinformation firmly and publicly so you shouldn't be afraid to correct misunderstandings and directly tackle unhelpful rumours, as well as refute feedback that's simply wrong.

Don't be afraid to repeat key messages and good advice, and to communicate via a number of methods including via email, text, on the school website, and so on.

It's important during a fast-moving crisis to date-stamp all content because messages change quickly, and you will want to make sure everyone is acting on the latest advice. Regularly review and update information shared via your website to ensure it is kept up to date.

End Matter

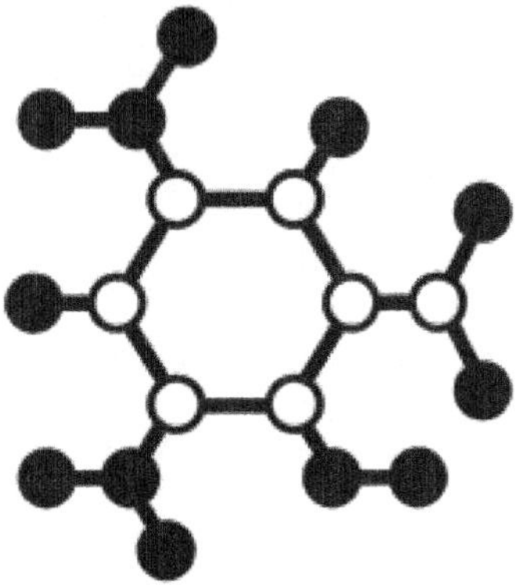

Conclusion

That's all, folks! We've reached the end, not only of this book, but of the whole series on *School and College Curriculum Design*. If you've read all three books, that's nearly 400,000 words you've digested. Frankly, you deserve a medal. But you'll have to make do with my sincere thanks instead.

I hope you have found the series to be of use and, although I don't expect you to agree with every word of it, I do hope it has challenged your thinking, ignited some sparks and started some conversations.

I also hope that you have taken something away with you that will lead to a tangible change in your school or college which, in time, has a positive impact on your learners. That's why I write, after all.

If you do put some of my advice into practice, I'd love to hear about it. You can contact me via Twitter @mj_bromley, email admin@bromleyeducation.co.uk or through my website www.bromleyeducation.co.uk.

Before you go and lie down in a dark room, which is certainly where I'm headed, here is a 'coffee break' summary of what we have learned in this book...

Defining 'impact'

In Book One of this series, I shared a process for approaching curriculum *intent*. I argued that a curriculum is not a single entity; rather, it is a composite of at least four facets: the national, the basic, the local, and the hidden curriculums. I explored what a broad and balanced curriculum might look like in practice. I considered the true purpose of education and, by so doing, articulated the intended outcomes of an effective school curriculum.

I also examined *why* designing a knowledge-rich curriculum was important and discussed *what* knowledge mattered most to our pupils' future successes and how to identify the 'clear end-points' of a whole-school – and indeed subject-specific – curriculum. I discussed ways of ensuring our curriculum was ambitious for all, including by adopting a mastery approach rather than reducing the curriculum offer or 'dumbing down' for some. I talked, too, of modelling the same high expectations of all, albeit accepting that some pupils will need additional and different support to reach that destination.

In Book Two, I turned my attention to curriculum *implementation*. I explained that Ofsted want to see how teachers enable pupils to understand key concepts, presenting information clearly and promoting appropriate discussion; how teachers check pupils' understanding effectively, identifying and correcting misunderstandings; and how teachers ensure that pupils embed key concepts in their long-term memory and apply them fluently.

I emphasised these key points again in this book because it's important to bear them in mind as we complete the trilogy and analyse what curriculum *impact* means in practice. Why? Because, at its heart, I think that 'impact' is about evaluating the extent to which we achieve all the above aims and ambitions.

Qualification outcomes are no longer the sole lens through which 'impact' is judged. Rather, 'impact' is about the extent to which pupils are prepared for the next stage of their education, employment and lives. An education is not solely about getting pupils through qualifications, though these are clearly important; it is about genuinely preparing pupils for what comes next.

In practice, this means that schools and colleges need to provide for pupils' broader development, enabling them to discover and develop their interests and talents. It means that the school curriculum needs to develop pupils' character including their resilience, confidence and independence, and help them keep physically and mentally healthy. It means that at each stage of education, schools need to prepare pupils for future success in their next steps and prepare them for adult life by equipping them with the knowledge and skills to be responsible, respectful, active citizens who contribute positively to society, developing their understanding of fundamental human values, their understanding and appreciation of diversity, celebrating what we have in common and promoting respect for all.

It stands to reason, I would suggest, that if the purpose of education is to prepare pupils for the next stage of their education, employment and lives, then the ways in which we measure 'impact' must go beyond mere outcomes.

Indeed, if we are to focus on the real substance of education, provide a broad and balanced curriculum that's ambitious for all and tackles social justice issues, then we should measure the impact of all this.

As such, in this book I have argued that the purpose of 'impact' is at least threefold:

1. To evaluate the effectiveness of the way in which the curriculum is designed
2. To evaluate the effectiveness of the way in which the curriculum is taught
3. To evaluate the pace of pupil progress, pupil outcomes, and pupils' preparedness for their next steps

Counting what counts

1. Evaluating the impact of curriculum planning

A good curriculum is a living organism, forever changing in response to reality. Curriculum design, therefore, should be a cyclical process.

A curriculum should not be designed then left to stagnate. Rather, we should design a curriculum, teach it, assess it to see if it's working as well as we had hoped, then redesign it in light of our findings and so on.

To help oil the wheel, so to speak, I think we should use assessment data to answer the following questions about our curriculum:

Is our curriculum ambitious enough?

Have we identified the right end points?

Have we planned and sequenced our curriculum effectively?

Does our curriculum help to tackle social justice issues?

At the heart of all these questions is a simple self-evaluative question: Is our curriculum working for all our pupils? Our assessment practices need, among other things, to answer this crucial question. And the outcomes of those assessments should be used to tweak our curriculum when – as will inevitably be the case from time to time – the answer is 'no'.

2. Evaluating the impact of curriculum teaching

As well as using assessment to evaluate the effectiveness of our curriculum planning – or *intent* – we should also use our impact assessments to evaluate the effectiveness of our teaching. To achieve this aim, it might help to ask the following questions:

Do teachers have expert knowledge of the subjects they teach?

Do teachers enable pupils to understand key concepts, presenting information clearly?

Do teachers ensure that pupils embed key concepts in their long-term memory and apply them fluently?

Do teachers use formative assessment to check pupils' understanding in order to inform their planning and their teaching, and to help pupils embed and use knowledge fluently and develop their understanding?

In addition to the above, I would suggest you also ask yourselves: how do we assess the effectiveness of the way in which our curriculum is taught so that pupils transfer key concepts into long-term memory and can apply them fluently and what do we do with the findings?

3. Evaluating pupil outcomes and preparedness for the next stage

As well as evaluating the effectiveness of our curriculum planning and teaching, we want our impact assessments to measure eventual outcomes so that we can determine what pupils have achieved and also the extent to which our curriculum planning and the way in which we have translated those curriculum plans into classroom practice have enabled pupils to achieve what we intended for them to achieve and that we have not perpetuated or opened any attainment gaps.

Ultimately, we should measure the impact of our curriculum by the extent to which we prepare all our pupils for their next steps – do they make good progress through our curriculum and go on to achieve positive destinations? Do our pupils leave us as well-rounded, cultured, inquisitive, caring, kind, resilient, knowledgeable human beings ready to make their own way in the world? And do we, as a consequence, make the world a better place one pupil at a time – for this surely is a measure of true success?

Sense-checking assessments

When we are clear *why* we assess, we need to ensure *how* we assess is the best possible way of doing so and that it results in useful and useable data. I would suggest we need to ensure that all our assessment decisions in school or college are sense-checked for three things:

Purpose

As a handy rule of thumb, whenever we ask teachers to engage in any form of assessment, we should ask ourselves: Why? What is the point of this assessment? How will this assessment - and the data we collect from it - help pupils to make better progress and improve the quality of education at our school?

Process

As well as considering the purpose of assessment, we should think about the process by which teachers are expected to assess, input data, and report the outcomes of assessment. Here, it is useful to ask ourselves whether the process is as efficient as it can be or if it is unnecessarily burdensome.

Validity

Finally, we should consider how valid the data we garner from assessments will be. By this, I don't mean how useful the data will be (we covered this under 'purpose') but rather how accurate and useable it will be. In other words, although we may have confidence that the data will be very useful in helping pupils to make better progress (for example, by identifying 'at risk' pupils who require additional interventions, and by 'stretching' higher-performing pupils to high grade achievement), the actual data we mine might not be as accurate as we hope and so all our subsequent actions may be futile or misguided.

Making marking meaningful, manageable and motivating

Once we have sense-checked our assessment practices for their purpose, process and validity, I think we need to ensure that all the marking and feedback that takes place in our schools and colleges are meaningful, manageable and motivating.

1. Meaningful marking and feedback

To my mind, marking and feedback have but one purpose: to help pupils make better progress and achieve good outcomes. They might do this directly by providing cues to the pupil about what to improve, and they might do it indirectly by providing assessment information to the teacher to guide their planning and teaching. Marking and feedback carried out for any other purpose are not, in my view, meaningful activities and – as well as being a waste of a teacher's precious time – can distract and indeed detract from this important goal.

Consistency is important but this does not mean unvarying practice. Whilst having a set of shared expectations regarding marking and feedback will help everybody to be clear about what is required of them, each subject discipline should be allowed to determine the detail of the policy for their areas, responding to the different workload demands of their subject and to the differences inherent in each phase and key stage of education.

The nature and volume of marking and feedback necessarily varies by age group, subject, and what works best for the individual pupil and for the particular piece of work being assessed. As such, teachers should be encouraged to be pragmatic, adjusting their approach according to context.

Schools also need to remember that marking looks different in different subjects. As such, departments should be allowed to decide what effective marking and feedback looks like for them.

2. Manageable marking and feedback

A teacher's job is a complex one and it would be possible to work twenty-four hours a day, seven days a week and still not feel that the job is done. And yet there are only so many hours in the day. It is important that, whatever approach schools take to marking and feedback, they ensure they protect teachers' wellbeing because tired teachers do not perform as well and burn-out can lead to issues with teacher retention, and staff shortages seriously impede pupils' progress.

Marking and feedback should, therefore, be proportionate. Any expectation on the frequency of marking should take into account the complexity of marking and the volume of marking required in any given subject, qualification type, and phase and key stage of education.

There is no doubt that feedback is valuable, but we need to decide which one of all the valuable things teachers do is more worthwhile than the others and focus on the areas of biggest impact for the smallest investment of teacher time and energy. Put simply, if teachers are spending more time marking and giving feedback than pupils are spending on a piece of work then your priorities are somewhat skewed.

3. Motivating marking and feedback

Marking can help motivate pupils to make progress. Short verbal feedback is often more motivational than long written comments on pupils' work. Indeed, some pupils find written comments demotivating because they ruin the presentation of their work and are confusing or overwhelming.

Too much feedback is not only harmful to teacher workload, but it can also become a disincentive for pupils because there is too much information on which to focus and respond. What's more, too much feedback can reduce a pupil's long-term retention and harm resilience. To build retention and resilience, pupils need to be taught to check their own work and make improvements *before* the teacher marks it and gives feedback. Feedback should also prompt further thinking and drafting, perhaps by posing questions on which the pupil has to ruminate and act, as opposed to ready-made suggestions and solutions.

Feedback can be more motivating if it requires pupils to think. For example, we might use comment-only marking more often as this engages pupils because it requires them to take action. Rather than correcting a pupil's spelling, punctuation and grammar, for instance, the teacher might place a letter in the margin for each error in that line using G for grammar, S for spelling, P for punctuation, and so forth. For the higher-performing pupils, the teacher could simply put a dot in the margin for each error. Feedback of this kind gives pupils something to do and therefore makes them think. By thinking, they are more likely to remember the feedback and avoid repeating the same mistakes.

Whole school v subject specific assessment

Some curriculums are linear, following a neat line between the starting point and the destination as pupils build on prior knowledge and make progress. But many curriculums are neither linear nor neat. They may be spiral or helical in shape; they may zigzag. Accordingly, it is crucial that subject specialists are afforded autonomy in deciding what their key concepts look like and how these might be planned and sequenced over time and then used as a form of assessment.

Before we can agree a subject-specific assessment system, I think we should write, consult upon and agree and articulate an assessment policy. From this point forwards, the assessment policy should be our guiding light; everything we do to develop an assessment system should support the delivery of our policy.

Once a new assessment policy is in place, each subject team needs to decide what unit of measurement they will use. In other words, how will teachers describe pupils' learning and progress in that subject? Whatever measure a team decides to use, it must successfully quantify learning and progress in that subject and must do so in a meaningful way.

Subject teams should start by engaging in a process of detailed curriculum planning before they set about designing a system of assessment. Assessment should be the servant and not the master; the curriculum should be king. After all, how can you decide on your assessment criteria before you know what it is that you're assessing? How we teach our curriculum and how pupils respond to it should form the basis of any new assessment system.

A team's first task should be to design a curriculum with clear end-points or bodies of knowledge which describe what will be taught and when, and what learning will result. This kind of detailed curriculum planning – perhaps using my six steps of curriculum intent as a guide – is necessary if a subject team is to successfully develop assessment criteria. Teams should not make the mistake of rushing into designing a new assessment system before they've considered how their curriculum will be taught in practice.

A subject team's second task, then, is to understand how a pupil's knowledge and skills in those parts of the subject covered in a particular module or scheme of work will accumulate over the course of a term, year or key stage into a holistic understanding of the concepts, key ideas, and capabilities learnt in the subject. As such, curriculum plans need to be progressive in nature, developing gradually over time.

Only once everyone is clear about how pupils' knowledge and skills will develop over the course of time, can a subject team move on to the third and final task: to develop a means of describing and quantifying what pupils are learning as they move through the curriculum.

A mastery learning approach is founded on the belief that all pupils will comprehensively know and understand the core content from each topic or module before moving on to the next. Progress, therefore, tends to be non-linear and tailored to meet the needs of each pupil. At the very least, it is likely to look different to how progress looks in other subject disciplines and thus must be bespoke.

'Progress' is a complex concept – a dotted line used to summarise the overall path taken along the mountainside, snaking towards the peak, which may go up as well as down as pupils find the right terrain and get a solid foothold in the rock. However, statistically speaking, we can estimate the average grade that a pupil is capable of achieving based on their prior performance and this information can be used to notify us if pupils fall below expectations.

Intended learning outcomes or objectives provide a good starting point for tracking pupil progress because they summarise what is taught in each lesson or unit and they are already widely used in lesson planning and delivery. Teachers routinely write and share objectives with pupils at the start of lessons and use them to measure progress in lesson plenaries.

As long as intended learning outcomes cover all the key concepts (end points) that must be learnt, then tracking and recording pupils' acquisition of them should provide a cumulative assessment log which will quantify their progress at any given point.

Making marking motivating

Learning intentions and criteria for success

One of the five key strategies of formative assessment is clarifying and understanding learning intentions and criteria for success.

The notion here is simple: if pupils do not know what they are supposed to be learning and how their work will eventually be judged, then their ability to learn and make progress will be stymied. Obviously, we want pupils to know what we want them to learn and to understand what successful outcomes will look like.

This talks to the three processes that are central to formative assessment:

1. Establishing where pupils are in their learning
2. Establishing where they are going
3. Establishing how they're going to get there

As we have seen, learning intentions are also helpful in that they can provide a starting point for tracking pupil progress because they summarise what is taught in each lesson or unit.

However, the use of learning intentions and success criteria does not mean that every lesson must start with a set of objectives scribed on the board which pupils have to copy down. And learning intentions are not the same as activities. Setting out what pupils will *do* is therefore not particularly helpful; rather, we should focus on what pupils are expected to *think* about and *learn*.

I would suggest that learning intentions are measurable statements which articulate what pupils should know and/or be able to do by the end of a lesson or sequence of lessons.

Sharing learning intentions and success criteria helps pupils to understand how what they're learning today fits into the 'bigger picture' and how they will be assessed. Sharing the big picture is about connecting learning, too; and making explicit the purpose of learning - articulating why pupils need to achieve the learning goals we're setting for them and of what use their learning will be to them in the future. As such, it can increase pupils' levels of motivation and engagement.

Classroom discussions and questioning

Once we know what we want our pupils to learn and how that learning will be assessed, we need to gather evidence about pupils' progress toward these goals. One 'low stakes' way we can do this is by planning effective classroom discussions and questions. In many ways, the art of asking good questions is what good teaching's all about. Indeed, Socrates argued that "questioning is the only defensible form of teaching".

Activating pupils are instructional resources for each other

Slavin, Hurley, and Chamberlain (2003) argue that activating pupils as instructional resources for each other leads to large gains. But there are two important conditions that must be met: Firstly, pupils must work *as a* group not just *in a* group; secondly, every pupil must be responsible for his or her own contribution to the group.

A simple way of activating pupils as instructional resources for each other is to ensure that all work is peer-assessed before it is handed to the teacher. Self- and peer-assessment can often be effective strategies – particularly because we want our pupils to become increasingly metacognitive in their approach to learning – because these strategies: give pupils greater responsibility for their learning; allow pupils to help and be helped by each other; encourage collaboration and reflection; enable pupils to see their progress; and help pupils to see for themselves how to improve.

However, such strategies come with health-warnings. Firstly, pupils need to be helped to develop the necessary skills and knowledge to be able to assess and give feedback. Secondly, we need to provide pupils with time in lessons to process, reflect upon and respond to peer-feedback.

Activating pupils as owners of their own learning

According to Deci et al (1982), when teachers are told they are responsible for pupils' progress, the quality of their teaching deteriorates, as does their pupils' learning. However, when pupils are told to take a more active role in monitoring and regulating their own learning, the pace of their progress increases.

A simple method to help pupils take ownership of their own learning is to give each pupil a laminated card, green on one side and red on the other. At the start of the lesson, the card is placed on the pupil's desk with the green side facing upwards. Once the teacher has given an explanation, if the pupil doesn't understand it, they flip the card over to red. As soon as one pupil flips the card to red, the teacher selects a pupil who is still showing green, and that pupil goes to the front of the class and answers a question that the pupil who's showing red wants to ask.

This is an example of metacognition. Metacognition describes the processes involved when pupils plan, monitor, evaluate and make changes to their own learning behaviours. Metacognition is often considered to have two dimensions:

Metacognitive knowledge refers to what learners know about learning. This includes:

- The learner's knowledge of their own cognitive abilities (e.g., 'I have trouble remembering key dates in this period of history')

- The learner's knowledge of particular tasks (e.g., 'The politics in this period of history are complex')
- The learner's knowledge of the different strategies that are available to them and when they are appropriate to the task (e.g., 'If I create a timeline first it will help me to understand this period of history').

Self-regulation, meanwhile, refers to what learners <u>do</u> about learning. It describes how learners monitor and control their cognitive processes. For example, a learner might realise that a particular strategy is not yielding the results they expected so they decide to try a different strategy. Put another way, self-regulated learners are aware of their strengths and weaknesses, and can motivate themselves to engage in, and improve, their learning.

I have found that metacognition and self-regulation are best developed in the classroom when we follow a 6-step process as follows:

1. Thinking aloud - The teacher makes explicit what they do implicitly and makes visible the expertise that is often invisible to the novice learner. The best thinking aloud occurs when the teacher is modelling excellence. Modelling and thinking aloud should not be too specific as this may inhibit pupils' reflection.

2. Thinking hard – The teacher needs to set an appropriate level of challenge if they are to help develop pupils' metacognition and self-regulation because if pupils are not given hard work to do – if they do not face difficulty, struggle with it and overcome it - they will not develop new and useful strategies, they will not be afforded the opportunity to learn from their mistakes and they will not be able to reflect sufficiently on the content with which they are engaging. Moreover, if pupils are not made to think hard, they will not encode new information into long-term memory and so learning will not occur.

3. Thinking efficiently - As well as thinking hard, pupils need to think efficiently if they are to cheat the limitations of working memory. Yes, pupils must be challenged and must struggle with new concepts if they are attend to them actively and therefore encode them into long-term memory, but if the work's *too* hard, they're likely to hit cognitive overload whereby they try to hold too much information in working memory at one time and therefore thinking fails. The trick, then, is to ensure the work is hard but achievable. The work must be beyond pupils' current capability but within their reach. They must struggle but must be able to overcome the challenge with time, effort and support.

4. Thinking positively - Research suggests that an important factor in the effective use of metacognitive strategies is the ability to delay gratification. In other words, pupils who are better able to delay rewards in favour of studying are better at planning and regulating their learning, and vice versa. To improve metacognition, we can share the 'big picture' with them. For example, we can explain how today's lesson connects with yesterday's lesson and how the learning will be extended or consolidated next lesson, as well as how it will be assessed at a later stage. We can explain how this learning will become useful in later life, too. And we can connect the learning in one subject with the learning in other subjects, making explicit the transferability of knowledge and skills and the interconnectedness of skills in everyday life.

5. Thinking together - Our job as teachers is to help pupils move from novice to expert. Part of this process is to ensure our pupils become increasingly independent over time. In short, we need to begin with lots of scaffolds in place but slowly remove those scaffolds as pupils develop their knowledge and skills. Asking challenging questions and guiding pupils with verbal feedback, prompting dialogue, and productive 'exploratory' talk is a great way to do this. In practice, the teacher might achieve this by encouraging pupils to think in advance of a task about what could go wrong then, afterwards, to discuss what they found hard about the task. 'Dialogic teaching' is a particularly effective method of managing classroom interactions because it emphasises dialogue through which pupils learn to reason, discuss, argue, and explain.

6. Thinking alone - As pupils move from novice towards expertise, they become independent learners and, with a greater degree of autonomy, make active choices to manage and organise their own learning. But even as pupils become independent, they need their teachers to provide them with timely feedback and to help them to plan, monitor, and evaluate their progress. The teacher, as the expert, initially takes responsibility for monitoring progress, setting goals, planning activities and allocating attention for example. Gradually, though, the responsibility for these cognitive processes is given over to the learner. The learner becomes increasingly capable of regulating his or her own cognitive activities.

Ensuring equity

The causes and consequences of disadvantage

Sadly, as much as I wish it were not so, we do not live in an egalitarian society and thus not all children are equal. They do not enter school equal, and they will not leave school equal. Whether we put this inequality down to nature or nurture, or perhaps, and as seems most likely to me, a nuanced combination of the two, we know that children start school with different levels of knowledge and skills and with different abilities and capabilities to know and do more.

No matter what we do to 'level the playing field', we are unlikely ever to do so. We can certainly improve awareness of the situation, and, above all, we can try to stop the gaps from widening as children travel through our education system. And we must truly believe in the transformative power of education and in our own capacities and – dare I say – duties, as educators, to improve the life chances of all those children in our charge including, perhaps especially, those who start their lives at a disadvantage. To think otherwise is to accept that a child's birth will also be their destiny; that success or failure are preordained.

But, put simply, there are too many complex factors at play, and too many ingrained inequalities in society, for schools and colleges alone to close the gaps and achieve absolute equality. Here are my main concerns with the 'closing the gap' narrative...

Firstly, the phrase 'closing the gap' is, I think, the language of a deficit model. In other words, it focuses on what is missing and what is 'wrong' with some pupils, rather than on what differences exist and what we can do to help all pupils access and achieve within an ambitious curriculum.

It also encourages us to fall into the trap of assuming that there is such a thing as an 'average' pupil, a bell-curve against which we can plot ability and thus determine the 'more able' and the 'less able'.

And yet 'ability', if that is the right term, is far more complex than this. Let's assume Pupil A is verbally articulate and yet struggles to commit their thoughts to paper whereas Pupil B struggles with oracy but is articulate when wielding the pen. Who is the more able and who is the less able of the two? Or imagine Pupil C is skilled at football but not so adept at cricket whereas Pupil D is a cricketing marvel but can't dribble a football for love nor money. Who is the more able sportsperson?

Not only does a deficit model focus on what's missing, it assumes that there are some more able, or higher-performing, pupils, and some less able, or lower performing, pupils. And yet ability – and indeed performance – is not binary. Some pupils will perform well in some subject disciplines but not others, and some pupils will perform better in some aspects of some subject disciplines but not others.

Every pupil is an individual and must be treated as such. We must not fall into the trap of thinking that Pupil A is disadvantaged and therefore is destined to fail. But nor should be assume that because Pupil A is deemed to be 'disadvantaged' and does indeed face some barriers to learning that they are uniformly less able to achieve in every unit and every subject they study in school and college and thus require additional interventions and support in order to 'catch up' with their peers.

Secondly, and related to this latter point, we are too obsessed, I think, with labels. Whether those labels pertain to socio-economic deprivation, such as Free Schools Meals (FSM) or Pupil Premium (PP), or to ethnicity and social status and gender, such as 'white working-class boys', or indeed to special educational needs and disabilities, such as 'speech, language and communication needs (SLCN), they can be problematic.

I am not suggesting that labels have no place in education. They can be a useful shorthand and thus help us report on generic attainment gaps at whole-school and national levels. They can help us to identify trends and to tackle endemic discrimination. And, in the case of medical diagnoses such as dyslexia or autism, they can explain why a child finds some aspects of school-life more challenging than their peers and they can open doors to specialist support, and not least to the money with which to buy that specialist support.

Yes, labels have a place in our system. But the problem with labels arises when they are used by schools and teachers to determine expectations of what a child can achieve – or, more likely, cannot achieve – and to ascertain what additional support will be provided.

A further problem with labels, I would argue, is when those labels are used to describe a cohort of pupils and thus stereotype children. Labels can mask significant individual differences within a cohort. There is no such thing, for example, as a typical 'Pupil Premium child' or a typical 'SEND child'. The mere notion is ridiculous. Every pupil is a human being, and every human being is different from every other human being in myriad ways. There may be some shared characteristics, of course; but labels lack nuance and lead us to assume that the problems faced by each child with the same label are exactly the same and that, as such, the solutions must also be the same.

Put simply, there is a difference between causes and consequences: The *cause* is the label. The *consequence* is what this means in practical terms for each child in each situation.

For example, the fact a pupil is eligible for the Pupil Premium – and thus is often labelled 'Pupil Premium child' – might tell you a little about their context. Perhaps they are eligible for free school meals and thus, you may know that they are categorised as living in poverty. But that, in and of itself, tells you little about what, if anything, they may find difficult at school and thus what you can do to help them. To help the child in school, we need to convert the cause, the label, into a consequence in order to better understand what the label means in practice. And the first point to make loud and clear is that it might mean absolutely nothing! Just because a child is eligible for free school meals doesn't mean they are in any way academically disadvantaged at school. Likewise, just because a child is NOT eligible for free school meals does not mean that they are not academically disadvantaged.

Furthermore, a label does not mean that a pupil will be uniformly disadvantaged at school or college. Which is to say, that whilst a pupil may find some aspects of school more difficult than some of their peers, they are unlikely to find EVERY aspect of school difficult and may even find some aspects easier than most of their peers. Labelling pupils leads to lazy decisions. It was common some years ago – and still happens in some schools today – to demand that teachers label pupils eligible for the Pupil Premium on their registers, to design 'strategic seating plans' (whatever they are!) and to provide evidence of what they do differently for these Pupil Premium children.

Why? Such a practice only serves to discriminate against pupils, and to define pupils – and publicly brand them – as being 'poor' and thus 'less able' and in need of help. Being eligible for the Pupil Premium, as I have said, might mean absolutely nothing in terms of a pupil's abilities in a subject or indeed in every subject. And even if it did, the generic 'PP' label tells us nothing about what to do.

The three-point plan

I have developed a three-point plan for supporting pupils with additional and different needs, including those eligible for the Pupil Premium, which is as follows:

Step 1: Identify the barriers - Before we can put in place intervention strategies aimed at supporting disadvantaged or vulnerable pupils, we must first understand why a gap exists between the attainment of disadvantaged pupils and non-disadvantaged pupils. In short, we need to ask ourselves: What are the consequences of disadvantage faced by my pupils? What barriers might their disadvantage pose in class? How does their disadvantage translate itself, if at all, in terms of their ability to access the ambitious curriculum I am teaching and to achieve in line with their peers?

Step 2: Plan the solutions - Once we have identified the barriers our disadvantaged pupils face towards learning, we need to plan the solutions. In so doing, we should ensure our strategies promote an ethos of attainment for all pupils, rather than stereotyping disadvantaged pupils as a group with less potential to succeed. We should take an individualised approach to addressing barriers to learning and emotional support and do so at an early stage, rather than providing access to generic support as pupils near their end-of-key-stage assessments. We should focus on outcomes for individual pupils rather than on providing generic strategies for whole cohorts. We should deploy our best staff to support disadvantaged pupils; perhaps develop existing teachers' and TAs' skills rather than using additional staff who do not know the pupils well. We should make decisions based on frequent assessment data, responding to changing evidence, rather than use a one-off decision point. And finally, we should focus on high quality teaching first rather than on bolt-on strategies and activities outside school hours and outside the classroom.

Step 3: Agree the success criteria - Once we have identified the barriers to learning faced by our disadvantaged pupils and have planned the best solutions to help them overcome these barriers, we need to be clear about what success will look like. We should ask ourselves: what do I expect to see as an outcome? What is my aim here? For example, is it to: Raise attainment; expedite progress; improve attendance; improve behaviour; reduce exclusions; improve parental engagement; or expand upon the number of opportunities afforded to disadvantaged pupils...? Whatever our immediate goal is, ultimately, we should be seeking to diminish the difference between the attainment of disadvantaged pupils in our school and non-disadvantaged pupils nationally, as well as narrowing our within-school gap. As such, if our initial aim is pastoral in nature, for example to improve behaviour and attendance, or reduce exclusions, then we must take it a step further and peg it to an academic outcome.

When interventions work best

When setting the success criteria, it's important to consider the best individual approach. For example, evidence suggests that interventions work best when they are short term, intensive, focused, and tailored...

Short term - The best interventions help pupils to become increasingly independent over time. In other words, the scaffolds slowly fall away. Interventions should, therefore, be planned to run for a finite amount of time, ideally less than a term. Of course, if the evidence shows the intervention is working but that further improvement is needed, then the intervention can be extended, but to slate an intervention for a year, say, is often misguided.

Intensive - Similarly, interventions should be intensive, perhaps with three or more sessions a week rather than just one. And those sessions should also be intensive in the sense of being short, say 20 to 50 minutes in length rather than an hour or more.

Focused - Interventions should be keenly focused on a pupil's areas of development rather than be generic. For example, rather than setting a goal of, say, 'improving a pupil's literacy skills', an intervention strategy should be focused on a specific aspect of literacy such as their knowledge of the plot of Stone Cold or their ability to use embedded quotations in an essay.

Tailored - Interventions need to be tailored to meet the needs of those pupils accessing them. They must be as personalised as any classroom learning and not be 'off the peg' programmes. Assessment data should be used to inform the intervention and to ensure it is being pitched appropriately to fill gaps in the pupil's knowledge.

Quality first teaching

Although intervention strategies can prove very effective, we must never forget that the best way to improve outcomes for pupils with additional and different needs is through quality first teaching because, if we improve the quality of timetabled teaching in the classroom, all pupils will make better progress.

A study by Hanushek and Rivkin (2006) found that teacher effectiveness had more impact on outcomes than anything else - pupils in the classroom of the most effective teacher out of a group of fifty teachers took just six months to make the same amount of progress that pupils taught by the least effective teacher out of fifty took two years to achieve – in other words, between the most and least effective teacher out of fifty, there was eighteen months' wasted time.

What's more, Hamre and Pianta's research (2005) showed that, in the classrooms of the most effective teachers, socio-economic differences were null and void - in other words, pupils from the most disadvantaged backgrounds made the same progress as the least disadvantaged.

In Book Two of this series, I argued that quality first teaching occurs when we introduce pupils to new curriculum content in four distinct stages:

1. Telling

2. Showing
3. Doing
4. Practising

Ultimately, though, whatever form it takes, 'quality first teaching' should ensure that all pupils, including those with additional and different needs:

- Are engaged - in the sense of being active participants in the process of learning not passive recipients of information
- Are highly motivated to learn and enthusiastic about learning
- Are challenged by hard work and know that making mistakes is an essential part of learning
- Receive effective feedback about where they are now, where they need to go next and how they will get there
- As a result of feedback, make progress over time and become increasingly independent and resilient learners.

The golden triangle

I advocate forming a 'golden triangle' which connects the following aspects of school management:

1. Quality assurance
2. Performance management
3. Professional development

Apex 1: Quality assurance

When it comes to quality assurance – or, as I prefer, quality *improvement*– I believe that we should measure the quality of education (note: not the quality of *teachers* or *teaching* necessarily) in a holistic rather than an isolated way.

An effective quality assurance process might, therefore, consist of three stages:

1. A professional conversation about subject purpose and intentions
2. A range of quality assurance activities (on which more below)
3. An action planning meeting to agree next steps

And the second stage should take myriad forms which, when triangulated, paint a holistic picture of performance. I'd suggest at least these four cornerstones:

1. Lesson observations
2. Work scrutiny
3. Review of planning
4. Review of resources

Apex 2: Performance management

When it comes to performance management – or, as I prefer, performance *development* – my philosophy is simple: it is no one's vocation to fail. In other words, no one wakes up in the morning determined to do the worst job they possibly can; no one opens their eyes, stretches and yawns, looks themselves up and down in the mirror and vows to fail as many pupils as they can before nightfall. But, despite the best of intentions, sometimes some people don't perform as well as they can or as well as we'd like.

When teachers under-perform, they need to be given time and support – including appropriate training – in order to improve.

For a long time and in too many cases, teacher performance management in schools and colleges was synonymous with an annual lesson observation. The lesson judgment – which usually took the form of a single number from 1 to 4, modelled on the Ofsted rating system – determined whether or not a teacher passed the appraisal cycle successfully and thus could escape the sanctions of 'capability' and – where relevant – be rewarded with pay progression.

Thankfully, this is much less common today than it once was, say, five or ten years ago. But it is not unheard of and even if *graded* lesson observations have ended, for too many teachers, appraisal cycles are still won or lost in a lesson observation. This is problematic because lessons observations alone – no matter how professionally and pragmatically they are carried out – do not enable us to accurately judge a teacher's effectiveness in the classroom, let alone their entire professional contribution.

The main thrust of my argument with regards performance management is simple: we should move away from performance *management* and towards performance *development*. In other words, we should avoid instigating a pass/fail system of appraisal that assumes teachers are either good or bad. Instead, we should strive for a system that recognises the complexity of the job, accepts that people have good and bad days, that many more factors affect pupils' progress and outcomes than an individual teacher, and that the goal is to help everyone – no matter their career stage – improve over time (whilst acknowledging that everyone is human, and no one is perfect).

Let me emphasise those key points again...

Performance management should:

- Recognise the fact that teaching and learning are highly complex and cannot be reduced to a checklist or rubric
- Accept that a teacher's performance isn't uniform – they have good and bad days, and an ineffective lesson does not mean they have failed
- Acknowledge that pupil outcomes are affected by many factors beyond a teacher's control
- Aim to help every teacher in a school to improve, no matter their career stage or training needs
- Promote collaboration rather than competition, and incentivise team-working and joint practice development

So, put simply, it is my belief that performance management – if it is to 'measure' anything – should measure a teacher's willingness to engage in professional development activity and improve over time. As a natural progression from this, it is reasonable to assert that an appraisal system could consist quite simply of one professional development target per year and be reviewed at the end of the cycle on the extent to which a teacher has engaged in CPD activity, tried new approaches and evaluated their impact. Talking of which...

Apex 3: Professional development

Professional development works best, I find, when it is worthwhile, sustained and evaluated.

Firstly, CPD should provide opportunities for external expertise to be injected into a school and so take the form of INSET events led by a guest speaker. This is important because schools must not become isolated from the outside world. If they do, they are in danger of becoming 'sausage factories' which keep churning out the same results precisely because they keep putting in the same ingredients.

External speakers, trainers and advisors can help schools to challenge the status quo, to question hitherto unquestionable practices, and to sense-check their work against other schools. They can also provide a new way of thinking about ideas and approaches.

Secondly, I think CPD should also be external in the sense of teachers accessing conferences, training courses and networking events outside the school gates. Such events provide an opportunity for teachers to stop, think and reflect on their current practices and to talk to colleagues from other settings and thus share ideas.

Thirdly, I think CPD should take myriad forms and not be limited to formal training courses. CPD can include engaging with academic research, networking online, and trying out new strategies in the classroom then evaluating their impact. In the case of vocational teachers in FE settings, CPD can – and indeed should – take the form of workplace visits to ensure their industry knowledge is kept up-to-date and relevant.

Fourthly, I think CPD should be teacher-led and thus afford teachers the opportunity to share best practice with colleagues from their own departments and schools and seek help and advice from colleagues who teach in the same setting. Peer-observations and peer-teaching are particularly helpful here. A note of caution, though: It is important that there is a structure and a clear focus for any teacher-led CPD in order to avoid it becoming simply a 'talking shop'.

And finally, CPD should perform the twin functions of *innovation* and *mastery*. In other words, professional development should not just be about learning new ways of working – professional development for innovation – although this is undoubtedly important. Rather, it should also be about helping teachers to get better at something they already do – professional development for mastery. Professional development for mastery is about recognising what already works well and what should therefore be embedded, consolidated, built upon, and shared.

The new normal

Ethical leadership

Ethical leadership in education is driven by a respect for values and an unfaltering belief in the dignity and rights of others. Ethical leaders build school cultures governed by fair, clearly articulated expectations, rather than cultures driven by personalities or politics.

In an ethically led school, there is a clear vision and mission, and a set of shared values and principles, that are understood and owned by everyone who works there.

Every action that is taken is sense-checked against this vision and mission – if completion of said action would not aid the pursuit of the vision and mission, it isn't deemed important; as well as against these values and principles – if completion of said action would not uphold the values and principles, it isn't considered valid.

Every element of the school, from performance management appraisals to staff professional development, from expectations of pupil behaviour to the resourcing of the curriculum, reflects this vision and mission, and these values and principles.

Ethical leaders cannot pick and choose which situations call for moral judgment or leave their principles at the door whenever it's convenient; an ethical code provides the very foundations on which these schools are built and function day-to-day.

In practice, ethical leadership is, I think, anchored in five principles:

1. Honesty
2. Justice
3. Respect
4. Community
5. Integrity

Above all else, I think, ethical leaders are kind leaders...

Ethical school leaders routinely recognise and reward success. For ethical leaders, celebrating others' achievements is an everyday part of what they do rather than an afterthought or rarity. Ethical leaders also give quality time to people, have an open-door policy – which does not mean being available twenty-four hours a day, but rather being able to meet with staff as soon as possible and listening and responding to what they have to say. Ethical leaders are protective of their staff, showing empathy, respecting people's privacy, remembering birthdays, and granting personal leave – without question – when staff have important or urgent personal matters to attend to such as family funerals. They also set as their default position a genuine belief that everybody wishes to do well and will try their best, rather than assuming the worst of people.

Parental engagement

Let's consider a few starting principles...

Firstly, **parental communication needs to start early** and continue throughout a pupil's journey through school. The parents of pupils moving from nursery to primary school, or from primary to secondary, will not want to receive information halfway through the summer holiday at which point it will be deemed too late. Schools need to engage with parents early and clearly set out their expectations and requirements.

Secondly, **parental communication needs to be a two-way process**: as well as the school staying in touch with parents, parents also need a means of keeping in contact with the school. One way to do this is to create a frequently asked questions (FAQ) page, as well as a Q&A facility and a parents' forum on the school's website. This will need to be monitored carefully, of course, or perhaps pass through a 'gatekeeper' in order to be vetted before comments are made 'live'. In order for it to be viewed as worthwhile, the school will also need to communicate its response to parental comments and suggestions, perhaps through a 'You Said, We Did' page.

Thirdly, **parental communications need to be appropriately timed, relevant and useful** and one way to do this is to utilise the experience and expertise of pupils and their parents. For example, the parents of current Reception or Year 7 pupils will be able to share their thoughts on what information they needed when they went through the transition process with their child not so long ago, as well as when they needed it most, whilst current Reception or Year 7 pupils will be able to offer their advice about how to prepare for primary or secondary school by, to give but two examples, providing a reading list for the summer and sharing their advice on how to get ready for the first day of school.

Fourthly, **parental communication should take many forms and embrace new and emerging technologies**. The use of technologies such as email, texting, websites, electronic portfolios and online assessment and reporting tools can make communication between parents and teachers more timely, efficient, productive and satisfying.

Of course, doing all of this effectively takes time and yet it is important to balance the needs of parents with those of hard-working teachers. You do not want the unintended consequence of effective parental engagement to be an unworkable teacher workload.

Crisis management

The Covid-19 pandemic has provided school and college leaders with a crash-course in crisis management. Although I'm sure we all hope we don't have to use these new-found skills any time soon, I think it is worth unpacking what we've learned because crises, though certainly not commonplace, do inevitably plague us from time to time.

During my tenure as a senior school and college leader and as a headteacher, I had several crises to deal with including the murder of one pupil by another, the sudden death of a much-loved colleague, fires and floods, bomb threats, and of course 'snow-day' closures. None of these crises compares with the scale of the Covid pandemic, of course, and I have nothing but admiration and respect for every colleague who's worked hard to keep their schools calm and orderly and to protect their pupils over the last year or so.

So, what can school and college leaders do to help prepare for the unexpected and to manage a crisis as it unfolds?

Many organisations use a *prevention, preparation, response, recovery* model (PPPR) of crisis management which describes three levels of intervention:

1. Primary intervention, which consists of activities devoted to preventing a crisis from occurring (this would equate to *prevention* in the PPPR model)

2. Secondary intervention or the steps taken in the immediate aftermath of a crisis to minimise the effects and keep the crisis from escalating (this would equate to *response*)

3. Tertiary intervention, which involves providing long-term follow-up assistance to those who have experienced a severe crisis (this would equate to *recovery*)

There are two key actions I would recommend taking by way of preparation for an emergency:

1. Write a crisis management plan
2. Put together a crisis management team

And here are some tips for mitigating some of the worst effects of a crisis and to help others cope with an emergency as it unfolds...

Be empathetic - Appreciate that, during a crisis, staff, pupils and parents/carers will be under immense stress and as such may not always act as professionally or courteously as you'd like or expect them to do, and they may occasionally take their frustrations out on you. It is not personal; you must not take it to heart. You are a figurehead, a community leader, and it is what you represent, not who you are, that sometimes makes you a target for their vitriol.

Be patient and forgiving - You also need to be understanding if some parents/carers don't want to follow the party line. Some parents will disagree with you whatever decision you take during a crisis, and some will feel the need to vent their anger publicly. Others will simply ignore your advice or direction and undermine you.

Be visible - It's tempting at times of heightened stress to descend to your bunker. And you'll certainly need time to think through and make important decisions, as well as to craft regular communications to all your stakeholders. But people really need your leadership during a crisis and that means you need to lead from the front. So be visible, be available, and be kind. If it's possible, get out and walk the floor.

Keep communicating - People will need to know what's happening and they will need to feel informed and involved. Regular, measured communications are therefore vital during this crisis. You should try to sound human in your written communications so don't just copy and paste the official line; rather, put it into friendly language that reflects your local context and sounds like you.

About the author

Matt Bromley is an education author and advisor with over twenty years' experience in teaching and leadership including as a secondary school headteacher and principal, FE college vice principal, and MAT director. He also works as a public speaker, trainer, and school improvement lead, and is a primary school governor. He remains a practising teacher, currently working in secondary, FE and HE settings.

Matt writes for various newspapers and magazines and is the author of numerous best-selling books for teachers. Matt's education blog, voted one of the UK's most influential, receives over 50,000 unique visitors a year.

He regularly speaks at national and international conferences and events, and provides education advice to charities, government agencies, training providers, colleges and multi-academy trusts. He works as a consultant and trainer with several companies and also provides a wide selection of direct-to-market consultancy and training services through his own company, Bromley Education, which he founded in 2012.

You can follow him on Twitter: @mj_bromley.

You can find out more about him and read his blog at www.bromleyeducation.co.uk.

Also by the author

The IQ Myth
The Art of Public Speaking
How to Become a School Leader
Teach
Teach 2
Making Key Stage 3 Count
The New Teacher Survival Kit
How to Lead
How to Teach
How to Learn
School & College Curriculum Design Book 1: Intent
School & College Curriculum Design Book 2: Implementation

About the publisher

PUBLISHED BY

Spark Education Books UK

ISBN: 9798722688484

Printed in Great Britain
by Amazon

20177241R00261